Painting
and Poetry

Painting and Poetry

Form, Metaphor, and the Language of Literature

Franklin R. Rogers

with the assistance of Mary Ann Rogers

Lewisburg
Bucknell University Press
London and Toronto: Associated University Presses

Associated University Presses
440 Forsgate Drive
Cranbury, NJ 08512

Associated University Presses
25 Sicilian Avenue
London WC1A 2QH, England

Associated University Presses
2133 Royal Windsor Drive
Unit 1
Mississauga, Ontario
Canada L5J 1K5

The paper used in this publication meets the minimum
requirements of the American National Standard for Permanence
of Paper for Printed Library Materials Z39.48-1984.

Library of Congress Cataloging in Publication Data

Rogers, Franklin R.
  Painting and poetry.

  Bibliography: p.
  Includes index.
  1. Ut pictura poesis (Aesthetics)   I. Rogers, Mary Ann.
II. Title.
N66.R64   1985   700'.1   83-46175
ISBN 0-8387-5077-X (alk. paper).

Printed in the United States of America

For Bruce

Shall I take thee, the Poet said
To the propounded word?
Be stationed with the Candidates
Till I have finer tried—

The Poet searched Philology
And when about to ring
For the suspended Candidate
There came unsummoned in—

That portion of the Vision
The World applied to fill
Not unto nomination
The Cherubim reveal—

—Emily Dickinson

Contents

Color illustrations appear as a group between pages 128 and 129.

Preface

That the figurative plays a role in verbal metaphor has long been a tenet of traditional literary criticism—"figurative," that is, not in the "ornamental" sense, but rather in the sense of a reference to visuo-spatial images. And the general acceptance of that tenet has almost traditionally been conjoined with another widely held assumption that there is a vital link between the painter and the poet. But the precise nature of that link and the insights it affords into the formation of the figurative in verbal metaphor and consequently into form in literature have never been fully explored, perhaps because inquiry has been forestalled by the general acceptance of yet another assumption, the one derived from Lessing's famous statement of the limitations of the two arts in contrast to each other, the assertion in the *Laokoön* that painting is limited to single visual impressions, thus achieving a unity and coherence impossible of achievement in literature, whereas literature is uniquely capable of presenting narrative sequences extending through time and space.

And, at first glance, Lessing's assertion seems true enough, and he, as dramatist, that is, as practitioner of the art of literature, would seem an unimpeachable authority. But an imposing number of other poets, in insisting that poetry and metaphor are one (*poetry* here designating all works of art using words as a medium), insist in effect that through the figure the poem makes, as Robert Frost phrased it, the poet achieves just such an immediate single unified impression by means closely related to those of the painter. Thomas Hardy, among others, was even more direct in his assertion when he wrote, "Probably few of the general body denominated the reading public consider, in their hurried perusal of novel after novel, that, to a masterpiece in story there appertains a beauty of shape, no less than

9

to a masterpiece in pictorial or plastic art, capable of giving to the trained mind an equal pleasure."*

The present study explores this concept. It assumed its first coherent shape as a series of lectures at the University of Paris-Sorbonne (Paris IV) in 1975–76. Its inception, however, was in a perception first gained in the writing of *Mark Twain's Burlesque Patterns* (1960) and pursued in the editing of *Mark Twain's Satires & Burlesques* (1967), the perception of Twain's dependence upon what in the latter volume was described as a "matrix," a ready-made verbal structure for his larger fictions. The encounter in 1969–71 with reports in the scientific journals of the work of Roger W. Sperry and others on the functional asymmetry of the human brain led to precisely that refocusing from the verbal toward the visuo-spatial which the phrase "the figure a poem makes" seems to suggest. The neurophysiological evidence, as it bears upon the use of language and the perception and re-creation of the visuo-spatial, permitted the bridging of the gap between painting and poetry insofar as the question of form is concerned and led to a redefinition of verbal metaphors as a phenomenon parallel to, indeed identical with, the visual metaphors of the pictorial and plastic arts.

Midway in the Paris lectures, Mrs. Mary Ann Rogers and I became aware of the recently advanced topological "catastrophe theory" propounded by the distinguished French mathematician René Thom of the Institut des Hautes Études Scientifiques and published in his book *Stabilité structurelle et morphogénèse* (1972). Thom's theory not only provided confirmation, by extension of the principles therein set forth, of the conclusions suggested by our own work but also furnished the tools necessary for more precise demonstration and analysis—this particularly in respect to verbal metaphor as we had defined it. The conjunction of the two lines of investigation, explored during a memorable afternoon in Professor Thom's study, led to the presentation at his request of a seminar at the Institut des Hautes Études Scientifiques devoted to the links between his theory and our analysis of metaphor and the literary work of art. The conjunction led as well to a recasting of our study into its present form.

It seems only fitting that mathematics should thus contribute so substantially to a study of metaphor and of the language of literature, for if the word *mythos* as used in classical Greek from the time of Pindar generally meant the same as the Latin *fabula,* that is, specifically denoted fiction, and if Thom is correct in translating the

Life and Art, ed. Ernest Brennecke, Jr. (New York: Books for Libraries Press, 1968), p. 68.

Heraclitean *logos* (the post-Pindaric antonym of *mythos*) as "form," *mythos* and *logos*, manifested as art and mathematics, become the perfect complementaries.* The concept is of profound significance, for if *mythos* and *logos* are two contiguous† complementary forms, the correlatives in language, poetry and discourse, become in their turn contiguous complementary forms susceptible like all forms of a topological description and analysis by virtue of the discontinuity which constitutes the contour between them. In its present form, this study is an exploration of that concept: It addresses itself strictly to the formal (in the topological sense of that word) aspect of literature and literary words, not to the discursive. It is to be hoped that this extensive address to a single but fundamental aspect of the phenomenon known as literature will contribute somewhat to a resolution of the hermeneutical problem posed by literature, for if the human brain is capable of conceptualizing in visuo-spatial forms, as the poets have maintained for centuries and neurophysiological research of the last decade confirms, and further if discursive language *(logos)* may interact with form—much as the cubist painter uses words and form—and the result is the literary language *(mythos),* the position taken by philosophical hermeneutics, especially that taken by Martin Heidegger and Hans-Georg Gadamer, must be considerably revised before it can be applied to works of literature.‡ Heidegger's metaphor for language, "house of being," itself illustrates the point, as indeed for centuries has the art of the Chinese and the Japanese poet-calligraphers. Indeed, Heidegger's metaphor is closely akin to one exploited by the T'ang dynasty poet Yüan Chen (779–817) in his poem "Temporary Palace" in which the emperor's travel-palace, used just once and crumbling now from old age and disuse, is juxtaposed to the palace woman, locally recruited, also used once and crumbling now from old age and disuse. The point which philosophical her-

---

*"I have twice allowed myself to translate the Heraclitean λοϑος as 'form.' Allowing that to Heraclitus the *logos* is the formal structure that assures for any object its unity and its stability, I am convinced that this particular use of the word 'form' (meaning the equivalence class of structurally stable forms) in this book is a reasonably good approximation." Thom, *Structural Stability and Morphogenesis*, trans. D. H. Fowler (Reading, Mass.: W. A. Benjamin, 1975), p. 329 n.5.

†*Contiguous* is here used in the sense given it by the physicist and the mathematician, i.e., touching along most or the whole of one or more surfaces.

‡"We can only think in a language, and just this residing of our thinking in a language is the profound enigma that language presents to thought [Das eigentliche Rätsel der Sprache ist aber dies, dass wir das in Wahrheit nie ganz können. Alles Denken über Sprache ist vielmehr von der Sprache schon immer wieder eingeholt worden]." Hans-Georg Gadamer, "Mensch und Sprache," in *Kleine Schriften* (Tübingen: J. C. B. Mohr [Paul Siebeck], 1967), 1 : 95; "Man and Language," in *Philosophical Hermeneutics*, trans. and ed. David Linge (Berkeley and Los Angeles: University of California Press, 1976), p. 59.

meneutics misses is visually present in the poem in the fact that seven of its twenty characters contain the "roof" radical, a radical which visually conjoins palace and woman: the palace is the place of her being, and hers is the being of the palace. The point is also visible in a pattern revealed by studies of Japanese stroke victims who before their strokes were able to read and write both in the *kanas* (phonetic characters) and *kanji* (ideographic characters). Commonly such victims, after suffering trauma in the left hemisphere language centers with consequent comparable aphasia, show such differentiated language impairments in the *kanas* and *kanji* as to indicate two separate modes of word processing or of access to semantic content, either phonological (the *kanas*) or figural *(kanji)*. That is to say, typically such stroke victims experience devastating losses in their abilities with the *kanas* whereas their abilities with *kanji* are considerably less impaired, and these impairments are to a large extent due to impaired motor control of the right hand and arm.* Such evidence suggests the danger of attempting to exclude the figural as visuo-spatial phenomenon from the consideration of language—and especially from the consideration of the literary language.

The topological approach to literary form and its creation has dictated the presentational form of the study, for if *logos* and *mythos* are indeed contiguous complementary forms they are then essentially no different from those forms with which the painter or sculptor deals in the formation of his art object. Thus, so it has seemed to us, the most expeditious route to the question of significance is through that consciousness of form essential in the creation of all art but most immediately manifest in the visuo-spatial formulations of the painter, through that consciousness of form to that consciousness of significance which is the reader's as consequence of the perception of poetic form.

It may be argued that in the discussion of the painter's consciousness of form the focus is too preponderantly upon comments by Picasso and Matisse. To a certain degree such a focus is enforced, for these two artists more than any others among Western artists have struggled directly with the question central to this study and in addition have commented more articulately than their fellows upon both the struggle and the question. To a further degree, the focus is delib-

---

*See Simiko Sansanuma and Osamu Fujimura, "An Analysis of Writing Errors in Japanese Aphasic Patients: Kanji versus Kana Words," *Cortex* 8 (1972): 265–82; and "Selective Impairment of Phonetic and Non-Phonetic Transcription of Words in Japanese Aphasia Patients: Kana *vs.* Kanji in Visual Recognition and Writing," *Cortex* 7 (1971): 1–18.

erate because these two artists in their art constitute contiguous complementary manifestations of the essential matter of the study: Both concerned themselves more than most painters with the formal relationship between line, color, and value on the one hand and the word on the other, but in their explorations and experiments, the two went in diametrically opposite directions, Picasso toward the multiple perspectives of his cubistic and postcubistic work, which thrust the concept of contour and thus of form into a dimensionality somewhere beyond the three of ordinary perception, and Matisse toward the simplicity of his *découpages,* the severe and precisely limited perspective of a contour reduced to a dimensionality which in truth may be said to be somewhat less than two of the ordinary three. The very scope embraced by the two in their juxtaposition makes the more valuable their unanimity in respect to the question of artistic form which is central to this study. These two painters thus present visually the characteristics which make the works of Wallace Stevens and Robert Frost, likewise, two contiguous complementary manifestations of the essential matter of this study. And it is for this reason that in the discussion of the poet's art a preponderance of the evidence has been drawn from the comments of these two poets. It is hoped, however, that enough has been drawn from the comments of other artists, both painters and poets, to indicate that the phenomena discussed are more universal than idiosyncratic.

In the course of a work so wide-ranging, we have incurred a quantity of debts which cannot possibly be catalogued in a formal list of acknowledgments; among them, however, is a number which no amount of gratitude can adequately repay: The detailing of them here is to record a permanent obligation. As the previous comments indicate, chief among these latter is one owed to René Thom, not only for the revelations afforded by his work but also for the warmth and enthusiasm with which he encouraged our own. We are indebted as well to Roger W. Sperry of the California Institute of Technology for guidance and generous advice in our attempts to cope with the sometimes deceiving and paradoxical complexities of research in the functional asymmetry of the human brain and the so-called "split-brain" phenomenon. And to my former colleague and our good friend Roger Asselineau of the University of Paris-Sorbonne is owing, as a consequence of his faithful performance of the vital function of "censeur ami," a substantial portion of whatever force our argument may have. He it is as well who undertook during the later stages of work on the manuscript to act as our agent in Paris in seeking out photographs essential to the documentation of the study. In the field of prehistoric studies, valuable assistance in interpretation came from André Leroi-Gourhan, Professeur de Préhistoire at the Collège de France and Conservateur du Musée de l'Homme, Paris. Alain Roussot, Conservateur du Musée d'Aquitaine, Bordeaux, took precious time from his excavations at the Maison Forte de Tayac to give us a much-needed orientation preliminary to our personal inspection of prehistoric art in the valleys of the Dordogne and the Lot. His "programme de voyage" permitted us to realize the maximum profit from a limited time. An acknowledgment must go to M. Jean Guichard, Conservateur du Musée de la Préhistoire, Les Eyzies de Tayac, for permission to study in detail several items in the collection. A special acknowledgment and grateful thanks must go as well both to M. Max Sarradet, Conservateur de la Grotte de Lascaux, for his permission to carry out our studies in Lascaux, and to the guardians of the various caves whose specialized knowledge of their particular caves proved indispensable. Worthy of special mention are Mme Paulette Daubisse, Gardienne de la Grotte de Font-de-Gaume, and M. Claude Archambeau, Gardien de la Grotte des Combarelles. Much of the information gleaned from the studies of prehistoric art *in situ* would be useless without adequate photographic documentation, and for much of this we are indebted to the kindness and generosity of the scholar-photographer Jean Vertut, who placed at our disposal his vast collection of photographs and permitted us free use of those we have chosen for reproduction in this volume. In respect to Japanese art and calligraphy, valuable assistance came from our good friend Yorimasa Nasu of Doshisha University, Kyoto, who verified for us a number of details in various Japanese libraries and also furnished translations from the Japanese for key passages cited in the text. Throughout the long work a number of graduate assistants have contributed materially to the progress of the study by sharing with us the necessary drudgery of library searches and note taking and by serving from time to time as guinea pigs. Chief among these are Mrs. Sally Houck and Mrs. Sophia Andres, who, we hope, are none the worse for the experience. A special recognition is owing Philippe and Marie-Paul Lefort, former students, now professors of English, Quimper, France, who gave of their valuable time during a brief California vacation to verify and occasionally to rectify our many translations from the French of both painter and poet. And finally a most grateful acknowledgment must go to Professor James H. Bunn, Department of English, State University of New York at Buffalo, whose sensitive and sympathetic reading of an earlier stage of the manuscript resulted in advice and recommendations leading to the strategy of presentation adopted in this text. To all these we owe much—except the errors and flaws, which remain our own.

Franklin R. Rogers
Mary Ann Rogers

A Note on Translations

Unless otherwise specifically indicated in the notes, all translations from the French are those of the author and his assistant. To signify the fact that commentary has been based upon the original French, the French text is presented first with the English translation following in brackets. Wherever practicable, in the case of comments by German artists, the original German text is included. To signify the fact that the author and his assistant have relied upon the English translation, the English is presented first, the German following in brackets.

Acknowledgments

The author wishes to express appreciation to the following for permission to reprint copyrighted material:

Oxford University Press for permission to quote from William Blake, *The Complete Writings of William Blake*, edited by Geoffrey Keynes, 1966.

Princeton University Press for permission to quote an excerpt from Samuel Taylor Coleridge, *The Notebooks of Samuel Taylor Coleridge*, edited by Kathleen Coburn, Bollingen Series 50, Vol. 2: 1804–1808, copyright © 1961 by Princeton University Press.

The Estate of Joseph Conrad and Richard Underwood Withers, Solicitors, for permission to quote from Joseph Conrad, *Prefaces to His Works* (London: J. M. Dent & Sons, Ltd., 1937).

Little, Brown and Company for permission to quote poem #1071 by Emily Dickinson from *The Complete Poems of Emily Dickinson*, edited by Thomas S. Johnson, copyright 1914 by Martha Dickinson Bianchi, copyright renewed © 1942 by Martha Dickinson Bianchi.

Harvard University Press for permission to quote poems #76 and #1126 by Emily Dickinson, reprinted by permission of the publishers and the Trustees of Amherst College from *The Poems of Emily Dickinson*, edited by Thomas H. Johnson, Cambridge, Mass.: The Belknap Press of Harvard University Press, copyright © 1951, © 1955, 1979, 1983 by the President and Fellows of Harvard College.

The University Press of Virginia for permission to quote from William Faulkner, *Faulkner in the University*, edited by Frederick L. Gwynn and Joseph Blotner (Charlottesville: University Press of Virginia, reprinted 1977).

McGraw-Hill Book Company for permission to quote from Françoise Gilot and Carlton Lake, *Life with Picasso*, 1964.

Benno Schwabe & Co., Verlag, for permission to quote from Paul Klee, *Das bildnerische Denken* (1956) and to reproduce from the same work Paul Klee's diagram illustrating the dynamics of a line.

Lund Humphries Publishers, Ltd., for permission to quote from Paul Klee, *The Thinking Eye*, edited by Jurg Spiller (1964), and for their concurrence in the reproduction of Paul Klee's diagram illustrating the dynamics of a line.

Chuokoron Bijutsu Shuppan for permission to quote from Tokuzo Masaki, *Hon'ami Gyojoki*, 1965.

Random House, Inc., for permission to quote from Gertrude Stein, *Lectures in America* (1935), and to reprint an excerpt from "In Memoriam, M.A.S." and the complete poem "Air Raid across the Bay at Plymouth" by Stephen Spender, from *Collected Poems: 1928–1953* (1955).

Faber and Faber Publishers for permission to reprint from poems by Stephen Spender the first seven lines from "Seascape. In Memoriam M.A.S." in *Poems of Dedication* (1947) and a revision in *Collected Poems: 1928–1953* (1955); also "Air Raid Across the Bay at Plymouth" in *Collected Poems: 1928–1953* (1955). Faber and Faber has also granted permission to quote extensively from Wallace Stevens, *The Necessary Angel: Essays on Reality and the Imagination* (1951).

Alfred A. Knopf for permission to quote extensively from Wallace Stevens, *The Necessary Angel: Essays on Reality and the Imagination* (1951); and for permission to reprint a seven-line excerpt from "Peter Quince at the Clavier" and a seven-line excerpt from "The Idea of Order at Key West" from *The Collected Poems of Wallace Stevens* (1955).

The Hogarth Press and the Literary Estate of Virginia Woolf for permission to quote from Virginia Woolf, *A Writer's Diary, Being Extracts from the Diary of Virginia Woolf*, edited by Leonard Woolf (1954).

Harcourt Brace Jovanovich, Inc., for permission to quote from Virginia Woolf, *A Writer's Diary, Being Extracts from the Diary of Virginia Woolf*, edited by Leonard Woolf (1954).

Jonathan Cape, Ltd., and the Estate of Robert Frost for permission to reprint "Pertinax" from *The Poetry of Robert Frost*, edited by Edward Connery Lathem (1969).

Holt, Rinehart and Winston, Publishers, for permission to reprint "Pertinax" from *The Poetry of Robert Frost*, edited by Edward Connery Lathem, copyright 1936 by Robert Frost, copyright © 1964 by Lesley Frost Ballantine, copyright © 1969 by Holt, Rinehart and Winston. Reprinted by permission of Holt, Rinehart and Winston, Publishers.

Painting
and Poetry

1

The Painter: Vision and
Transformational Perception

*D*uring his early years in Paris, Ernest Hemingway lived at 74, rue Cardinal Lemoine, just around the corner from Place de la Contrescarpe and only a short distance by way of Place du Panthéon, Rue Soufflot, and the gardens, from the Palais du Luxembourg, which at that time housed the collection of Impressionist paintings later moved to the Jeu de Paume. Habitually, after putting in the allotted time writing in his apartment, he walked to the Palais: "I went there nearly every day for the Cézannes and to see the Manets and the Monets and the other Impressionists that I had first come to know about in the Art Institute at Chicago. I was learning something from the painting of Cézanne that made writing simple true sentences far from enough to make the stories have the dimensions that I was trying to put in them. I was learning very much from him but I was not articulate enough to explain it to anyone. Besides it was a secret."[1] Despite the secrecy, it is fairly obvious he was doing what Gertrude Stein had done some fifteen or sixteen years earlier: learning from Cézanne how to see, how to write—in her words—with his eyes. His aim, implicit here in his word *dimensions*, was stated much more explicitly through the autobiographical Nick Adams: "He wanted to write like Cezanne painted. . . . He, Nick, wanted to write about country so it would be there like Cezanne had done it in painting. You had to do it from inside yourself. There wasn't any trick. Nobody had ever written about country like that. He felt almost holy about it. It was deadly serious. You could do it if you would fight it out. If you'd lived right

23

with your eyes."² As one reads a mature work by Hemingway the question he should ask himself is not the one so often asked—"What did he do?"—but rather the same one with which Hemingway faced Cézanne's canvases: "How did he see?" Rephrased in more general terms, the question is central to the whole relationship between painting and poetry: Precisely how is the artistic vision formed and precisely how does it inform the work of art?

Among his various counsels to the would-be painter, Leonardo included a bit of advice for those moments when the imagination seems to fail, when the spring of invention suddenly, inexplicably, and frighteningly dries up, as it has the distressing habit of doing from time to time: "I shall not fail to include among these precepts a new discovery and aid to reflection which, although it seems a small thing and almost laughable, nevertheless is very useful *stimulating the mind* to various discoveries. This is: look at walls splashed with a number of stains or stones of various mixed colors. If you have to invent some scene, you can see there resemblances to a number of landscapes, adorned in various ways with mountains, rivers, rocks, trees, great plains, valleys and hills. Moreover, you can see various battles and rapid actions of figures, strange expressions on faces, costumes and an infinite number of things which you can reduce to good integrated form."³ Leonardo flattered himself with what he thought was the discovery of something new, but as everyone knows who has seen a figure in a piece of driftwood, a face in the grain of wood or stone, it is a game of human perception not particularly unique to the artist and surely not new at the time Leonardo thought he had discovered it. Some four centuries earlier and a world away, Sung Ti, the eleventh-century Chinese artist, offered a critique of Ch'ên Yung-chih's landscape paintings and with it advice for the improvement of the artistic vision, advice which is the same as that which Leonardo offered:

> The technique in this is very good but there is a want of natural effect. You should choose an old tumbledown wall and throw over it a piece of white silk. Then, morning and evening you should gaze at it until, at length, you can see the ruins through the silk, its prominences, its levels, its zig-zags, and its cleavages, storing them up in your mind and fixing them in your eyes. Make the prominences your mountains, the lower part your water, the hollows your ravines, the cracks your streams, the lighter parts your nearest points, the darker parts your more distant points. Get all these thoroughly into you, and soon you will see men, birds, plants, and trees, flying and moving among them. You may then ply your brush according to your fancy, and the result will be of heaven, not men.⁴

And again a world away, although a century later, Kōetsu Hon'ami recorded in his journal the visit of his friend Shikibu Makanuma (pseud. Shojō Shokado):

> One day Shojoo saw my newly built tea room, and said, filled with wonder, what a variety of bird and animal patterns the walls presented. He always hesitated to ask permission from others to copy such patterns when he happened to notice them on their walls, because he knew these others had no aptitude for painting. "It was good fortune, because this is your house and you, unlike them, have a special taste for painting." And he sojourned one night at my house and throughout the next day was completely absorbed in drawing many different pictures after the wall-patterns. He was so kind as to give me one. I think I have a knack for painting somehow, but am not so good at it as to find like him patterns in a rough wall as a model of what a good painting ought to be. Of course, it has been told from ancient times that pictures appear on rough walls: until then I felt suspicious about it but, by my own experience watching Shojoo copy them from the rough walls of my room, my doubts about it have been dispelled.[5]

Indeed there is ample evidence to show that prehistoric man as much as 35,000 years before the Christian era also knew the device and used it as Leonardo, Sung Ti, and Shojō did to stimulate his imagination in the creation of his cave paintings. In a passage which in several essential respects is remarkably similar to those already cited, Annette Laming-Emperaire describes the cave walls upon which prehistoric man painted the vast majority of his works: "Cette roche jamais préparée, jamais aplanie, est toujours utilisée telle quelle, comme un support presque vivant dans lequel les aspérités, les bosses, les découpures, les corniches, les jeux des creux et des reliefs, loin de gêner l'artiste, l'ont comme guidé et inspiré. Car, c'est la roche, avec ses formes naturelles, évoquant tantôt une croupe, tantôt un ventre, tantôt une trompe, tantôt un animal presque entier, qui souvent semble avoir fait naître la représentation [This rock, never prepared, never smoothed, was always used just as it was, as an almost living support in which irregularities, outcroppings, depressions, ledges, the interplay of hollows and reliefs, far from hampering the artist, guided him as it were and inspired him. For, it is the rock, with its natural forms, evoking sometimes a croup, sometimes a belly, sometimes a trunk, sometimes almost an entire animal, which often seems to have given rise to the representation]."[6]

The stimulating effect of the rock forms upon the imagination of prehistoric man appears, for example, in the remarkable group of

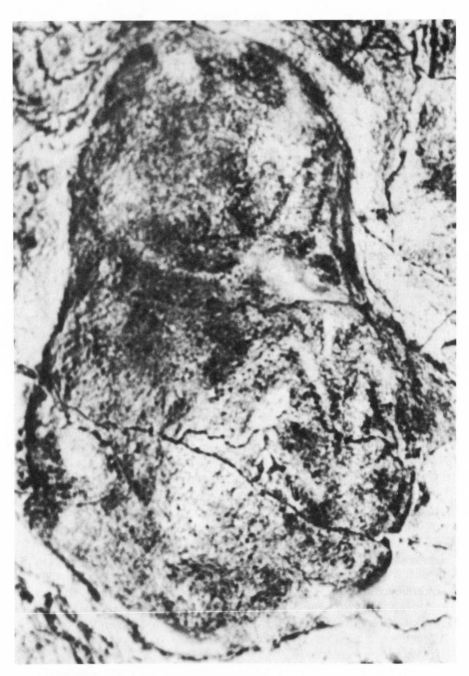

The natural protuberance on the ceiling of Altamira. The original configuration which stimulated the artist's imagination has to some extent been recaptured by means of black and white photography and retouching.

crouching, kneeling, or sleeping bison, painted in polychrome (see color plate), in the grand hall at Altamira. This group had its origin in a cluster of natural protuberances on the ceiling, the forms of which needed but little addition to transform them into the bison now seen. The nature of the percept image experienced by the prehistoric artist becomes more apparent when the artist's additions to one of the protuberances are suppressed by black and white photography and a slight retouching. Another fine example is found not far from Altamira in the cave of El Castillo. At the rear of the principal chamber, on the right-hand wall one finds a stalagmite, the shape of which furnishes the hump, back, and one rear leg of a bison painted in black. That the stalagmite form dictated the bison is clear from the fact that the bison is represented as standing up on its hind legs.[7] Another excellent example is a red-ochre horse in Gallery 3 of Le Portel whose general orientation on the wall, line of the back, hindquarters, and hind leg are furnished by the natural configuration of the rock. In addition, the horse's eye is a rock nodule. In the case of another example, the spotted horses on the left-hand wall of the great chamber in Pech-Merle (see color plate), there is some dispute. Ucko and Rosenfeld assert, "Examples such as the spotted horses at Pech Merle . . . , in which the outline of the rock is said to have formed a first version of the horse's head, whereas the flatwash neck and tiny 'duck-bill' heads were a later addition, are less convincing."[8] That the head-shape is indeed there in the rock shape is quite apparent to any person who looks at the painted panel: the eye of the present-day observer cannot fail to assimilate the head-shaped rock formation into the painted horse, to see the "flatwash neck and tiny 'duck-bill' heads," in the case of the right-hand horse, as mane and forelock. The only question is whether or not prehistoric man so saw it. Failing the testimony of the artist who drew the outlines, one cannot say with assurance insofar as the horse painting itself is concerned. But when one considers the series of black dots outside the body which echo the linear movement of the outlines at belly, forelegs, neck, and chest, it becomes quite apparent that, at least to the prehistoric man who made the dots, the rock-shaped head was indeed part of the composition, for at the jaw, cheek, and muzzle, the dots follow the contours, not of the "flat-wash neck" and "duck-bill head," but of the natural rock-shaped head. Another interesting example is to be found in the Grand Hall of the Bulls at Lascaux, in the figure of the third bull clockwise from the "Unicorn." This painting differs from all the others in the Hall in that the chest and belly have been shaded by pouncing with powdered manganese. When one looks closely one discovers why: discernible within the pounced area is a small brown

bear, its muzzle, forehead, ears, and back formed by the natural irregularities of the rock.

Such examples as these require little or no imagination on the part
of modern man to trace the play of prehistoric man's imagination.
Other instances are less definite, less demonstrable, unless one goes
into the caves with a light similar to that which prehistoric man had, a
feeble and flickering flame. In such instances wherever the faint rays
of the light fall, the cave walls become literally alive, magically transformed on all sides into the shapes of animals: bison, horses, antelopes. Only upon closer examination with, perhaps, a stronger light
does one discover that prehistoric man too had seen at least some of
these shapes and had reinforced the shadow-forms with black and
ochre: ". . . Neither drawing nor photograph can ever do justice to the
evocative power of the rock walls of a cave. Without having spent long
hours at a stretch in Palaeolithic caves examining the surfaces of the
walls by the uncertain gleam of some fitful light and allowing one's
whole being to be overcome by the silence and the dark, it is impossible to realize the extent to which the caves themselves guided the
hands and fired the imaginations of those Quarternary artists. Some
evocative projection, some play of shadow on the rock-face, has often
been a decisive factor in the selection of a subject and its position."[9] At
such moments one feels, through a common imaginative experience,
that inexpressible thrill of a communion which telescopes some
35,000 years of man's time on earth and links the prehistoric with the
modern consciousness in a common humanity. At such moments, one
realizes that in this respect at least prehistoric man was in no essential
way different from oneself and that both, in looking not only at rock
shapes but, like Shakespeare's Antony, at the clouds, are subsumed in
an all-embracing "we":

> Sometime we see a cloud that's dragonish,
> A vapour sometime like a bear or lion,
> A towered citadel, a pendent rock,
> A forkéd mountain, or blue promontory
> With trees upon 't, that nod unto the world
> And mock our eyes with air.
> (*Antony and Cleopatra*, 4.14.2–7)

"We people," so Robert Frost told the students of Amherst, "are thrust
forward out of the suggestions of form in the rolling clouds of nature." The evidence of the cave paintings is that Paleolithic man, too,
was thus thrust forward, and the continuation of Frost's statement

points to the wider significance of the phenomenon of perception visible in the cave paintings: "The artist, the poet, might be expected to be the most aware. . . , but it is really everybody's sanity to feel it and live by it."[10] The cave paintings attest to our common sanity, Paleolithic man's and ours, and unite us in a common consciousness of form which erases time.

One's insight into Paleolithic man's artistic sophistication is deepened by those cave markings called "meanders" or "macaronis," marks formed by running two or three fingers, or a two- or three-pronged instrument over the cave wall in random, convoluted, over-lapping "free forms."[11] Many of them give evidence—since nothing "comprehensible" came of them—either of abortive experiment or merely of the sheer delight which prehistoric man took in the free, undirected sweep and movement of his arm as he made "doodles" on the soft clay walls and ceilings, as, for example, at Rouffignac. Within the tangled lines of others, however, one can discern various forms, as for example in the meanders traced on the ceiling of the great cham-ber at Pech-Merle where one can find several human female repre-sentations and some mammoths. A certain amount of ambiguity is involved in such instances, however, for although undoubtedly the figures are there, present to the perception of a modern viewer, one can not say with certainty that, apparently accidentally formed as they were in the random markings, they ever were perceived by the prehis-toric man who made the marks. But in two other instances, a delibera-tion on the part of the artist is much more clearly perceivable. At Gargas, in the course of making random marks, or impelled by ran-dom marks already present, the artist set about making the head of a bovine creature, using the same finger-trace technique as for the other marks in the same area of the cave. At La Baume-Latrone, the "meanders" are in a different technique: instead of finger-tracings in soft clay, the artist here dipped his fingers in a liquid colored with red ochre and swept them across the rock face. The results are quite interesting, for they seem to combine the characteristics of the marks at Pech-Merle ("found" figures, but no assurance that prehistoric man found them) and at Gargas (a constructed figure made in the same finger-tracing technique as adjacent meanders): The prehistoric artist at La Baume-Latrone, in the process of making free-flowing lines on the cave walls, developed from the marks so made the forms of sev-eral mammoths. The animals are considerably distorted because of their "found" quality, but they are recognizable (see color plate). An even more striking instance of such found figure development is at Altamira: on the ceiling of the right-hand gallery, a prehistoric artist made a rather extensive field of meanders and then, as a consequence of these marks, either he or some subsequent artist found near the right end of the field a quite accidental linear formation suggestive of a bull's head. A few additional touches sufficed to provide the tip of the muzzle and the nostril, a better delineation of the eye, and a horn which, since it crosses over all other lines in its course, was obviously the last stroke in that portion of the drawing.[12] This bull's head is a clear-cut instance of meanders functioning as a stimulus for the artist's imagination in a manner identical to the stimulation provided by the suggestive rock formations in the examples described earlier.

The "meander" technique at either La Baume-Latrone or Altamira is even more remarkably modern in that it anticipates by some thirty millennia the essence of Max Ernst's *frottage* technique, which, according to his own account, Ernst "discovered" quite by accident: ". . . Happening to be at a seaside inn in wet weather I was struck by the way the floor, its grain accentuated by many scrubbings, obsessed my nervously excited gaze. So I decided to explore the symbolism of the obsession, and to encourage my powers of meditation and hallucination I took a series of drawings from the floorboards by dropping pieces of paper on them at random and then rubbing the paper with blacklead. As I looked carefully at the drawings that I got in this way—some dark, others smudgily dim—I was surprised by the sudden heightening of my visionary powers. . . ."[13] The random samples of wood-grain pattern obtained with the rubbings served to stimulate Ernst's imagination as the meanders at Altamira did the prehistoric artist's. Max Ernst was as convinced as Leonardo that he had made a new discovery, but not only Leonardo, prehistoric man, Sung Ti and Shojō, but also Victor Hugo had made the "discovery" before him. Hugo's awareness of the technique is evident, for example, in a letter to Paul Foucher, written while Hugo was vacationing at his uncle's farm, La Miltière, at Sologne in 1825: "Je suis pour le moment dans une salle de verdure attenante à la Miltière; le lierre qui en garnit les parois jette sur mon papier des ombres découpées dont je t'envoie le dessin, puisque tu désires que ma lettre contienne quelque chose de pittoresque. Ne va pas rire de ces lignes bizarres jetées comme au hasard sur l'autre côté de la feuille. Aie un peu d'imagination. Suppose tout ce dessin tracé par le soleil et l'ombre et tu verras quelque chose de charmant. Voilà comment procèdent des fous qu'on appelle les poètes [I am for the moment in a room of greenery adjacent to La Miltière; the ivy which furnishes the walls throws on my paper sharp cut shadows, the drawing of which I send to you because you wish my letter to contain something picturesque. Don't set yourself to laughing at these strange lines thrown as by hazard on the reverse side of this sheet. Use a little imagination. Suppose the whole drawing traced by the sun and shadow and you will see something charming. That is how they operate, the madmen called poets]."[14] Hugo also, in his own version of the "meander field" technique, deliberately created the "meander field" to establish the conditions necessary for the finding of forms. In what in essence is a version of the Rorschach ink-blots, Hugo spent hours splotching ink on paper either with random movements of a fully loaded pen or by folding the paper across a blot, "finding" the consequent form, and then elaborating it with additional pen strokes more deliberately controlled. The literally hundreds of such drawings preserved at the Bibliothèque Nationale and the Maison de Victor Hugo on the Place des Vosges, in Paris, attest to the seriousness with which he applied himself to this procedure. But, of course, this technique of meander field creation was not new with Hugo. According to Leonardo, Botticelli used the device in a slightly different form in order to create landscapes: reportedly he would throw a paint-filled sponge against a wall to find in the resulting splotch a fine landscape which then could be developed to a painting.[15] And the English landscapist Alexander Cozens, from whom, indeed, Hugo may have learned his technique, published a book in 1765 entitled *A New Method of Assisting the Invention in Drawing Original Compositions of Landscape.* The "new" method was the use of ink-blots and the finding of forms in the random marks thus made.

One is tempted to suppose that prehistoric man, like Hugo, Botticelli, or Cozens made his meander fields with equal deliberation, but unfortunately none of the prehistoric artists has left any sign through which his intentions may be clearly read: if he had, the study of the cave paintings would be considerably easier. One could, indeed, argue that the infrequency of forms unquestionably developed from meander fields strongly suggests a lack of deliberation: If prehistoric man generally knew the technique, why did he not use it more frequently? A possible answer is that the already present meander field of the rock walls themselves was sufficient. Indeed, one could build an at least superficially valid thesis to the effect that the deliberately created meander field increases in frequency with the shift from such grounds as cave walls to those of paper and stretched canvas. In any event, although the technique is visible as far back as the cave paintings, it is not commented upon as a deliberate technique until the modern era, and the movement in painting known as *Tachisme* or "Action Painting" elevates it to the level of dogma.

The extent to which Picasso was dependent upon such "found"

forms is evident in his astonishment that marble ever became a medium for art:

> It seems strange to me that we ever arrived at the idea of making statues from marble. I understand how you can see something in the root of a tree, a crevice in a wall, a corroded bit of stone, or a pebble. . . . But marble? It stands there like a block, suggesting no form or image. It doesn't inspire. How could Michelangelo have seen his *David* in a block of marble? If it occurred to man to create his own images, it's because he discovered them all around him, almost formed, already within his grasp. He saw them in a bone, in the irregular surfaces of cavern walls, in a piece of wood. . . .[16]

The nature of "inspiration" manifest in Picasso's comment and in the history of art from prehistory to the present day is most succinctly stated in Georges Braque's famous words, "The senses deform, the mind forms." But, as the evidence of the meander field indicates, Braque's statement gives only a middle and a terminal step in the creative process. The process begins with a recept image: the cave wall *as cave wall*, illuminated by prehistoric man's flickering lamp, or the meanders or doodles traced by his fingers on the walls—again *as meanders or doodles,* or Leonardo's, Sung Ti's, or Shojō's walls or Hugo's leaf shadows or ink-blots: all of these as objects Absolute in Emily Dickinson's terms in a poem focused upon precisely this stage in the process:

> Perception of an object costs
> Precise the Object's loss—
> Perception in itself a Gain
> Replying to its Price—
> The object Absolute—is nought—
> Perception sets it fair
> And then upbraids a Perfectness
> That situates so far—

> (Poem #J1071)

At this point presumably all elements in the receptible environment which can possibly register are present to the retinae as potential stimuli. In the next stage, the formation of the percept image, some of the elements of the object Absolute are filtered out, others retained in a selection-construction process governed to a great extent by a memory image. In the present context memory images of "cave wall," "meander," "stained wall," "leaf-shadow," or "ink-blot" rise to fuse with the recept images of the corresponding objects Absolute to form the meander fields which seem to be objectively present to the senses.

Almost simultaneously, but nevertheless clearly a separate and subsequent step, occurs what may best be termed a "transformational perception." That is to say, certain elements of the percept image are reperceived as, potentially, elements of something else which the present percept definitely is not. In the case, for example, of that one rock protuberance at Altamira, all in being perceived as rock protuberance in its totality of receptible and perceived elements, it is also, as a consequence, perceived as containing in its contour a portion which is transformable into hump, back line, and rump of a bison in a certain position; an adjacent crack in the ceiling is equally perceived as transformable into neck and a portion of the head in outline; a segment of another crack is potentially the muzzle, while two arclike indentations allow transformations into shoulder and haunch. In the transformational stage, then, elements, but not the whole, of the perception are recognized (*re*-cognized) as potentially portions or elements in another image, another memory image, of a distinctly different order of objects Absolute: the form fragments of the percept are seen as transferable to sections of a transformational memory image, based on another order of percepts. It is important to remember at this point that although now the artist's attention is focused upon the transformable elements, the contrary or useless elements of the percept are still present to his senses: the artist has merely chosen to ignore them. The transformational stage thus merges almost imperceptibly into the deformational stage, the first half of Georges Braque's "the senses deform, the mind forms."

Only after the percept has thus been reduced to scattered and disjointed transformable form fragments is the artist's imagination ready to proceed with the next step, in which, as Braque asserts, "the mind forms." For, once abstracted from the percept, the form fragments must now be reassembled with other elements from the image memory to form the artistic image. Georges Rouault speaks of this stage of the creative process when he says, "In truth, I have painted by opening my eyes day and night on the perceptible world, and also by closing them from time to time that I might better see the vision blossom and submit itself to orderly arrangement."[17] Henri Matisse rather clearly describes the process from perception through the deformation to the reformation in his description of how he accomplished the painting of a woman's body: "J'ai à peindre un corps de femme; d'abord, j'en réfléchis la forme en moi-même, je lui donne de la grâce, un charme, et il s'agit de lui donner quelque chose de plus. Je vais condenser la significance de ce corps, en recherchant ses lignes essentielles. Le charme sera moins apparent au premier regard, mais

il devra se dégager à la longue de la nouvelle image que j'aurai ob-
tenue, et qui aura une signification plus large, plus pleinement
humaine [I am to paint a woman's body; first, I reflect her form
within me, I give grace to it, charm, and there is also the question of
giving something further. I am going to condense the signification of
this body, in seeking out its essential lines. The charm will be less
apparent at first glance, but it cannot fail to emerge in good time from
the new image which I will obtain, a new image which will have a
larger, more fully human significance]."[18] Such testimony and the visible traces of the process in the cave paintings, especially the drawings
developed from meanders, attest to the essential truth in Bachelard's
definition of the imaginative process: "On veut toujours que l'imagination soit la faculté de *former* des images. Or elle est plutôt la faculté
de *déformer* les images fournies par la perception, elle est surtout la
faculté de nous libérer des images premières, de *changer* les images.
S'il n'y a pas changement d'images, union inattendue des images, il
n'y a pas imagination, il n'y a pas d'*action imaginante* [Always one
would have it that the imagination is the faculty of *forming* images. But
it is rather the faculty of *deforming* the images furnished by perception; it is above all the faculty of liberating ourselves from the initial
images, of *altering* images. If there is no change in the images, no
unanticipated union of images, there is no imagination, there is no
imaginative process]."[19]

The artist's image memory, then, is the decisive factor in the transformation of a percept into an artistic image: the deformation and the
reformation—the alteration and the unanticipated union of images—
are achieved by means of the image memory operating simultaneously in two separate orders of memory images, for it is not the
rock protuberance itself which becomes bison—this would be hallucination—but rather the memory image of certain form fragments
from the rock protuberance. This image fuses with the schematized
memory image "bison." At this stage the operation has shifted from
an interplay between receptible environment and the psyche to an
interplay of images within the painter's consciousness, a fact amply
illustrated by the emphasis placed by artists upon training the image
memory and relying upon it rather than upon observation at precisely
this stage in the formation of the work of art. This essential image
interplay is the *raison d'être* in the best art instruction for the exhaustive training in drawing from models, in learning the anatomy not just
of the human figure but of the whole world: so that one is not com-
pelled to run to look again at a bison for assurance that a portion of
rock contour indeed resembles hump, spine, and rump. "Par coeur!

Par coeur! [By heart! By heart!]" Delacroix was fond of exclaiming and thus said as much as Sabartés and Brassaï in their long conversation about Picasso's image memory. Sabartés commented first on the fact that Picasso's memory for the forms of the world about him was so good that he no longer needed models. "He knows them all by heart—their contours, their singularities, everything that makes them unique." Agreeing with him, Brassaï suggested that Picasso's image memory reminded him of Balzac, who also was "so impregnated" with the forms of the world that he, too, had no need "to document" himself to create his characters. Sabartés found the comparison a just one: "Yes, your comparison with Balzac seems right to me. With Picasso too, it's a matter of an extraordinary impregnation. At any instant all the forms of the real are at his disposition. What he has seen once, he retains forever. But he himself does not know when and how it may take form again. So when he places the point of a pen or a pencil on the paper, he never knows what will appear. . . ."[20] This "extraordinary impregnation"—happy phrase—gives birth to both orders of memory images (rock protuberance and bison) which rise in the artist's consciousness to meet and merge in the moment's transformational perception. It is the source, too, of that "idea of the object" which for Picasso made abstract art impossible: "There is no abstract art. You must always start with something. Afterward you can remove all traces of reality. There's no danger then, anyway, because the idea of the object will have left an indelible mark. It is what started the artist off, excited his ideas, and stirred up his emotions." The concept expressed by the phrase "idea of the object" is a complex one to which we will later return; for the moment, insofar as it constitutes in one aspect an "explanation of the object," it is the manifestation of that "real memory" to which Matisse refers in a context parallel to that of Picasso's remark: "On peut dire . . . qu'aujourd'hui s'il n'est plus besoin, en peinture, d'expliquer par la constitution physique il est pourtant nécessaire qu'un artiste qui exprime l'objet par synthèse tout en ayant l'air de s'en écarter ait *en lui,* porte *en lui,* l'explication de cet objet. Il doit finir par l'oublier nécessairement mais, je le répète, il faut qu'il ait profond *en lui,* le souvenir réel de cet objet et des réactions de cet objet dans son esprit [One may say . . . that today, if it is no longer necessary in painting to explain by physical constitution it is nevertheless necessary that an artist who expresses the object by synthesis, even while appearing to deviate from it, have *within himself,* carry *within himself,* the explanation of that object. He must end, necessarily, in forgetting it, but I repeat, he must have deep *within himself,* the real memory of that object and of the reactions of that object in his mind]."[21] The two comments lead deep within the artistic imagination, close to that point where distinctions between poetry and painting cease to exist and only artistic vision remains.

But for the moment, still pursuing the insights afforded by painting, it is necessary to notice one last factor in the formation of the artistic image. Speaking of the artist's percept and of what should be done with it, Georges Braque said, "The goal is not to be concerned with the *reconstitution* of an anecdotal fact, but with *constitution* of a pictorial fact."[22] The comment as reaffirmation of those by Picasso and Matisse adds nothing to our insight, but one may, as well, apply it to the schematized memory image which rises to meet the form fragments from the percept. That is, the second-order image (e.g., bison) evoked by the percept and toward which the form fragments tend in transformational perception is not evoked in a reconstitution of itself. Instead it too undergoes a deformation and transformation in a movement toward the transformational elements of the percept. Both images move from sources in their individual orders toward an unanticipated union which, for reasons to be discussed fully in later chapters, is best described as occurring on a "surreal" plane—in the case of Braque, Matisse, Picasso, the canvas surface; in the case of the prehistoric artist, the cave wall. Again, the rock protuberance at Altamira furnishes a clear and visible illustration: The rock, as already noted, needs a suppression of some of its elements, an emphasis upon others, and some additions in order to become the form of a bison. But—and at this point most important—the memory image of a bison needs modification in order to fit the transformational form fragments provided by the outcropping: bison and other bovines do not normally kneel or crouch in the fashion depicted—the contours are those of a bison, but the position itself is more the rest position of either a dog or a cat.[23] Indeed, the neck of a bison is not long enough to permit its flection downward and backward to the extent that the jaw may rest upon the knees of the forelegs. And one must assume that the prehistoric artist, dependent for his very survival upon his knowledge of the animals around him, was fully aware of, and accepted with equanimity, such a deviation from anecdotal fact. The point is even more obvious in such cases as the stalagmite in El Castillo which likewise was transformed into a bison: again some elements of the rock form, retained in the artist's vision, become head, hump, back, rump, and hind leg; other elements were suppressed, as for example, an extension of the stalagmite which would make a good feline tail but which was ignored in favor of a paint-supplied bison's tail, and other elements were added, elements derived from the memory image of a bison. But, because of the total configuration of the stalagmite, the bison must of necessity be represented as standing upright on its hind legs. Again the memory image of a bison has undergone a certain amount of deformation in order to move toward the percept image. Such evidence as this is infinitely more significant for the study of the artistic image than is the stylization characteristic of any one movement in art, such as cubism, or the modifications necessitated by the characteristics of the medium itself, for it permits the direct observation of the artistic image in formation. It also, as a consequence, permits a fairly precise definition of the artistic image, which, thus, is a composite image resulting from the fusion of transformable form elements in a percept image with transformable form elements in a memory image of a different order of objects, the fusion occurring under a transformational impulse in the artist of sufficient strength to remove the composite image to a plane clearly detached from the "real" of the receptible environment. The same image fusion is discernible in van Gogh's account of how he discovered the flesh tone which appears in the *Potato-Eaters.* He had been working from the models and in doing so had used the "academic" flesh-tone mix of white with yellow and red ochres, but this color proved to be much too light. To correct the flaw, he set to work from memory and the result was a "flesh-tone" which he recognized as the color of potatoes: "I have painted this *from memory on the picture itself.* In the picture I give free scope to my own head in the sense of *thought* or imagination, which is not the case in studies where no creative process is allowed, but where one finds food for one's imagination in reality, in order to make it exact. This is the second time that a saying by Delacroix has meant much to me: the first time it was his theory about colours; now it is his theory about the *creation* of a picture. He pretended that the best pictures are made from memory. 'Par coeur!' he said."[24] The reciprocal centripetal movement of the transformable elements imparts to the artistic image its distinctive quality in contradistinction to the simple memory or percept image.

In a letter to Anton Ridder van Rappard, written while he was still in his dependency upon the model—before, that is, he had learned fully the lesson in Delacroix's "Par coeur!"—van Gogh described the creative process as he was then experiencing it and in the process recorded his discovery of how his subject could move from anecdotal to pictorial fact. The description begins, if one rearranges the comments to put them in order of occurrence, with an indication of what is best termed the "meander" stage of the process: "I am very much pleased to have you notice that of late I have been trying to express the values of crowds, and that I try to separate things in the dizzy whirl and chaos one can see in each little corner of Nature."[25] The separation of elements from the dizzy whirl and chaos involves a feeling which van Gogh calls "the feeling of my subject," a feeling which may be drawn in several variations, each modeled from nature: "When I once get *the feeling of my subject,* and get to know it, I usually draw it in three or more variations—be it a figure or a landscape— only I always refer to Nature for every one of them and then I do my best not to put in *any detail,* as the dream quality would then be lost. . . ."[26] The separation of a subject from the meander field, then, not only isolates a feeling of the subject but also involves several selections of form fragments from which to constitute the three or more variations. These variations entail as well suppressions of definitive details—the deformative process—in order to preserve a "dream quality." At this point, an earlier comment in the letter becomes apropos: "I *seldom work from memory.* . . . When I have a model who is quiet and steady and with whom I am acquainted, then I draw repeatedly till there is one drawing that is different from the rest, which does not look like an ordinary study, but more typical and with more feeling."[27] The suppression of definitive, particularizing detail, then, permits the formulation of the "drawing that is different from the rest," the "more typical" drawing, the drawing which, no longer anecdotal fact, is now pictorial fact. "HOW IT HAPPENS [sic] THAT I CAN EXPRESS SOMETHING OF THAT KIND?" van Gogh asks and answers, "because the thing has already taken form in my mind before I start on it. The first attempts are absolutely unbearable. I say this because I want you to know that if you see something worth while in what I am doing, it is not by accident but because of real intention and purpose."[28] Thus van Gogh's account reveals again the level of artistic vision and the unanticipated union *(union inattendue)* of images of which Bachelard speaks. It reveals as well the paradoxical nature of the union, that it both embodies and is under the impulsion of that feeling which is the indissoluble link between motif and emotion, that "typified" feeling which shapes the vision before the artist even begins to shape the art object.

Here, then, is the *typos* at the heart of the artistic vision, that which is both the striking or the impressing and, simultaneously, the imaging, the modeling: what Picasso called, as we have seen, "the idea of the object [which] has left an ineffaceable imprint . . . [,] the thing that aroused the artist, stimulated his ideas, stirred his emotions." In this context, Picasso's phrase "idea of the object" immediately evokes Émile Bernard's *"synthètisme,"* a descriptive label both for the art movement of which Bernard was champion and for the essence of the artistic process as Bernard saw it, best exemplified in Gauguin's pictorial facts, his *cloisonnisme*. Behind, inextricably embodied in, the synthesis which is the art object, is the synthesis of images, Bachelard's unanticipated union of images again, and the "idea of the object" as form:

> Puisque l'idée est la forme des choses recueillies par l'imagination, il fallait peindre non plus devant la chose, mais en la reprenant dans l'imagination, qui l'avait recueillie, qui en conservait l'idée, ainsi l'idée de la chose apportait la forme convenable au sujet du tableau ou plutôt à son idéal. . . . La mémoire ne retient pas tout, mais ce qui frappe l'esprit. Donc formes et couleurs devenaient simples dans une égale unité. En peignant de mémoire, j'avais l'avantage d'abolir l'inutile complication des formes et des tons. Il restait un schéma du spectacle regardé [Because the idea is the form of things gathered by the imagination, it was no longer necessary to paint before the object, but instead to recapture it in the imagination, which had gathered it, which preserved the idea, thus the idea of the object brought the form suitable to the subject of the painting or rather to its ideal. . . . Memory does not retain all, but only what strikes the spirit. Thus forms and colors became simplified in an even unity. Painting from memory, I had the advantage of abolishing the useless complications of forms and tones. There remained a schema of the scene viewed].[29]

One must not fail to notice the reiteration here of Coleridge's caution that the word *idea*, "in its original sense as used by Pindar, Aristophanes, and in the gospel of St. Matthew, represented the visual abstraction of a distant object, when we see the whole without distinguishing its parts."[30] Nor must one fail to notice the affirmation here that the artist's "ideas" are of a vastly different order from the ideas of the philosopher or the psychologist. The idea of the object is the form of the artistic vision, what Max Ernst called the "first cause." In describing how he discovered "frottage," he said, "I was struck by the way the floor, its grain accentuated by many scrubbings obsessed . . . my gaze." As already noted, he scattered sheets of paper randomly about the floor and took rubbings: "I stress the fact that, through a series of suggestions and transmutations arrived at spontaneously like hypnotic visions, drawings obtained in this way lose more and more of the character of the material being explored (wood, for instance). They begin to appear as the kind of unexpectedly clear images most likely to throw light on the first cause of the obsession, or at least to provide a substitute for it."[31] If one makes adequate allowance for the specifically Freudian bias which Ernst intends behind the word *obses-*

sion, one nevertheless finds oneself at what is indeed the "first cause" of the art object, at what is in Paul Klee's words "the cosmogenetic moment, . . . a point in chaos . . . concentrated in principle . . . [which] lends this point a concentric character of the primordial. The order thus created radiates from it in all directions [Der kosmogenetische Moment ist da. Die Feststellung eines Punktes im Chaos, der, prinzipiell konzentriert, nur grau sein kann, verleiht diesem Punkte konzentrischen Urcharakter. Von ihm strahlt die somit erweckte Ordnung nach allen Dimensionen aus]."[32]

2
The Poet: Vision and Transformational Perception

*H*orace's *ut pictura poesis* has been echoed across the centuries in many different ways by both painters and poets. One finds it, for example, in the advice which Antoine Coypel gave in his discourse before L'Académie Royale de Peinture et de Sculpture (1741): "The painter in the grand manner must be a poet; I do not say that he must write poetry, for one may do that without being a poet; but I say that not only must he be filled with the same spirit that animates poetry, but he must of necessity know its rules, which are the same as those of painting. . . . Painting must do for the eyes what poetry does for the ears."[1] One finds it as well in a comment by Picasso recalled by Françoise Gilot: "Painting is poetry and is always written in verse with plastic rhymes, never in prose."[2] From the poets' side Horace finds a modern voice in Wallace Stevens, who asserts, "No poet can have failed to recognize how often a detail, à propos or remark, in respect to painting applies also to poetry. The truth is that there seems to exist a corpus of remarks in respect to painting, most often the remarks of painters themselves, which are as significant to poets as to painters."[3]

The precise nature of the complementarity is adumbrated by what is surely the most durable of all artistic precepts. Four centuries before the *ut pictura poesis* of Horace, Simonides is reputed to have said painting is silent poetry and poetry, speaking painting. The durability of the precept is measured by echoes to be found in the words of Leonardo da Vinci in the fifteenth century and of e. e. cummings in the twentieth. Leonardo wrote, "Painting is a poetry that is seen and

41

not heard and poetry is a painting which is heard and not seen."[4] e. e. cummings, who was himself both an accomplished painter and a poet, characterized himself in his preface to *CIOPW* as an "author of pictures, draughtsman of words" and described the process of creation as "hearing such paintings, seeing such poems." It is indeed this complementarity which was dramatically present in the rich interplay between painter and poet in the relationship between Picasso and Gertrude Stein, an interplay out of which she evolved her own extension of Simonides' precept: "A writer should write with his eyes, and a painter paint with his ears."[5]

The intimacy of the link between painting and poetry is most immediately manifest in the shared vocabulary of the two arts: a novelist as well as a painter "sketches." For example, in describing how he handled the characters in *Fathers and Sons*, Turgenev wrote, "Let me say one thing: I sketched these characters as I would have sketched mushrooms, leaves, or trees; they hurt my eyes and I began to draw."[6] In this respect, Russian and French parallel the English of Washington Irving, for example, with his title *The Sketch Book*. Painter and poet share such words as *delineate, portrait, landscape, draw*—the point is so obvious it hardly needs demonstration. To be sure, one may object that such a vocabulary is, insofar as poetry is concerned, little more than an affectation which becomes almost too evident in Irving's pseudonym, Geoffrey Crayon, an affectation which is at best but "figurative," suggestive of no more than Stephen Spender's analogy with the word *palette* when he says of the poet, "He should be able to think in images, he should have as great a mastery of language as a painter has over his palette. . . ."[7] But the evidence afforded by artists who were both painter and poet or poet and painter indicates that the shared vocabulary reflects something much more immediate and direct than similitude or mere "manner of speaking." A great many Western artists have on occasion dabbled in the sister art; Turgenev, for example, had a facility for quick pen-and-ink portraits which the German journalist and illustrator Ludwig Pietsch described appreciatively:

> He had the ability to draw forth from his imagination and put down on paper—in simple outline, without faltering or correcting— human profiles, especially men's, which were extraordinarily lifelike and showed a great consistency of formal development and the sharp imprint of a definite individuality, a firmly pronounced personality.[8]

But despite the traces of it in his comments about the character-portraits in *Fathers and Sons*, such drawing as drawing always remained for Turgenev a pastime: For the serious work of artistic expression, he much preferred sketching with words. Similarly Pablo Picasso dabbled in literature, writing a *jeu d'esprit,* the play entitled *Le Désir attrapé par la queue,* in a French which strongly resembles Gertrude Stein's "cubistic" English poetry or prose. Although its first—and apparently only—production, a private one at Picasso's apartment in Paris on 16 June 1944, was highly auspicious, directed as it was by Albert Camus and numbering in its cast such figures as Jean-Paul Sartre and Simone de Beauvoir, there is no indication that the pen as writing instrument ever seriously threatened to replace Picasso's brush and paint box. With others, however, the attraction of the sister art has been much stronger, attaining sometimes the intensity of a first love as in the case of Thackeray or John Updike, both of whom studied painting at some length and for a time, at least, seriously envisaged a career as painter before turning instead to literature. Victor Hugo exhibited a tendency in the opposite direction: although writing, his first love, remained dominant throughout his life, he also sketched and drew with an intensity and mastery that imparted to many of his drawings a permanent artistic value. Théophile Gautier could rightly say of him, "If he were not a poet, Victor Hugo would be a painter of the first order. . . ."[9] Similarly, D. H. Lawrence turned to painting, apparently with as much seriousness as Hugo, after having thoroughly established his credentials as a novelist—with, as a result, "enormous profit" for his artistic vision: "I not only acquired a considerable technical skill in handling water-colour . . . ; but also I developed my visionary awareness. And I believe one can only develop one's visionary awareness by close contact with the vision itself: that is, by knowing pictures, real vision pictures, and by dwelling on them, and really dwelling in them."[10]

Lawrence's comment is directly applicable to the thesis and strategy suggested here, for it is the vision itself which is the essential, the necessary link between painting and poetry, a point upon which Wyndham Lewis was categorical: When asked by Louise Morgan if his painting helped him in his writing, he replied, "It must of course do that. The habit of thinking of things in plastic and pictorial terms must have its influence upon the writer's art, when you practice both as I do. First of all I *see!* The first—and last—thing that I do is to use my eyes."[11] That which Lewis asserts and which his own artistic career illustrates is even more directly exemplified by the careers of such painter-poets as Dante Gabriel Rossetti or, ultimately, by William Blake, for whom the words *painter* or *poet* no longer have meaning, so inextricably mingled are the two modes of expression. All, indeed, that one can say of Blake is that he was a *seer.* His art is neither painting nor poetry but vision, a word which indeed was his other word for imagination: "The Nature of Visionary Fancy, or Imagination, is very little Known, & the Eternal nature & permanence of its ever Existent Images is consider'd as less permanent than the things of Vegetative & Generative Nature; yet the Oak dies as well as the Lettuce, but Its Eternal Image & Individuality never dies, but renews by its seed; just so the Imaginative Image returns by the seed of Contemplative Thought; the Writings of the Prophets illustrate these conceptions of the Visionary Fancy by their various sublime & Divine Images as seen in the Worlds of Vision."[12]

Blake's art—even if Blake were the only artist to have practiced it—would be sufficient proof of the link between painting and poetry. But other artists, both painters and poets, have practiced the same art and, more important, have through their comments brought greater insight into the phenomenon which is the art of William Blake. Matisse expressed the relationship between the two arts with the word *équivalent* and exemplified his understanding in the books which he designed, or better, "painted," so that the totality of the book, the print as form, the white space of the pages, the drawings and the sense of the words, all combine to form, like the chapel at Vence, a single and whole work: His editions of Mallarmé's poetry, the *Pasiphaé* of Montherlant, *Visages, Poésies de Ronsard,* James Joyce's *Ulysses,* the *Poèmes* of Charles d'Orléans, *Le Requin et la mouette* are examples of a total art. What he attempted in such works appears in a comment addressed to Raymond Escholier: "Je trouve juste votre distinction du livre illustré et du livre décoré. Le livre ne doit pas avoir besoin d'être complété par une illustration imitatrice. Le peintre et l'écrivain doivent agir ensemble, sans confusion, mais parallèlement. Le dessin doit être un équivalent plastique du poème. Je ne dirai pas: 1er violon and 2e violon, mais un ensemble concertant [I find correct your distinction between the illustrated book and the decorated book. The book must not have need of completion by an imitative illustration. The painter and the writer must act together, without confusion, but in parallel. The drawing must be a plastic equivalent of the poem. I will not say 1st violin and 2nd violin, but a concerted *ensemble*]."[13] The phrase "concerted *ensemble*," a first and second violin playing in concert, expresses with beautiful exactitude what, at least according to Elizabeth Sewell, Ezra Pound accomplished in Cantos LI to LXXXIV through the interweaving of a defining text and various Chinese ideographs: "All this could have been said in words, our Western kind of words, I mean. Pound, however, adds the ideograms at this point, as if to compel us to look at figuring in the form of image, not just at concept or principle. The figure is not a picture or illustration; it is part of the process which is going on, the operation of the poetic mind, where image, idea and language do their work together."[14] To be sure, as Cyril Birch has pointed out, "The picturesqueness of Chinese script forms tends to impress itself more vividly on the foreign student than on the native," and "Ezra Pound is the egregious example of the translator who, overconscious of elements still visible in the script, attempts to incorporate whole etymologies into the English realization of a Chinese word."[15] But, as dubious as such a procedure may be from a scholarly standpoint, Pound's emphasis upon the graphic quality of Chinese writing and upon what we might call "image etymologies" reveals his understanding of the "concerted *ensemble*" which word and drawing make. Nor is Pound's procedure as far removed from the spirit of Chinese art as his unscholarly etymologies might make it seem, for it is the pictorial aspect of calligraphy which in Chinese and Japanese art links painting and poetry. The point is perhaps best illustrated with the more purely Japanese calligraphy, the *Wayo* style, as practiced by such masters as Kōetsu Hon'ami, Konoe Nobutada, and Shojō Shokado who, in the early Edo period, brought Japanese calligraphy to its peak of artistic perfection. Their art consisted of a blending of painting, poetry, and writing, the writing at once embodying the poetry and participating in the painting. Kōetsu, for example, to produce one of his calligraphic works, began with a paper made to his own specifications on which he painted in silver and gold pigments a ground decoration complementary to the poem to be written. Upon this ground he then disposed the characters and lines of the poem, using primarily the Japanese *kana* (cursive characters) instead of the more rigid *kanji* (Chinese characters), in such a manner that visually the characters and lines of the poem blended with the ground painting, the whole effect further enhanced by a careful modulation of line and intensity of ink in the formation of the characters. The difference between this (see color plate) and the purely ornamental use of *kana*, especially the *hiragana*, in the *uta-e* (literally, "poem picture") is precisely the distinction which Matisse made between the decorated and the illustrated book. The *uta-e* is one variety of a style of landscape painting called *ashide* (literally, "reed hand") in which a riverside or lakeside scene containing reeds displays a text, some of whose characters, written to resemble reeds, are mingled with the depicted reeds and participate in the representation. As this style developed, characters were similarly used to represent the streaks of a current in the water, birds, rocks, and so forth.[16] But such an ornamental use of the characters exploits the purely representational at the expense of the compositional. The great calligraphic artists avoided this imbalance in a perfect interweaving of painting and word—the word both as form and sign—in a total signification. Insofar as the poem is writing *(graphē)* and the painting is drawing (also *graphē)* and the two together constitute *kallos* (beauty), the result is *calligraphy.* Ezra Pound, for all his errors in etymology, was true to the Oriental sense of art, and his use of the ideogram as a graphic complement to his word-images both corroborates and illustrates the *équivalence* of the two arts, an *équivalence* directly expressed by the Chinese painter who in describing his activity habitually speaks not of "painting" but of "writing" a picture.[17]

The meeting of poetry and painting in a calligraphic complementarity fully justifies Picasso's interchange of the verbs *write* and *paint* when he declared, "after all the arts are all the same; you can write a picture in words just as you can paint sensations in a poem."[18] Indeed, according to Jaime Sabartés, Picasso maintained that "if I were born Chinese, I should not be a painter, but a calligrapher. I should write my pictures."[19] Although perhaps less succinct, Henry James was no less definite: ". . . The analogy between the art of the painter and the art of the novelist is, so far as I am able to see, complete. Their inspiration is the same, their process (allowing for the different quality of the vehicle) is the same, their success is the same. They may learn from each other, they may explain and sustain each other."[20] The words "explain and sustain," in the context of complementarity, permit a greater precision in understanding that assertion by Vlaminck which so misled Etienne Gilson: "When a picture can be explained, when it can be made to be understood or felt, by means of words, it has nothing to do with painting." Gilson derived from Vlaminck's remark the proposition that "it is as impossible to paint by means of words as it is to speak by means of paintings."[21] But the essence of the matter is that although the one art may through its complementarity "explain" the other by means of an equivalency, it may never *substitute* for the other. The image in James's word *sustain* illustrates the point: one must see the two arts as two stems of the same plant equivalent but not identical, each stem transmitting sustenance through the common root system to the other. The image reveals a truth about painting and poetry which is already implicit in the discussion of the word *calligraphy.* A common error, to which Gilson fell victim, holds that painting is a plastic art allied with sculpture; the evidence is that it is one of the two complementary forms of writing, more precisely of *graphē.* The distinction here is that which informs Paul Klee's discrimination between material and ideal means in art: Material means are for sculpture; ideal means are for painting and poetry. The word *ideal,* it should be noted, involves the same figural whole which Coleridge found behind the word *idea*. For the painter:

> The choice of means should be undertaken with great restraint. This, more than profusion of means, makes for orderly intelligence. Material means (wood, metal, glass, etc.): massive use of material means is above all to be avoided here.
>
> Ideal means (line, tone, value, color): ideal means are preferable. They are not free from matter; if they were, it would be impossible to "write" with them. When I write the word wine with ink, the ink does not play the primary role but makes possible the permanent fixation of the concept wine. Thus ink helps us to obtain permanent wine. The word and the picture, that is, word-making and form-building are one and the same.
>
> [Die Wahl der Mittel ist in letzter Beschränkung vorzunehmen. Das ermöglicht geordnete Geistigkeit besser als die Fülle der Mittel. Materielle Mittel (Holz, Metall, Glas usw.): Materielle Mittel in Massigkeit sind vor allem hier zu vermeiden.
>
> Ideelle Mittel (Linie, Helldunkel, Farbe): Ideelle Mittel sind zu bevorzugen.
>
> Sie sind nicht frei von Materie, sonst lässt sich nicht damit "schreiben". Wenn ich das Wort Wein mit Tinte schreibe, so spielt dabei die Tinte nicht die Hauptrolle, sondern ermöglicht die dauernde Fixierung des Begriffes Wein. Also Tinte verhilft zu Wein auf Dauer. Schrift und Bild, das heisst Schreiben und Bilden, sind wurzelhaft eins.][22]

In his critical study of Proust, Samuel Beckett wrote, "For Proust, as for the painter, style is more a question of vision than of technique. Proust does not share the superstition that form is nothing and content everything, nor that the ideal literary masterpiece could only be communicated in a series of absolute and monosyllabic propositions. For Proust the quality of language is more important than any system of ethics or aesthetics. Indeed he makes no attempt to dissociate form from content. The one is a concretion of the other. . . ."[23] The statement is essentially the same as Paul Klee's, and the two reassert the central importance of that concept embodied in the word *calligraphy*. In doing so, they strongly suggest that the cosmogenetic point for the literary art object is the same as that for the drawn and painted one. The poet gives verbal definition to that which the painter would depict with line and color: The two, each in his own fashion, project the form of that which the artist ceaselessly seeks, "the one image that will connect or embody two points," to use Flannery O'Connor's words, two points of which, in her particular vision, "one is a point in the concrete, and the other is a point not visible to the naked eye, but believed in by him firmly, just as real to him, really, as the one everybody sees."[24] The result, in O'Connor's case, was a transformational vision which as a consequence of her religious ardor was more properly a vision of Transfiguration. But her words express a truism about the art of those less dogmatically ardent, a truism more succinctly expressed in Gertrude Stein's "I write with my eyes not with my ears and my mouth. . . . As a matter of fact as a writer I write entirely with my eyes."[25] The poet's words both form the vision and grow out of the "visionary awareness" which, as we have seen, D. H. Lawrence discovered could only develop through "close contact with the vision itself."

Very few poets, those of the Chinese, Japanese, and other calligraphic traditions excepted, have overtly manifested the awareness in the other graphic form as did Blake, Rossetti, Hugo, Lewis, Lawrence himself. But as Robert Graves indicates, visual acuity is the very essence of poetry: "A poet should be aware of the way in which he looks at the world (in the most literal optical sense) and takes in what he sees; if he finds that he has contracted visual habits which prevent him from seeing things clearly or wholly, he should study to correct them."[26] Virginia Woolf recorded in her diary a long conversation with Max Beerbohm in which by implication they both affirmed the importance for the writer of good vision. The implication appears in Beerbohm's criticism of George Moore: "George Moore never used his eyes. . . . He got it all out of books. Ah I was afraid you would remind me of *Ave atque Vale.* Yes; that's beautiful. Yes, it's true he used his eyes then."[27] The most comprehensive and unequivocal statement about the role of a visuo-spatial image in the inspiration for and the construction of a novel—the most comprehensive and unequivocal I have yet found—is a declaration by Angus Wilson, made during his Ewing Lectures at the University of California, Los Angeles, 1960. Embarking upon a protest against the "paramount importance" given to social, moral, and similar thematic or intellectual significances of the novel, he asserted his wish to end with his own experience that "the impulse to write a novel comes from a momentary unified vision of life":

In my original conception of *Hemlock and After,* for example, I saw Mrs Curry, obese, sweet and menacing, certain in her hysteric sense of power that she can destroy a good man, Bernard Sands; and because my vision is primarily ironic, I saw Bernard painfully thin, bitter, inward-turning, defeated and destroyed, not, as Mrs Curry thought, by her knowledge of his private life but by his own sudden impulse of sadism as he witnessed the arrest in Leicester Square. A momentary powerfully visual picture of a fat woman and a thin man. The whole of the rest of the novel, for good or bad, is simply an extension needed, as I thought, to communicate this very visual ironic picture to others. In this way I could analyse the impulse that started all my novels.[28]

There is, then, a doubled significance to James's report about how a story began for Turgenev. James wrote: "I have always fondly remembered a remark that I heard fall years ago from the lips of Ivan Turgenieff in regard to his own experience of the usual origin of the fictive picture. It began for him almost always with the vision of some person or persons, who hovered before him, soliciting him, as the active or passive figure, interesting him and appealing to him just as they were and by what they were. He saw them, in that fashion as *disponibles,* saw them subject to the chances, the complications of existence, and saw them vividly, but then had to find for them the right relations, those that would most bring them out; to imagine, to invent and select and piece together the situations most useful and favourable to the sense of the creatures themselves, the complications they would be most likely to produce and to feel."[29] The procedure was the same as in Turgenev's portrait game except that in the game Turgenev furnished the players with a pen-and-ink sketch from which the players were to derive a personality and a story or history. In his novels or stories, he sketched with the same pen and ink, but in words, not lines. A further significance appears in the manner of James's assertion: that such a vision is "the origin of the fictive picture." At this point James, possibly drawing from an image already projected by Turgenev, envisioned not only the origin but also the finished art object as a visuo-spatial image. Calligraphically James's critical preface leads from the vision origin in Turgenev's imagination, through the "fictive picture" which is the totality of Turgenev's verbal projection, to the work for which James wrote the preface, the work entitled *The Portrait of a Lady*. That the apparent multiplicity of the total literary art object may be subsumed in a single holistic image every bit the equivalent of a single finished painting is a point to be developed later. For the present, suffice it to notice James's and Turgenev's concurrence that the "fictive picture" has its origin in a single image which may be represented equally well in either calligraphic form.

As with the painter, such images for the poet come from the "dizzy whirl and chaos of life" or, as Robert Frost put it:

> Let chaos storm!
> Let cloud shapes swarm!
> I wait for form.
>
> ("Pertinax")

With life itself as the cloud banks, Frost plays here substantially the same game that prehistoric man played in the caves as he watched the shifting shapes on the walls both revealed and produced by the flickering flame of his lamp. And the reverse then would seem equally true: outside his cave, looking at the sky and the world around him, prehistoric man, too, let cloud shapes swarm and waited for form. For both, the images emerged from the intertwined, convoluted, entangled "meander field" which is the presence to the senses of the receptible environment, emerged as indeed they did for van Gogh and as well for both James and Turgenev: "As for the origin of one's wind-blown germs themselves," wrote James, "who shall say, as you ask, where *they* come from? We have to go too far back, too far behind, to say. Isn't it all we can say that they come from every quarter of heaven, that they are *there* at almost any turn of the road? They accumulate, and we are always picking them over, selecting among them. They are the breath of life—by which I mean that life, in its own way, breathes them upon us. They are so, in a manner prescribed and imposed—floated into our minds by the current of life."[30] "They accumulate, and we are always picking them over . . ."—the phrase recalls vividly the painter's sketchbook, or perhaps more specifically the little room at the far end of Henry Moore's smaller studio "where," so Moore says, "I put all the odds and ends that I have collected, bits of pebbles, bits of bone, found objects, and so on, all of which help to give one an atmosphere to start working. . . ."[31]

Such echoes of the found figure in the painter's meander technique permit a deeper penetration into that moment when "inspiration" comes to the poet, James's phrase "the breath of life" and the image of inspiration which it projects carry with them implications of a certain passivity on the artist's part, seemingly to some extent visible behind Frost's "I wait for form." But Frost's title "Pertinax" (persevering, unyielding, stubborn) asserts, paradoxically, an active quality in the waiting most succinctly expressed in John Keats's phrase "Negative Capability." Viewed from the painter's angle of vision, the phrase proves to be most happily chosen, for on the one hand it negates deliberation while on the other hand it asserts endeavor: one does not deliberately focus a search, but one watches, even hungrily, ready to seize (*capability* is from the Latin *capere,* "to seize"). In an experience which itself illustrates the process, Keats fell upon his term in the course of a "disquisition" with an acquaintance during which "several things dove-tailed in my mind, and at once it struck me what quality went to form a man of achievement, especially in literature, and which Shakespeare possessed so enormously. I mean," Keats continued, "*Negative Capability,* that is, when a man is capable of being in uncertainties, mysteries, doubts, without any irritable reaching after fact and reason." To clarify his meaning and to define further the state he wished to describe, he went on to assert that Coleridge, insofar as he was incapable of waiting, insofar as he sought to know, did not possess this capability: "Coleridge, for instance, would let go by a fine isolated verisimilitude caught from the Penetralium of mystery, from being incapable of remaining content with half-knowledge."[32] Coleridge's dejection consequent upon his failure to capture a fine isolated verisimilitude from the Penetralium of mystery is, of course, the occasion for "Dejection: An Ode." But that he did frequently experience transformational perception is evident not only from his poetry but also from a specific instance during his voyage to Malta, recorded in a long notebook entry, when Coleridge played the role of Frost's Pertinax:

> Saturday late Evening, about 8 °clock—I was gazing to the Starboard on the Clouds & was musing that in this Bay of Biscay I had observed that the great masses on the Horizon split themselves into more Heads, & those more deeply cleft, chimneys, obelisks, Turrets, & chiefly those larger loftier forms that have the Peak of the Mountain with the breadth & Proportions of the Tower. Yesterday I saw a strong resemblance of the most striking five Segments of Glencoe the right hand side as you go *to* Ballachulish & this Evening exactly over the Convoy, with it beginning & with it ending, I saw a delightful mockery of a Fleet, masts & Sails & Pennants. While I was thus musing, I turn to the Larboard side of the Vessel, & my Heart did indeed leap up—Was it the Placefell Bank of Ulswater? Or the Benlomond side of Loch Lomond?—Or Lochness?—or rather that which I saw in late eve at Letter Findlay? Or was it not a new Mountain with a new Lake only so completely did the Sea between our Ship & and it become a Lake, and that black substantial Squall Cloud the Mountain that formed & rose up from its banks, that it would be a positive falsehood to say, it was like. It was utterly indistinguishable. . . .[33]

"Dejection: An Ode" records his reaction to the loss of such vision. Distracted by his "wan and heartless mood, / To other thoughts by yonder throstle wooed," he has gazed "with how blank an eye" at clouds, stars, and moon, but:

> My genial spirits fail;
> And what can these avail
> To lift the smothering weight from off my breast?
> It were a vain endeavor,
> Though I should gaze for ever
> On that green light that lingers in the west;
> I may not hope from outward forms to win
> The passion and the life, whose fountains are within.

The state which Keats described as "Negative Capability" and which Coleridge illustrated in both its presence and its absence is that which Robert Graves distinguishes from the "deliberate" on the one hand and the unconscious on the other.[34] It is the state which manifests what Proust called "involuntary memory," at least in Beckett's understanding of Proust's phrase: ". . . Involuntary memory is an unruly magician and will not be importuned. It chooses its own time and place for the performance of its miracle."[35] The paradox, caught in an active, almost imperious "let" is a deliberate suspension of deliberate design: I, pertinax,

> Let chaos storm!
> Let cloud shapes swarm!
> I wait for form.

In his comments on how the artist differs from the scholar, Frost makes the same point more discursively with, however, the same focus upon the word *let:*

> Scholars and artists thrown together are often annoyed at the puzzle of where they differ. Both work from knowledge; but I suspect they differ most importantly in the way their knowledge is come by. Scholars get theirs with conscientious thoroughness along projected lines of logic; poets theirs cavalierly and as it happens in and out of books. They stick to nothing deliberately, but let what will stick to them like burrs where they walk in the fields. No acquirement is on assignment, or even self-assignment. . . . A schoolboy may be defined as one who can tell you what he knows in the order in which he learned it. The artist must value himself as he snatches a thing from some previous order in time and space into a new order with not so much as a ligature clinging to it of the old place where it was organic.[36]

In a further paradox, the state is *positively* negative in that it requires a negative reaction to what at first glance is a most distressingly negative situation, that situation described by Paul Valéry when artistic achievement seems frustrated and negated by the distractions of "reality" and the consequent dispersion of mental effort. At such moments, precisely those of which Leonardo spoke in announcing his "new" discovery, instead of reacting "positively" with greater concentration and effort, the experienced artist reacts "negatively" by willingly submitting to the dispersion, confident that, such are his capabilities, from the chaos will emerge that which is wanting:

> ... This always imminent dispersion is important and even coöperates in production almost as much as concentration itself. The mind at work, struggling against its own mobility, against its constitutional restlessness and its own diversity, against the dissipation or natural deterioration of every specialized attitude, finds, on the other hand, in this very situation incomparable resources. The instability, the incoherence, the inconsistency of which I have spoken, and which are obstacles and limitations to the mind in its business of construction or sustained composition, are just as truly treasures of possibility whose riches the mind can sense in its environs the moment it reflects upon itself.[37]

Mark Twain made the same discovery in learning to cope with those moments when a story, once begun, runs out of momentum and the writer is tempted to force invention. In his autobiographical dictations of 1906, he said of his method of writing, "I was a faithful and interested amanuensis and my industry did not flag, but the minute that the book tried to shift to *my* head the labor of contriving its situations, inventing its adventures and conducting its conversations, I put it away and dropped it out of my mind." He learned to do this willingly or even willfully while writing *The Adventures of Tom Sawyer:* When he was well into the manuscript, "the story made a sudden and determined halt and refused to proceed another day." He was "disappointed, distressed and immeasurably astonished," but despite his efforts the story would not develop further. For two years, according to his testimony, the manuscript was ignored while he concerned himself with other things. Then one day, he took it out, read the last chapter he had written and discovered that he could now go on quite easily: "It was then that I made the great discovery that when the tank runs dry you've only to leave it alone and it will fill up again in time, while you are asleep—also while you are at work at other things and are quite unaware that this unconscious and profitable cerebration is going on." He learned thus to adopt a policy of deliberate nondeliberation when creativity failed him, a policy which he pursued with equanimity during the rest of his writing career.[38]

It might be objected that both Twain and Valéry refer to problems which occur after the cosmogenetic moment during the elaboration of the vision into the finished work, whereas both Frost and Keats refer to the process by which the vision itself is formed. But, as Twain's experiences in the composition of *Pudd'nhead Wilson* show, what superficially may seem to be two different situations are actually two separate manifestations of the same phenomenon, for in either event the essence of the matter is a question of transformational perception. Twain's novel had its origin in a visuo-spatial image, the perception of the famous Siamese twins, Chang and Eng. In the compositional sequence which eventually produced *Pudd'nhead Wilson*, this percept fused successively in three different affective modes—the comic, the serio-comic, and the satiric-tragic—with three different memory images, as Negative Capability worked its magic, to produce three successive transformational images which may be labeled respectively "the ties that bind," "split personality," and, to use Lincoln's image, "a house divided." The process produced three successive art objects: "Personal Habits of the Siamese Twins" (1869), "Those Extraordinary Twins" (1894), and *Pudd'nhead Wilson* (also 1894).[39]

The vision comes then for poet as well as painter as a consequence of an unanticipating expectation: the readiness is all. When it does come, as it surely will sooner or later, it is in Matisse's words a bolt of lightning: "Quelquefois je m'arrête sur un motif, un coin de mon atelier que je trouve expressif, même au-dessus de moi, de mes forces et j'attends le coup de foudre que ne peut manquer de venir [Sometimes I halt upon a motif, a corner of my studio which I find expressive, even beyond me, beyond my strength, and I await the thunderbolt which will not fail to come]."[40] The image is evocative. Who has not caught his breath in wonder at the brief, vivid glimpse of another world which comes with a flash of lightning?—such a moment of sudden, comprehensive vision as that described by the third-century Chinese poet Lu Chi:

The dawn of [the poet's] mood grew brighter and brighter. . . .

[And]

He was seeing the past and the present in a moment of time, he was touching the Four Seas in one blink of an eye.[41]

The passage adds to, or even one may say in defiance of diachrony, continues Frost's triplet into the moment when the perseverance of

Pertinax has been rewarded, continues Matisse's image beyond the bolt, and adds overtones of cosmic creation. With his phrase "transmuted perception" Siegfried Sassoon emphasizes the same miraculous quality in the vision: "I have never been fond of ideas for their own sake. In fact they have played a comparatively unimportant part in my literary life. My thoughts—if one can call them that—have been a series of mental pictures. Thinking in pictures is my natural method of self-expression. I have always been a submissively visual writer. . . . Mind-sight eliminates what is inessential, and achieves breadth and intensity by transmuted perception."[42] As well, he makes explicit what is implicit in Lu Chi's comment, the same paradox which struck van Gogh with wonder: the fact that, instead of imposing narrower limitations, an elimination of detail, a selectivity, provides through the transformational process what van Gogh recognized and treasured as the "more typical" drawing—a paradox which Henry James captured in the word *inclusive* when he wrote, "Art is essentially selection, but it is a selection whose main care is to be typical, to be inclusive."[43]

In an interplay between the words *essential* and *typical,* Sassoon, van Gogh, and James provide sharper definition for the nature of the visionary process and for Georges Braque's summation in "the senses deform, the mind forms." The interplay appears in a comment by Flannery O'Connor: "In a work of art we can be extremely literal, without being in the least bit naturalistic. Art is selective, and its truthfulness is the truthfulness of the essential that creates movement."[44] The role of movement in transformational perception is a subject for the next chapter. Here it is important to notice that the selection is both of the essentially typical and of the typically essential with, in either instance, in both instances, the word *typical* carrying its most basic values: of or pertaining to type, figure, outline, schema. The total transformational process is, then, again in O'Connor's words, a matter of a "delicate adjustment" of *typos* and essence: "When we talk about the writer's country we are liable to forget that no matter what particular country it is, it is inside as well as outside him. Art requires a delicate adjustment of the outer and inner worlds in such a way that, without changing their nature, they can be seen through each other."[45] As in the case of the rock protuberance in Altamira and the superimposed bison painting, the formal or "typical" of the receptible environment fuses with the essential elements of the inner world, the world of being, in a delicate adjustment which in the very transformation, nevertheless, preserves the identity of both worlds.

The image so shaped, the artistic vision, is beautifully characterized by Paul Valéry: "Thus we have on one hand the *undefinable,* on the other a necessarily finite act; on one hand a condition, sometimes a single sensation producing value and impulsion, a condition the sole character of which is that it corresponds to no finite term of our experience; on the other, an *act,* that is to say essential determination, since an act is a miraculous escape from the closed world of the possible and an introduction into the universe of fact. And this act is frequently produced in spite of the mind with all its precisions; it escapes from the unstable, like Minerva, produced full-armed from the mind of Jupiter, an old image still full of meaning."[46] What Valéry describes is given phenomenological presence in Wallace Stevens's poem "Anecdote of the Jar": The poet places a jar on a hill, and it "made the slovenly wilderness / Surround that hill."

> The wilderness rose up to it,
> And sprawled around, no longer wild.

The jar is the concretized, objectified imaginative shape, the cosmogenetic point, which imposes "essentially typical" form upon the "chaos without." The result is what for Wallace Stevens the poet sings on the blue guitar, that world freshly created by the "other solitary singer" in "The Idea of Order at Key West":

> She was the single artificer of the world
> In which she sang. And when she sang, the sea,
> Whatever self it had, became the self
> That was her song, for she was maker. Then we,
> As we beheld her striding there alone,
> Knew that there never was a world for her
> Except the one she sang and, singing, made.

Or, in the words of Lu Chi, who in his image of the hub anticipated Paul Klee's cosmogenetic point by some sixteen centuries, "[The writer], taking his stand at the hub of the universe. . . , [traps] heaven-and-earth within a visible form, forcing all creation onto the tip of his brush."[47]

The total process, here pieced together from numerous sources and paralleled with the creative process in painting, is summarized by Henry James in one of the most complete statements by any writer: his description of how *The Spoils of Poynton* began. The initial image, what James called the germ, came to him in the midst of dinner-party chatter one Christmas Eve: ". . . When I was dining with friends: a lady beside me made in the course of talk one of those allusions that I have always found myself recognizing on the spot as 'germs.' The germ, wherever gathered, has ever been for me the germ of a 'story,' and most of the stories straining to shape under my hand have sprung from a single small seed. . . ." One must see as vividly as possible the dizzy whirl and chaos in the scene that must have been present to James's senses: the table itself with its white cloth and possibly flowers, the dishes and the place settings, wine glasses and water glasses, all gleaming in the glow of the lamps; a servant or perhaps two passing the dishes, the animation of service, and heads inclined in the chatter of small-talk. Then suddenly in the midst of it all, indeed while it all continues, that "stray suggestion," that which, like the motif in the corner of Matisse's studio, arrests the attention in anticipation of the thunderbolt: "Such is the interesting truth about the stray suggestion, the wandering word, the vague echo, at touch of which the novelist's imagination winces as at the prick of some sharp point: its virtue is all in its needle-like quality, the power to penetrate as finely as possible." In his own version of "the senses deform, the mind forms," James continues: "Strange and attaching, certainly, the consistency with which the first thing to be done for the communicated and seized idea is to reduce almost to nought the form, the air as of a mere disjoined and lacerated lump of life, in which we may have happened to meet it. Life being all inclusion and confusion and art being all discrimination and selection, the latter, in search of the hard latent value with which alone it is concerned, sniffs round the mass as instinctively and unerringly as a dog suspicious of some buried bone. The difference here, however, is that, while the dog desires his bone but to destroy it, the author finds in *his* tiny nugget, worked free of awkward accretions and hammered into a sacred hardness, the very stuff for a clear affirmation, the happiest chance for the indestructible."[48] James's view of the process appears as well in more fragmentary comments elsewhere in the various prefaces or in other of his critical writings. Despite the fact that they are fragmentary, in that they generally restrict themselves to single stages of the process, these other comments nevertheless complement this account especially in two respects. First of all, as evident in his comments about Turgenev, the "germ" was for James a single image, a picture. The other is that the consequence of the "happiest chance for the indestructible" is not "reality" but "a reality." Both of these appear in his anecdote of the manner in which an unnamed English novelist built a convincing impression of French Protestant youth:

I remember an English novelist, a woman of genius, telling me that she was much commended for the impression she had managed to

give in one of her tales of the nature and way of life of the French
Protestant youth. She had been asked where she learned so much
about this recondite being, she had been congratulated on her peculiar opportunities. These opportunities consisted in her having
once, in Paris, as she ascended a staircase, passed an open door
where, in the household of a *pasteur,* some of the young Protestants
were seated at table round a finished meal. The glimpse made a
picture; it lasted only a moment, but that moment was experience.
She had got her direct personal impression, and she turned out her
type. She knew what youth was, and what Protestantism; she also
had the advantage of having seen what it was to be French, so that
she converted these ideas into a concrete image and produced a
reality.[49]

The indefinite article, "*a* reality," is extremely significant, for it
brings us back once again to that other reality which is best called
"surreal," a "reality" which must be carefully distinguished from the
receptible.

In her diary, Virginia Woolf recorded the effect on her of Faith
Henderson's visit for tea, 14 March 1927. In her record of the event,
one can see to a remarkable extent the tension between the two
realities, the receptible furnished by the actual, the tea with Faith
Henderson, and the reality of what Virginia Woolf proposed to entitle
"The Jessamy Brides." As one reads the account one must keep present to the mind's eye the Faith Henderson, who, transmuted, becomes the "unattractive woman, penniless, alone" with novelistic
possibilities. One must also keep in view the English sitting room in
which the tea service occurs, the tea things, the small talk, and the
external presentation of Virginia Woolf herself "valiantly beating the
waters of conversation" while her imagination races away with the
image caught, the germ, as James would say:

> Faith Henderson came to tea; and, valiantly beating the waters of
> conversation, I sketched the possibilities which an unattractive
> woman, penniless, alone, might yet bring into being. I began im-
> agining the position—how she would stop a motor on the Dover
> road and so get to Dover; cross the channel etc. . . . Suddenly
> between twelve and one I conceived a whole fantasy to be called
> "The Jessamy Brides" . . . . I have rayed round it several scenes. . . .
> One can see anything (for this is fantasy). . . . Anyhow this records
> the odd horrid unexpected way in which these things suddenly
> create themselves—one thing on top of another in about an hour.
> So I made up *Jacob's Room* looking at the fire at Hogarth House; so I
> made up the *Lighthouse* one afternoon in the Square here.[50]

One must not fail to note Woolf's use of the word *rayed* in this account: "I have rayed round it [the initial perception, the germ] several

scenes. . . ." The image behind the word is essentially the same as that behind Lu Chi's "hub" or Paul Klee's "cosmogenetic point."

The exploration of the poet's experience with transformational perception brings us, then, to the same point as that experienced by the painter. In an essay entitled "The Relations between Poetry and Painting," Wallace Stevens, in addressing himself to the common assertion "that the origins of poetry are to be found in the sensibility," wrote:

> Yet if one question the dogma that the origins of poetry are to be found in the sensibility and if one says that a fortunate poem or a fortunate painting is a synthesis of exceptional concentration . . . , we find that the operative force within us does not, in fact, seem to be the sensibility, that is to say, the feelings. It seems to be a constructive faculty, that derives its energy more from the imagination than from the sensibility. . . . The mind retains experience, so that long after the experience . . . , that faculty within us of which I have spoken makes its own constructions out of that experience. If it merely reconstructed the experience or repeated for us our sensations in the face of it, it would be the memory. What it really does is to use it as material with which it does whatever it wills. This is the typical function of the imagination which always makes use of the familiar to produce the unfamiliar.[51]

The nature of the interplay among imagination, memory, and construction which Stevens touches upon here emerges more clearly in a comment by Stephen Spender in *The Making of a Poem,* a comment which may profitably be read as an expansion upon Stevens's remarks. Spender wrote, ". . . Memory exercised in a particular way is the natural gift of poetic genius. The poet, above all else, is a person who never forgets certain sense-impressions which he has experienced and which he can re-live again and again as though with all their original freshness." Neither he nor Stevens seems to have heard of the rather intense debate among cognitive psychologists over the nature of memory, for they assume that all who read them will understand the word *memory* and the assumptions lying behind it. But the evidence adduced about the nature of the artistic vision for both painter and poet strongly suggests that, in evoking the memory, Stevens and Spender are both evoking the same thing that Delacroix evoked with his exhortation "Par coeur, par coeur!" Spender goes on to assert, "Memory is the faculty of poetry, because the imagination itself is an exercise of memory." The concept of memory implicit in such a statement is one that John B. Watson denounced so vigorously in the first quarter of the century that until the 1960s American behaviorist psychology tended to deny the image any role whatsoever in thought or memory and to insist that such processes are uniquely verbal processes. For Spender, however, it is the pattern of rich associations in and among images which is the essence of poetry: "I have a perfect memory for the sensation of certain experiences which are crystallized for me around certain associations." The image associations are made on the basis of a "memory for the sensation" so that ". . . the memory is not exactly a memory. It is more like one prong upon which a whole calendar of similar experiences happening throughout years, collect. A memory once clearly stated ceases to be a memory, it becomes perpetually present, because every time we experience something which recalls it, the clear and lucid original experience imposes its formal beauty on the new experience."[52] The "construction" of which Wallace Stevens speaks is, for Stephen Spender at least, the same fusion of percept image and memory image which produced, say, the surreal bison on the ceiling of Altamira.

At the level of artistic vision, then, poet and painter merge, become one—the Artist. Again in the words of Wallace Stevens, "The point is that the poet does his job by virtue of an effort of the mind. In doing so, he is in rapport with the painter, who does his job, with respect to the problems of form and color, which confront him incessantly, not by inspiration, but by imagination or by the miraculous kind of reason that the imagination sometimes promotes."[53] Paul Klee used what he called "the parable of the tree" to characterize the creative process as the painter knows it, especially the transmutation accomplished as the artist's perception of the world passes through his vision to become the art object:

> Let me use a parable. The parable of the tree. The artist has busied himself with this world of many forms and, let us assume, he has in some measure got his bearings in it; quietly, all by himself. He is so clearly oriented that he orders the flux of phenomena and experiences. I shall liken this orientation, in the things of nature and of life, this complicated order, to the roots of the tree.
>
> From the roots the sap rises up into the artist, flows through him and his eyes. He is the trunk of the tree.
>
> Seized and moved by the force of the current, he directs his vision into his work. Visible on all sides, the crown of the trees unfolds in space and time. And so with the work.
>
> No one will expect a tree to form its crown in exactly the same way as its roots. We all know that what goes on above cannot be an exact mirror image of what goes on below.
>
> [Lassen Sie mich ein Gleichnis gebrauchen, das Gleichnis vom Baum. Der Künstler hat sich mit dieser vielgestaltigen Welt befasst,

und er hat sich, so wollen wir annehmen, in ihr einigermassen zurechtgefunden; in aller Stille. Er ist so gut orientiert, dass er die Flucht der Erscheinungen und der Erfahrungen zu ordnen vermag. Diese Orientierung in den Dingen der Natur und des Lebens, diese vielverästelte und verzweigte Ordnung, möchte ich dem Wurzelwerk des Baumes vergleichen.

Von daher strömen dem Künstler die Säfte zu, um durch ihn und durch sein Auge hindurchzugehn. So steht er an der Stelle des Stammes.

Bedrängt und bewegt von der Macht jenes Strömens, leitet er Erschautes weiter ins Werk. Wie die Baumkrone sich zeitlich und räumlich nach allen Seiten hin sichtbar entfaltet, so geht es auch mit dem Werk.

Es wird niemand einfallen, vom Baum zu verlangen, dass er die Krone genau so bilde wie die Wurzel. Jeder wird verstehn, dass kein exaktes Spiegelverhältnis zwischen Unten und Oben sein kann.][54]

Klee's image is equally applicable to the poet. Poetry and painting are two stems from a common root system: The same sap circulates in both, carries the same nourishment for growth to and from the leafy crowns. Because of their different orientations toward the light, the crowns themselves do indeed differ in their general configurations, but one must not, from the differences in configuration, draw erroneous conclusions—one must not forget that, because of the common root system, they are two stems of the same organic form, calligraphy.

3

Archetrope and Transformation

Gyorgy Kepes noted that the idea of art as mimesis has been supplanted by more modern knowledge about the relationship between art and perception. Specifically, he wrote, ". . . The traditional concept of an image as a mirror held in front of nature is now obsolete. . . . The patterns of nature's processes and our pictures of them are not identical and cannot be interchanged. A new vocabulary of visual thinking is suggested, focusing our attention on process and change and pointing to the fundamental significance of transformation."[1] His "new vocabulary," as we have seen from the evidence of prehistoric art and the statements of artists, both poets and painters, is as old as humankind, but his articulation of the concept permits a glimpse on the level of artistic vision of a twofold truth which all too frequently is obscured or totally unperceived in discussions of art as "imitation" of "reality." The mimetic concept, the concept of art as a mirror held up to nature, bestows the highest value upon congruence between the perception and the art object. It necessarily obscures the importance, even masks the presence, of the transformational process. Imitation is, as Wallace Stevens noted, "identity manqué."[2] The logic of mimesis demands that the mirror be as free as possible of defect or distortion. But the legacy of Altamira and the other prehistoric sites reveals the error. If he had had the opportunity, the prehistoric artist would undoubtedly have agreed with Philostratus, who, in his biography of Apollonius of Tyana, provides an interesting dialogue between Apollonius and his disciple, Damis, upon precisely this point. In India the two are awaiting an audience with the king. Having viewed some metal reliefs made in the Greek style at the time of Alexander the

Great, Apollonius asks, "Tell me, Damis, is there such a thing as painting?"

"Of course," Damis replies.

"And what does this art consist of?"

"Well," Damis says, "in the mixing of colors."

"And why do they do that?"

"For the sake of imitation, to get a likeness of a dog or a horse or a man, a ship, or anything else under the sun."

"Then," continues Apollonius, "painting is imitation, mimesis?"

"Well, what else? If it did not do that it would just be a ridiculous playing about with colors."

"Yes," says Apollonius, "but what about the things we see in the sky when the clouds are drifting, the centaurs and stag antelopes and wolves and horses? Are they also works of imitation? Is God a painter who uses his leisure hours to amuse himself in that way?"

The two agree that these cloud shapes have no meaning, that instead they occur by pure chance; it is instead, the perceiver who is prone to imitation and who imposes his vision on the clouds.

"But does this not mean," insists Apollonius, "that the art of imitation is twofold?"[3]

Through Apollonius, Philostratus exemplifies that phenomenological method which Bachelard chämpioned some two millennia later because "by obliging us to retrace our steps systematically and to make an effort toward clarity of awareness with respect to a poet's given image, the phenomenological method leads us to attempt communication with the creating consciousness of the poet."[4] The systematic retracing leads into the artist's imagination, to his "visionary awareness," in D. H. Lawrence's phrase, and to the perception that Philostratus long ago anticipated Lawrence: "The picture must all come out of the artist's inside awareness of forms and figures. We can call it memory, but it is more than memory. It is the image as it lives in the consciousness, alive like a vision. . . ."[5] Both Philostratus and Lawrence focus attention upon that image fusion (for Philostratus, percept of cloud and transformational images of centaurs, stag antelopes, wolves, and horses), that unanticipated union of images at the heart of the transformational process.

Lawrence, however, with the word *lives* and the phrase *alive like a vision*, adds a dimension which, in view of the evidence afforded by poets and painters alike, must be taken in a sense of near or actual kinesthesia. The words *motif* and *emotion*, indicative, in their conjunction, of a reciprocity in affectivity, form a parallel to the reciprocity in movement already discerned in the fusion of percept and memory images to form the artistic image. As we have already seen, Flannery O'Connor, who was quite perceptive in her comments about the creative process, summed up the lesson learned by van Gogh with the words, "Art is selective, and its truthfulness is the truthfulness of the essential that creates movement": that is to say a close analysis of the transformational process leads to a focus upon selected transformable elements which are, in terms of motion, that which makes the percept a motif.

The physiological aspect of what van Gogh called the "feeling of the subject" appears with insistent frequency in the comments of artists. Emily Dickinson once wrote, "If I read a book [and] it makes my whole body so cold no fire ever can warm me I know THAT is poetry. If I feel physically as if the top of my head were taken off, I know THAT is poetry. These are the only way I know it. Is there any other way. . . ?"[6] For Joan Miró, as well as for A. E. Housman and Hamada Shoji, the impact centers in the pit of the stomach. William Fifield reports the following exchange with Miró on the subject of the impulse to paint:

> [Fifield]: "The source?"
> [Miró]: "Oh—a mystery. Unknown. But it has relevancy to the primitive—long before Christ. I feel my work going back even further as I grow. Yes, it is like cavern art sometimes but, no, I did not see the cavern art first. I saw it after. It gave me a shock. I feel I am only beginning my true work now. *Now.* Oh, I might go on another five or six years."
> [Fifield]: "What do you seek?"
> [Miró]: "The shock. A shock: it gives you a shock—a tock on the stomach—something—and you start. The painting itself is rapid."[7]

Miró's word *shock* recalls the thunderbolt Matisse awaited when his eye fell upon a motif in the corner of his studio. A. E. Housman offers the same testimony: "Poetry indeed seems to me more physical than intellectual. . . . Experience has taught me, when I am shaving of a morning, to keep watch over my thoughts, because, if a line of poetry strays into my memory, my skin bristles so that the razor ceases to act. This particular symptom is accompanied by a shiver down the spine; there is another which consists in a constriction of the throat and a precipitation of water to the eyes; and there is a third which I can only describe by borrowing a phrase from one of Keats's last letters, where he says, speaking of Fanny Brawne, 'everything that reminds me of her goes through me like a spear.' The seat of this sensation is the pit of the stomach."[8] Further in the same context, Housman becomes even more precise about the relationship among the perception of the world around him, the appearance of lines of poetry in his thoughts, and the physiological sensation. The event, or perhaps the advent, occurred for Housman while he was engaged in aimless wandering both physical and psychological, a state which surely Keats would have recognized as Negative Capability:

> . . . I would go out for a walk of two or three hours. As I went along, thinking of nothing in particular, only looking at things around me and following the progress of the season, there would flow into my mind, with sudden and unaccountable emotion, sometimes a line or two of verse, sometimes a whole stanza at once, accompanied, not preceded, by a vague notion of the poem which they were destined to form a part of. Then there would usually be a lull of an hour or so, then perhaps the spring would bubble up again. I say bubble up, because, so far as I could make out, the source of the suggestions thus proffered to the brain was an abyss which I have already had occasion to mention, the pit of the stomach.[9]

Housman's comments find an echo in the definition of beauty offered by Hamada Shoji, the great Japanese potter. Reacting to the art critic Yanagi's use of the word *beauty* to express this feeling, Hamada said, "Beauty is not in the head or heart, but in the abdomen."[10] Such comments, though much more restrained, refer to the same physiological sensation as that which Picasso recognized in a comment by Cézanne, a comment with which, according to Françoise Gilot, Picasso heartily agreed: "Cézanne came closer than anybody else when he said, 'Painting is something you do with your balls.'"[11]

The Oriental theory of the artist's sensibilities, the theory dramatized in Natsume Kinnosuke's novel *Kusa Makura,* is that man reaches the height of artistic achievement only when he is most fully receptive to the universal rhythms of nature, only when he becomes a living unity with the trees, the flowers, the animals, the very rocks and cliffs around him. The aim of this discipline is to garner visions of the world not in terms of "realism" or "representation" but rather in terms of what the Chinese call "rhythmical vitality." By this is meant the essence of physical objects revealed through their characteristic and natural movement, the movement which is the essence of life. Man's structures must not obscure, but as art objects must enhance or preserve, this essential movement. The Japanese call the artistic achievement of this idea *Sei-do,* "living movement," manifest in the art object when, as a consequence of correctly formed lines and the vivid depiction, not of the subject but of the artist's sense of the subject's natural movement, the depiction itself seems on the verge of movement. It should be added that *Sei-do* is not achieved through "real-

istic" or *trompe l'oeil* effects. It is instead strictly a matter of
transformational perception translated primarily through the artist's
brush strokes.[12] In this respect a story is told about Sen no Rikyū, the
celebrated Japanese tea-master. Expecting the arrival of guests for
tea, he instructed his son to clean the garden. The young man carefully removed all litter, pruned and shaped the plants, rendered the
garden immaculate and as perfectly finished as possible. Rikyū examined the result disapprovingly and said, "This is not the way." He
then shook a tree that stood in the center of the perspective so that a
number of leaves detached and drifted to fall in a random pattern
across the path. Gyorgy Kepes, after recounting this anecdote, comments, "Thus, the man-made structural order of the garden was
joined with the natural order of living forms."[13] To be more precise,
Rikyū had provided at the very center of his garden the concrete
traces of a living, physical movement, of "leaf-drift," the movement
pattern invisible, but nevertheless present in the space between the
branches and the now scattered leaves. Robert Frost once said, "The
suggestion is all in poetry": Rikyū had provided the suggestion and
thus had transformed his garden into either a painting or a poem.
The nature of the suggestion appears again in another anecdote:
Having been invited to another person's tea ceremony, Rikyū and
some friends walked along a deserted lane overhung by "mukuju"
trees. Observing with fascination the drifted piles of leaves in the
gardens by the lane, Rikyū exclaimed, "How suggestive they are!" and
went on to say, "I guess the master of the house will clean away every
leaf from the garden because of his lack of sense." He was right;
coming back, they saw no leaves there: all had been thrown away.
"Look, I am right," he said. "And I will instruct you about how to treat
a lane. It is better for you to do your cleaning during the previous
night when you hold a morning tea ceremony, and when you hold a
noon tea ceremony, you should clean your garden in the early morning. In either case, you would rather leave leaves as they have fallen
there."[14] In short, the stories told of Rikyū illustrate what O'Connor
called the "truthfulness of the essential that creates movement." By
providing "leaf-drift" in his garden, Rikyū provided the essential elements which would transform the garden into motif and thus into
something capable of giving his guests the Oriental version of Lawrence's image living in the consciousness "alive like a vision."

In Rikyū's garden the "fusion" of movement at the center of the
transformational process is clear because the process is acted out in
the three-dimensional world: Rikyū's sense of "leaf-drift" moves
physically into the "image" to shake the tree, to realize or "make real"

the "leaf-drift" inherent in the tree, which in turn will meet and fuse with the guests' sense of "leaf-drift" as their eyes receive the image of tree and scattered leaves. The whole proceeding is an externalization of what is usually hidden within the artist's consciousness as he reacts to the motif to experience the vision and to produce the art object, an externalization, in this particular case, of what occurred within Sōseki to produce the haiku

> The winds that blow . . .
> Ask them, which leaf of the tree
> Will be the next to go!

In that which links the haiku and the anecdote of Rikyū's garden, one can discern the same process which motivated *La Danse,* painted by Matisse for Stschoukine:

J'aime beaucoup la danse. . . . Lorsqu'il m'a fallu composer une danse pour Moscou, j'ai simplement été au Moulin de la Galette le dimanche après-midi. Et j'ai regardé danser. J'ai regardé notamment la farandole. Souvent, au milieu ou en fin de séance, il y avait une farandole. Cette farandole était très gaie. Les danseurs se tiennent par la main, courent à travers la salle, entortillent les gens qui sont un peu égarés. . . . C'est extrêmement gai. Et tout cela sur une musique sautillante. Atmosphère que je connaissais très bien. Quand j'ai eu à faire une composition, je suis retourné au Moulin de la Galette pour revoir la farandole. En rentrant chez moi, j'ai composé ma danse sur une surface de quatre mètres, en chantant le même air que j'avais entendu au Moulin de la Galette, si bien que toute la composition, tous les danseurs sont d'accord et dansent sur le même rythme [I like the dance very much. . . . When I had to compose a dance for Moscow, I simply went to the Moulin de la Galette that Sunday afternoon. And I watched the dancing. Particularly, I watched the farandole. Often, either at the middle or the end of the séance, there was a farandole. This farandole was very gay. The dancers hold hands, run across the room, sweep up the spectators who get in the way. . . . It is extremely gay. And all that to a bouncy music. Atmosphere that I knew very well. When I had to make a composition, I returned to the Moulin de la Galette to see the farandole again. Returning home, I composed my dance on a surface of four meters, singing all the while the same air which I had heard at the Moulin de la Galette, so well that the entire composition, all the dancers are in tune and dance to the same rhythm.][15]

Matisse's account amply confirms the conclusions reached by Jean Piaget and his team in their study of the image and its role in the consciousness of the child. In essence Piaget observed what Matisse experienced and what Rikyū illustrated, that the image is not only an interiorized sensory-motor imitation in the presence of a model but also a generalized formulation of such imitations constructed in the image memory from the same or similar sensory-motor experiences: "L'image est donc à la fois imitation sensori-motrice intériorisée et esquisse d'imitations représentatives."[16] In fact, Piaget's studies of the image become of even more central importance at this point for the illumination they cast on the role played by the sense of motion or action in the construction of the artistic image. Piaget and Bärbel Inhelder, in their studies of children's mental images, discerned two major classes of images: "static" images and images of movement and transformation. The imagery characteristic of ages prior to seven or eight tends to be "static," that is, simply reproductive; whereas imagery in the later years becomes progressively more flexible, capable of representing movements and transformations, especially characterized by an anticipatory quality. This later imagery contains a stronger motor aspect than the former and may be conceptualized as internalized imitation. Thus the more mature imagery contains the implicit motor components of actual imitation in its capacity to symbolize movements and transformations. To this extent, as they indicate in their introductory comments, their results do little more than expand the documentation of what a number of investigators before them had already discerned.[17] Beyond the motor content of the image, Piaget's and Inhelder's essential contribution was to discern various classes of what they called *schèmes*. Among their general conclusions they stated, "Si nous appelons 'schème' un instrument de généralisation qui permit de dégager et d'utiliser les éléments communs à des conduites analogues successives, il existe des schèmes perceptifs comme des schèmes sensori-moteurs, des schèmes opératoires, etc.: et il existe aussi, en ce sens, des schèmes imagés en tant que permettant au sujet de construire des images analogues en des situations comparables [If we designate a *schème* as an instrument of generalization which permits us to disengage and to use the common elements in successive analogous behavior, there exist, as well as sensory-motor *schèmes*, perceptual *schèmes*, operative *schèmes*, etc.: and there exist also, in this sense, imaged *schèmes* inasmuch as they permit the subject to construct analogous images in comparable situations]."[18] The imaged *schème* fuses selected motor elements in the percept with comparable or analogous elements from the image memory to construct an imaged form of movement common to both the percept and the memory image or images. Such a fusion so closely parallels the fusion already discerned in the transformational process of art as to permit the hypothesis that the two are complementary aspects of the same thing: the artistic image is a visuo-spatial formulation of the "movement-form" characteristic of a particular imaged *schème*.

This hypothesis permits an even deeper penetration into the moment of artistic vision and leads to a further link with what is known experimentally of the processes of perception and cognition. On the basis of the hypothesis and the evidence leading to it, one may reconstruct the initial steps in the creative process in the following sequence: At the outset the artist is in a state of Negative Capability, deliberately nondeliberatively waiting as the "meander field" of the receptible environment swirls about him. A form captures his eye—or to be more precise, his attention is recalled to the form. Involved is a two-stage event: as the attention roves in the state of negative capability something in a fleeting recept triggers an almost involuntary reaction, bringing the attention back in a sharper focus upon the form. The *belated re*-cognition of transformable motive elements in the form recalls the attention in that sharper focus to accomplish the deformation and reformation of which Braque spoke. This analysis accords closely with Ulric Neisser's analysis of the process of attention in the cognition of a perception. Neisser also discerns two stages: the "preattentive process" and the process of "focal attention":

> Since the processes of focal attention cannot operate on the whole visual field simultaneously, they can come into play only after preliminary operations have already segregated the figural units involved. . . . I will call them the *preattentive processes* to emphasize that they produce the objects which later mechanisms are to flesh out and interpret.
> The requirements of this task mean that the preattentive processes must be genuinely "global" and "wholistic." Each figure or object must be separated from the others in its entirety, as a potential framework for the subsequent and more detailed analyses of attention.[19]

A trivial example of this two-stage process, one well within the range of ordinary experience, is the so-called "double-take," which occurs when, in a moment of abstraction or preoccupation, the senses "record" something which nevertheless does not receive attention until a perceptible moment later when the psyche and frequently the body or some of its members "turn back" with a heightened awareness. This heightened awareness manifests itself with the shock of recognition which Henry James speaks of as having "the effect of some particular

sharp impression or concussion."[20] In James's phrase one recognizes
again the physiological reaction spoken of by Dickinson, Matisse,
Housman, Miró, Cézanne, Picasso, and Hamada.

The "turning back" in accordance with this often literally physiological sensation is itself so nearly overtly physical as well as psychological that one is completely justified in denoting it as a tropism, if
not in the modern biological sense, certainly at least in the original
sense of the Greek root: *tropos*, "a turning." Such a use of *tropism* in the
context of art and the creative process represents a shift in emphasis
from the use which Gaston Bachelard made of the word in his study
of the dream of flight. His word occurs in his commentary upon the
first strophe of Keats's "I stood tip-toe upon a little hill," especially the
lines:

> I gazed awhile, and felt as light, and free
> As though the fanning wings of Mercury
> Had play'd upon my heels: I was light-hearted,
> And many pleasures to my vision started;
> So I straightway began to pluck a posey
> Of luxuries bright, milky, soft and rosy.

As Bachelard comments, the linking of lightness and freedom (". . .
and felt as light, and free . . .") is so traditional that one forgets to
examine the imaginative basis for the coupling, but as Keats's subsequent lines show, only the "dynamic imagination" can bring an understanding. Bachelard continues: "Seule l'imagination dynamique peut
nous faire comprendre cette synonymie. Ces deux impressions déri-
vent d'un même tropisme de l'imagination aérienne. On le voit, c'est
le tropisme, l'ouranotropisme du vol onirique qui entraîne tous les
rêveurs aériens [Only the dynamic imagination can bring to us a
comprehension of this synonymy. These two impressions derive from
the same tropism of the aerial imagination. As can be seen, it is the
tropism, the Urano-tropism of the oneiric flight which compels all
aerial dreamers]."[21] But the phenomenon of which Bachelard speaks
is not the "turning back" itself, that which I designate the tropism, but
rather that prior, deeper, and more immediate element in the experience which compels the turning back and in doing so provides a
strong sense of anticipation, that which is apparently the source, then,
of the "anticipatory pre-image" which Piaget and Inhelder discerned
in children's attempts to produce drawings of previously experienced
percepts: "La copie suppose donc une pré-image anticipatrice . . . qui
décompose et recompose le modèle, et guide la réalisation graphique
[The copy presupposes then an anticipatory pre-image . . . which

decomposes and recomposes the model, and guides the graphic reali-
zation]."[22] Thus two separate and distinct tropisms figure in the total
process, one a motor component, the other a motor consequence, the
two separated by an often distinctly perceptible gap in time, a hysteresis. First occurs the complex transformational perception with its
motor component, its link with a *schème;* second occurs the realization
and the "double-take," the tropism which is a turning back.
Bachelard's compression of the event into one word obscures, indeed
loses, the significance of the insight. Of the two, the first tropism, the
motor component in the transformational perception, is of such crucial importance that the term *archetrope* seems an appropriate designation: *trope,* because it is again either an overt or interiorized
movement; *arche-,* because it precedes and compels the "turning
back" and because, once the attention has turned back, it reveals itself
as the motive force in the transformational process which produces
first the artistic vision and then the art object. The movement, the
kinesthesia, the archetrope, is, then, the actual in the root sense of
actual. It is inherent in those elements of the percept which provide
the "truthfulness of the essential that creates movement": it is archetrope for any given art object or artistic vision both in that it is initial
and in that it initiates. It is manifest, of course, as that which impelled
Matisse: the dance both felt and seen, felt *as* seen, indeed performed—felt, remembered, experienced, produced—produced as
and *is* the painting which went to Stschoukine, *La Danse.*

The archetrope, then, sensible in the selected elements, the form-
fragments, of the percept, is the vital element in the processes of the
artistic imagination. It arises in fusion with that generalized dynamic
formulation in the image memory which Piaget and Inhelder called
imaged *schèmes;* visuo-spatial formulations of movement which in the
external three-dimensional world manifest themselves as Rikyū's garden with its "leaf-drift," Matisse's dance or his chapel at Vence, or
other art objects with three-dimensional interior space, as for example, the cathedral at Chartres. The physical movement in and
through three-dimensional space—and not only the walking but the
sensing, the seeing, the smelling—becomes one totality of motion, a
holism of synchronized leg, arm, and body-act, of sweep of eye and
intake and outlet of breath, so that in the words of Miss Rosa in
Faulkner's *Absalom, Absalom!,* we experience the very "substance of
remembering—sense, sight, smell: the muscles with which we see and
hear and feel—not mind, not thought: there is no such thing as memory: the brain recalls just what the muscles grope for: no more, no
less. . . ." Or in Wordsworth's remarkably similar terms, the arche-

trope is that "active power to fasten images" derived from what lay "like substances" on the mind "and almost seemed to haunt the bodily sense":

> While yet a child, and long before his time
> He had perceived the presence and the power
> Of greatness, and deep feelings had impressed
> Great objects on his mind, with portraiture
> And colour so distinct that on his mind
> They lay like substances, and almost seemed
> To haunt the bodily sense. He had received
> A precious gift, for as he grew in years
> With these impressions would he still compare
> All his ideal stores, his shapes and forms,
> And being still unsatisfied with aught
> Of dimmer character, he thence attained
> An active power to fasten images
> Upon his brain, and on their pictured lines
> Intensely brooded, even till they acquired
> The liveliness of dreams.
>
> ("The Pedlar"—1798 version)

Of this passage Mary Warnock says, ". . . The forms of things seen in his youth lay, still thing-like, in the pedlar's mind, and haunted his seeing in the future. Moreover, these substance-like images were in the first place impressed on his mind by deep feelings and could not later be separated from feelings, when they were recalled in the absence of their original objects."[23] But it would be even more accurate to say that forms and feelings are indistinguishable, so that forms are the feelings, the feelings are the forms—a form-feeling complex with substance-like presence which confers upon the pedlar an *active* "power to fasten images / Upon his brain. . . ." In "Lines Composed a Few Miles above Tintern Abbey," Wordsworth offers a more succinct phrase adaptable to the present purpose: ". . . A motion and a spirit, that impels. . . ."

Thus the archetrope of any one art object is that particular motion-form, manifested in elements of the percept, which are assimilable into an imaged *schème:* what is in common in motif and emotion insofar as both words have their origins in the Latin *motus,* past participle of *movere,* "to move." It is this that Umberto Boccioni, for example, sought, according to his declaration in the *Futurist Manifesto:* "Action in our works, will no longer be an arrested moment of universal dynamism. It will be, simply, dynamic sensation itself."[24] Boccioni like Leonardo flattered himself that he was making manifest something new, but like Leonardo he was mistaken. The manner of expression may have changed with him and the other Futurists, but what he sought to express is at least as old as Altamira. Fittingly enough Gertrude Stein, who was making similar discoveries about motion-form at the same time as Boccioni, was gaining some of her insights from one of the very masters Boccioni purported to reject, Leonardo himself. Of her experience, she wrote, "The first thing that ever interested me in that way as the picture moving was the Leonardo in the Louvre, the Virgin, the child and Saint Anne. Before this the moving in a picture was the effect of moving, but in this picture there was an internal movement, not of the people or light or any of these things but inside in the oil painting." What she observed in such instances led her to seek a similar embodiment of motion itself in her prose at first by the relatively simple process of eliminating nouns and adjectives (because "they are uninteresting") and restricting her vocabulary as much as possible to verbs and adverbs:

> . . . Any one can see that verbs and adverbs are more interesting than nouns and adjectives.
> Besides being able to be mistaken and to make mistakes verbs can change to look like themselves or to look like something else, they are, so to speak on the move and adverbs move with them and each of them find themselves not at all annoying but very often very much mistaken.[25]

One comes back, then, to James's "germ" and to Wordsworth's "recollected in tranquility." The archetrope is initial, is initiating—indeed, guides the whole process, but it must not be mistaken for the process. The distinction becomes clear in another comment by Matisse, this one apropos of a series of flying doves cut out of colored paper. As he cut, he imaged the flights of doves: "Ces vols successifs de colombes, leurs orbes, leurs courbes glissent en moi comme dans un grand espace intérieur. Vous ne pouvez pas vous figurer à quel point, en cette période de papiers découpés, la sensation du vol qui se dégage en moi m'aide à mieux ajuster ma main quand elle conduit le trajet de mes ciseaux. C'est assez difficilement explicable. Je dirai que c'est une sorte d'équivalence linéaire, graphique de la sensation du vol [These successive flights of doves, their circles, their curves glide in me as in a great interior space. You cannot imagine to what point, in this period of paper cut-outs, the sensation of flight which is released within me aids me to better adjust my hand while it guides the trajectory of my scissors. It is difficult to explain. I will say that it is a sort of linear, graphic equivalence of the sensation of flight]."[26] Despite his difficulty, Matisse has nevertheless left a most detailed account of how the archetrope motivates the artistic vision, controls the artist's work, and emerges, finally, embodied in the art object. Unfortunately, as is so often the case with artists other than poets or novelists, he has not given us a coherent, consecutive account in one narrative: one must piece together from a number of comments. But sufficient unity exists from comment to comment to justify the piecing together. Passing over the "double-take," the tropism, Matisse begins his account with the archetrope: "C'est du premier choc de la contemplation d'un visage que dépend la sensation principale qui me conduit constamment pendant toute l'exécution d'un portrait [From the first shock of the contemplation of a face depends the principal sensation which guides me constantly throughout the entire execution of a portrait]."[27] That this first shock and principal sensation are impulse and movement has already been illustrated with the anecdote about the doves and will again be illustrated later. For the moment it is sufficient to point out that subsequently the initial and initiating sensation serves as guide throughout the evolution of the painting. So much is this true that Matisse can say as have so many other artists, both painters and poets, that the pattern of the painting develops with almost a life of its own, independent of any preconceived plan: "En résumé, je travaille *sans théorie*. J'ai seulement conscience des forces que j'emploie et je vais, poussé par une idée que je ne connais vraiment qu'au fur et à mesure qu'elle se développe par la marche du tableau [In sum then, I work *without theory*. I am conscious only of the forces which I use and I proceed, impelled by an idea which I truly know only progressively as it develops through the progress of the painting]."[28] Exactly how this development is pursued throughout the various stages of the painting appears in a somewhat longer comment:

La réaction d'une étape est aussi important que le sujet. Car cette réaction part de moi et non du sujet. C'est à partir de mon interprétation que je réagis continuellement jusqu'à ce que mon travail se trouve en accord avec moi. Comme quelqu'un qui fait sa phrase, il retravaille, il redécouvre. A chaque étape, j'ai un équilibre, une conclusion. A la séance suivant, si je trouve qu'il y a une faiblesse dans mon ensemble, je me réintroduis dans mon tableau par cette faiblesse—je rentre par la brèche—et je reçonçois le tout. Si bien que tout reprend du mouvement et comme chacun des éléments n'est qu'une partie des forces (comme dans une orchestration), tout peut être changé en apparence, le sentiment poursuivi restant toujours le même.

[The reaction to a stage (in the painting) is as important as the subject. For this reaction originates in me and not from the subject.

Thus, it is on the basis of my interpretation that I continually react until my work finds itself in accord with me. As one makes his sentence, he reworks, he rediscovers.

At each stage, I have a balance, a conclusion. In the following session, if I find that there is a weakness in the whole, I reintroduce myself into my painting by this weakness—I re-enter by the breach—and I reconceive the whole. So well that the whole resumes its movement and, as each element is only a portion of the forces (as in an orchestration), the whole can be altered in its appearance, while the sentiment I pursue remains always the same.][29]

That the depiction in the painting may change, may evolve from stage to stage while the "forces," the "movement" remain constant is a point of considerable importance. Coleridge commented upon it in a notebook entry in May 1804: "Remember my repeated Memoranda—Dorothy, myself, &c in my Red Cottle Book. Does not this establish the existence of *a Feeling* of a Person quite distinct at all times, & at certain times *perfectly separable* from, the Image of the Person? And this Feeling forms a most important link of Associations—& may be combined with the whole Story of a long Dream just as well as with one particular Form no way resembling the true Image?"[30] Again, the separability of the archetrope and the depiction is evident in Conrad's account of how his novel *The Secret Agent* began, how it grew from two separate anecdotal acquisitions, one that furnished the beginnings of plot or depiction, the other that furnished impulse, movement. In a conversation with a friend which touched upon the bombing of the Greenwich Observatory by an anarchist, he was particularly struck by two brief sentences spoken by his friend, the only reference to the subject: "'Oh, that fellow was half an idiot. His sister committed suicide afterwards.'" Concerning the information thus gained, which later would furnish plot material, Conrad said, "Of the illuminating quality there could be no doubt whatever. One felt like walking out of a forest on to a plain—there was not much to see but one had plenty of light. No, there was not much to see and, frankly, for a considerable time I didn't even attempt to perceive anything. It was only the illuminating impression that remained. It remained satisfactory but in a passive way." But a week later, he came upon an obscure little book in which he found an anecdote told of Sir William Harcourt, the home secretary at the time of such anarchist bombings: a minor official, encountering Sir William in the lobby of the House of Commons, had passed on to him some intelligence about anarchist activity. Sir William had burst out angrily: "'All that's very well. But your idea of secrecy over there seems to consist of keeping the Home Secretary in the dark.'"

The effect of the metaphor "keeping the Home Secretary in the dark" was remarkable:

> ... All of a sudden I felt myself stimulated. And then ensued in my mind what a student of chemistry would best understand from the analogy of the addition of the tiniest little drop of the right kind, precipitating the process of crystallization in a test-tube containing some colourless solution.
>
> It was at first for me a mental change, disturbing a quieted-down imagination, in which strange forms, sharp in outline but imperfectly apprehended, appeared and claimed attention as crystals will do by their bizarre and unexpected shapes. One fell to musing before the phenomenon—even of the past: of South America, a continent of crude sunshine and brutal revolutions, of the sea, the vast expanse of salt waters, the mirror of heaven's frowns and smiles, the reflector of the world's light. Then the vision of an enormous town presented itself, of a monstrous town more populous than some continents and in its man-made might as if indifferent to heaven's frowns and smiles; a cruel devourer of the world's light. There was room enough there to place any story, depth enough there for any passion, variety enough there for any setting, darkness enough to bury five millions of lives.[31]

The metaphoric comment upon the kind of intelligence activity which, instead of enlightening, keeps one in the dark provided the archetropic "stimulation" and a sequence of visions, various images (crude sunshine, the sea and a vast expanse of salt water—no doubt glittering in the sunshine, heaven's smile, and a reflector of the world's light, these all conjoined with images of brutal revolutions and heaven's frowns—note carefully the word *revolutions*)—each image focused on the archetropic revolution from light to dark. The whole culminates in the vision of the monstrous town, "a cruel devourer of the world's light" containing "darkness enough to bury five millions of lives" and thus certainly enough to bury the life of the sister of a half-idiot anarchist. The archetrope thus joined with depiction, and the novel was born.

In her diary, in a sequence of entries about the origins of *The Waves*, Virginia Woolf provides the means by which one may perceive a process parallel to a remarkable degree to that described by Conrad. Her account is, however, even more remarkable in that it gives us a much more intimate view because in the first steps Woolf was as yet unaware that a new novel was a-borning. Late in September 1926 she wrote of her concern for herself, her concern because of her "procrastination and nerves," her staleness. In general she was feeling fatigue and a

sort of rebellion after a long stretch of steady application in the composition of *To the Lighthouse.* She wrote:

> As for the book—Morgan said he felt "This is a failure," as he
> finished the *Passage to India.* I feel—what? A little stale this last week
> or two from steady writing. But also a little triumphant. If my
> feeling is correct, this is the greatest stretch I've put my method to,
> and I think it holds. . . . This is only my own feeling in process. Odd
> how I'm haunted by that damned criticism of Janet Case's "it's all
> dressing . . . technique. *(Mrs. Dalloway). The Common Reader* has
> substance." But then in one's strained state any fly has liberty to
> settle and it's always the gadflies. Muir praising me intelligently has
> comparatively little power to encourage—when I'm working, that
> is—when the ideas halt. And this last lap, in the boat, is hard. . . . I
> am forced to be more direct and more intense. I am making more
> use of symbolism, I observe; and I go in dread of "sentimentality."
> Is the whole theme open to that charge?

The quotation is made deliberately long so that one may clearly see
here in Woolf's account that "dissipation or natural deterioration of
every specialized attitude" of which Paul Valéry spoke, that situation
in which, however, one finds "incomparable resources." On the following day, 30 September, she continued, "I wished to add some
remarks to this, on the mystical side of this solicitude; how it is not
oneself but something in the universe that one's left with. It is this that
is frightening and exciting in the midst of my profound gloom, depression, boredom, whatever it is. One sees a fin passing far out. What
image can I reach to convey what I mean? Really there is none, I
think. The interesting thing is that in all my feeling and thinking I
have never come up against this before."[32]
    What Woolf does not realize at this stage is that she has already
reached the image despite her assertion to the contrary. The image is,
of course, in the sentence preceding the question: "One sees a fin
passing far out." That this is indeed *the* image is clear from her diary
entry of 7 February 1931 in which she records the completion of *The
Waves.* She wrote, "Here in the few minutes that remain, I must record, heaven be praised, the end of *The Waves.* I wrote the words, O
Death fifteen minutes ago. . . . I mean that I have netted that fin in the
waste of water which appeared to me over the marshes out of my
window at Rodmell when I was coming to the end of *To the Lighthouse.*"[33] Somewhere in the interval between the entry of 1926 and that
of 1931, Woolf did the "double-take," turned back to the archetropic
image of "a fin passing far out," and built from it a novel entitled *The*

Waves in which the central character, Bernard, in a final interior monologue cries out as the end approaches, "This self now as I leant over the gate looking down over fields rolling in waves of colour beneath me made no answer. He threw up no opposition. He attempted no phrase. His fist did not form. I waited. I listened. Nothing came, nothing. I cried then with a sudden conviction of complete desertion, Now there is nothing. No fin breaks the waste of this immeasurable sea."[34] At the end, however, although it is not overtly stated, the fin does rise, and Bernard goes forward to meet it in a triumphant affirmation:

> "And in me too the wave rises. It swells; it arches its back. I am aware once more of a new desire, something rising beneath me like the proud horse whose rider first spurs and then pulls him back. What enemy do we now perceive advancing against us, you whom I ride now, as we stand pawing this stretch of pavement? It is death. Death is the enemy. It is death against whom I ride with my spear couched and my hair flying back like a young man's, like Percival's, when he galloped in India. I strike spurs into my horse. Against you I will fling myself, unvanquished and unyielding, O Death!"[35]

This final affirmation carries the reader back to the initial entry, the diary entry of 1926, and Woolf's statement then that "I feel—what? A little stale this last week. . . . But also a little triumphant." Depression—elation, a falling and a rising—or in Woolf's phrase in the next to the last paragraph of her novel: "Yes, this is the eternal renewal, the incessant rise and fall and fall and rise again." When one sees the cyclic conjunction of the waves—crest and trough; of the shark—the arching upward and sweeping downward; and of the human lot—life and death, one literally sees the archetrope upon which her novel was built. Almost as if to underscore the point, Woolf, after recording the last words, "O Death," in her diary on 7 February 1931, added a final sentence, a final image: *"The waves broke on the shore."*

What Matisse, Conrad, and Woolf recorded explains and illustrates what disturbed Henry James when he failed to recapture the origins of *The Tragic Muse:* "If it be ever of interest and profit to put one's finger on the productive germ of a work of art, and if in fact a lucid account of any such work involves that prime identification, I can but look on the present fiction as a poor fatherless and motherless, a sort of unregistered and unacknowledged birth. I fail to recover my precious first moment of consciousness of the idea to which it was to give form; to recognize in it—as I like to do in general—the effect of some particular sharp impression or concussion. I call such remembered glimmers always precious, because without them comes no clear vision of what one may have succeeded in doing."[36]

To return to Matisse and the archetropic technique illustrated by his comments, since all elements of the work are forces within the total movement, a weakness reveals itself at any one stage when a portion of the whole ceases to move, becomes dead and lifeless. At this point the next stage begins. The bringing to life of the one dead point may and probably does involve, since the whole is an orchestration of forces, a reorientation of the whole, but that does not matter because it is not the form schema, a depiction, but a formulated movement *schème* that is sought, and a great number of forms will formulate any given movement. What one observes in the origins of Virginia Woolf's *The Waves* and the finished novel amply illustrates the point, for after one perceives the archetropic impulse behind the central image of the novel one realizes that the word "waves" in the title no longer refers specifically to the movement of water in an ocean. It refers instead to the movement itself, the upward-downward-upward movement of a whole range of forms from ocean waves to the birth and death of human life, to, that is, the form of the novel itself.

Essentially then the poet and the painter share a context which endows the word *technique* with a meaning entirely different from its usual sense in discussions of art. The evidence indicates that the word must not be limited in reference to the manner of medium manipulation. It is, instead, best defined by e. e. cummings in his preface to *is 5:*

> At least my theory of technique, if I have one, is very far from original; nor is it complicated. I can express it in fifteen words, by quoting 'The Eternal Question And Immortal Answer of Burlesk,' viz, 'Would you hit a woman with a child?—No, I'd hit her with a brick.' Like the burlesk comedian I am abnormally fond of that precision which creates movement.

Robert Graves's comments about cumming's definition make the direct application: "Technique itself has taken on a different character; it is no longer the way a poem is presented to the reader, but the way its elements correspond in every respect with the governing sense."[37] But the precision which cummings valued requires the insistence that "the governing sense" is specifically a governing movement—the archetrope. Precision as well requires recognition that, despite Graves's assumption, this definition of technique is not, as cummings himself indicates, particularly new. Instead, as he said, it is "very far from original," and the evidence rather clearly supports him. Nevertheless it is useful to have Graves's more explicit statement of what Matisse, Conrad, Woolf, and Rikyū illustrate:

> In making a poem the poet may be said to be ruled by this [governing] sense, and in this foreshadowing, inevitable sense the poem exists even before it is recorded on paper, before the poet is aware of anything more definite than that there is a poem to be written. . . . Thus technique in the modernist definition is no code of rules by which a poem is written but an awareness of its evolutionary history. "The Eternal Question And Immortal Answer of Burlesk" are in literary terms: "Do you write poems with a prearranged technique?—No, I write them with a pen."[38]

Emily Dickinson said it much more succinctly: "After great pain a formal feeling comes. . . ."

4

The Literary Art Object: A Topological View

*T*he formation of the artistic image, that is to say, the fusion, in accordance with an archetropic impulse, of two deformed images to form a composite, documents the fact that to see as an artist sees is to compose. Indeed it is this direct link between seeing and composing that permitted Gertrude Stein to assert, "Nothing changes from generation to generation except the thing seen and that makes a composition."[1] In short it is but a single step from the archetropic image, that which is seen in the artistic vision, to the art object itself—and this, as Angus Wilson insisted, despite the seeming multiple steps in the sometimes long span of time filled with manipulations of the medium, paint or words, to achieve the embodiment of the art object. Speaking of the "momentary powerfully visual picture" with which each of his novels began, Wilson asserted:

> The novels . . . *are* those moments of vision. No didactic, sociological, psychological or technical elaboration can alter that significance for the novelist himself. Like any other artist's, the novelist's statement is a concentrated vision; he aims as much as any symbolist poet or impressionist painter at seizing the 'stuff' of life and communicating it totally; but, unlike the others he has chosen the most difficult of all forms, one that makes its own discipline as it goes along. We can never hope for the perfection, even with a Tolstoy, that other arts can achieve with a Piero della Francesca or a Bach. But any serious novelist who tries to describe aspects of his work and does not announce this vision as his central impulse is either playing down to some imaginary "plain chap" audience or

has forgotten his original true inspiration in the polemics of moral, social or formal purpose.[2]

Precisely this insight lay behind Matisse's experiments with cutouts. The intricate simplicity of such forms, the better observed because they are masses of cutout colored paper rather than outline forms filled in with color, amply illustrates the fact that the composition of the art object is something which precedes the cutting itself, is something inherent in the interior prefiguring, integral with the archetropic image. Matisse was emphatic on this point: "Pour moi, tout est dans la conception. Il est donc nécessaire d'avoir, dès le début, une vision nette de l'ensemble. Je pourrais citer un très grand sculpteur qui nous donne des morceaux admirables: mais, pour lui, une composition n'est qu'un groupement de morceaux, et il en résulte de la confusion dans l'expression [For me, all is in the conception. It is necessary to have, from the very outset, a sharp vision of the totality. I could cite a very great sculptor who gives us admirable pieces: but, for him, a composition is only a grouping of pieces, and this results in a confusion in the expression]."[3] Thus composition is both the integrative force, the "orchestration" in Matisse's vision of the farandole, and the result, *La Danse* which he sent to Stschoukine. Matisse's distinction here is, then, between what in structuralist terms would be a structure (composition) and an aggregate (disposition)—the same distinction implicit in what Gertrude Stein learned from her study of Cézanne's paintings. "Everything I have done has been influenced by Flaubert and Cézanne and this gave me a new feeling about composition. Up to that time composition had consisted of a central idea to which everything else was an accompaniment and separate but was not an end in itself, and Cézanne conceived the idea that in composition one thing was as important as another thing. Each part is as important as the whole and that impressed me enormously and it impressed me so much that I began to write *Three Lives* under this influence and this idea of composition. . . . It was the first time in any language that anyone had used the idea of composition in literature. . . ."[4] One cannot be too certain about her historical accuracy in these assertions: as far as painting is concerned, the evidence of Altamira, Font-de-Gaume, and Lascaux is to the effect that composition has existed since man first drew; the evidence to be adduced in subsequent chapters will strongly suggest that composition in this sense has been inherent in literature ever since man first poeticized. One of Stein's major and not inconsiderable achievements is the articulation of the concept not only for herself but also for that group of writers and painters gathered periodically at her apartment in the Rue de Fleurus, the articulation which undoubtedly sent Hemingway almost daily to the Musée du Luxembourg to learn from Cézanne how to "live right with his eyes."

Implicit then in this discussion of composition is a fact visible in Matisse's cutouts. In the composition of his flying doves, as Matisse's hand guided the scissors through the color of the paper sheet, the hand in turn guided by the sensation of interiorized flight, there was no outline, no sketch: the scissors-cut itself was the only manifested "line": "Le papier découpé me permet de dessiner dans la couleur. Il s'agit pour moi d'une simplification. Au lieu de dessiner le contour et d'y installer la couleur—l'un modifiant l'autre—je dessine directement dans la couleur, qui est d'autant plus mesurée qu'elle n'est pas transposée. Cette simplification garantit une précision dans la réunion des deux moyens qui ne font plus qu'un [Paper cutouts permit me to sketch in the color. It is for me a matter of simplification. Instead of drawing the contour and establishing the color within it—the one modifying the other—I draw directly in the color which is the more tailored in that it has not been transplanted. This simplification guarantees a precision in the conjunction of the two procedures which are now reduced to one]."[5] The event shows Matisse's desire to reduce and simplify the medium manipulations and consequently the time that intervenes between the vision and the realization of the art object, his effort to achieve in the making of the art object as close an approach as possible to the synchrony of the creative process. What he sought with his cutouts is the "strength and simplicity" of which Siegfried Sassoon spoke: ". . . I hope that I have said enough about the visual element in poetry to stimulate your interest in the subject, and also to remind you that simplification of visual imagery is essential to the best poetry. Strength and simplicity always go together. Good draughtsmanship means elimination of redundant detail, and so it is in writing. He who distracts and confuses the mind's eye by over-elaboration and congestion of illustrative language can never be memorable. And that is where imagination, when instinctively controlled, gets the better of contrived thought. For mind-sight eliminates what is inessential, and achieves breadth and intensity by transmuted perception."[6]

But perhaps the most incisive statement by a poet on that precision in form making visible in Matisse's cutouts is one by William Blake, whose poetic lines, indeed, are every bit as distinct, sharp, and wiry as any bounding line he ever engraved, or as any contour ever cut out by Matisse's scissors:

The great and golden rule of art, as well as of life, is this: "That the more distinct, sharp, and wirey the bounding line, the more perfect the work of art; and the less keen and sharp, the greater is the evidence of weak imitation, plagiarism, and bungling." Great inventors, in all ages, knew this: Protogenes and Apelles knew each other by this line. Rafael and Michael Angelo and Albert Dürer are known by this and this alone. The want of this determinate and bounding form evidences the want of idea in the artist's mind, and the pretence of the plagiary in all its branches. How do we distinguish the oak from the beech, the horse from the ox, but by the bounding outline? How do we distinguish one face or countenance from another, but by the bounding line and its infinite inflexions and movements? What is it that builds a house and plants a garden, but the definite and determinate? What is it that distinguishes honesty from knavery, but the hard and wiry line of rectitude and certainty in the actions and intentions? Leave out this line, and you leave out life itself; all is chaos again, and the line of the almighty must be drawn out upon it before man or beast can exist.[7]

Blake's incisiveness on the role of outline sharpens a most important point which emerges from Matisse's cutouts, a point concerning the concept of linearity which underlies either branch of the calligraphic art, but most particularly for the present purpose as far as literature is concerned, for creation by cutting directly into a color field manifests an alternative to that "geometry" of art most frequently assumed by viewer or reader. The alternative in turn reveals a major alternative in the concept of linearity, permitting as a consequence a significant reorientation in the "geometry" of the literary language. But first, lest it seem extravagant to speak of a geometry of language, one should recall, as the mathematician René Thom has pointed out, "S'il est vrai, comme l'a dit Paul Valéry, qu': 'il n'y a pas de géométrie sans langage,' il est non moins vrai—comme l'ont entrevu certains logiciens—qu'il n'y a pas de langage intelligible sans une géométrie, une dynamique sous-jacente dont ce langage formalise les états structurellement stables [If, as Paul Valéry said, 'There is no geometry without language,' it is no less true—as some logicians have foreseen—that there is no intelligible language without a geometry, an underlying dynamic whose structurally stable states are formalized by the language]."[8]

In drawing and painting, the word *outline* refers to a graphic indication of the outer limits of that which is concentric, the outer limits of that which has a common center. Although frequently used as a synonym for *contour,* the outline more properly is a two-dimensional abstraction of the contour of an object. Thus, despite the preposition *out* embedded in the word, outline in drawing or painting is essentially centripetal. In writing, however, the word is frequently understood as a reference to an orderly arrangement of topics and subtopics with an indication of coordination and subordination. In such common usage in reference to verbal composition, the word makes *composition* virtually indistinguishable from *disposition,* adding only slightly to the dimension of *disposition* in that *disposition* does not necessarily contain within itself an indication of linear direction in the arrangement of the elements: the conjunction of composition and outline in the terminology of writing introduces a specific linear direction explicit in the literal sense of the word *proposition,* a linearity derived from a concept of the universe as empty Euclidean space, defined by the three dimensions of the Cartesian coordinates. The fact is self-evident in that this linearity is the same as that of the Aristotelian beginning, middle, and end, the story "line" or "line of argument" which is the equivalent of the Archimedean "straight line," basal element of Euclidean geometry, "the shortest distance between two points," that Archimedean line which is both the Cartesian coordinates and the principle of their functioning.

The question raised by the difference in meaning of the word *outline* as one goes from painting to poetry is a question of the definition of form. Essentially, the drawn outline, the (Euclidean) geometrical form on a plane surface, is a projection. The exploration of this fact led James J. Gibson to ask, "Might it not be that the dynamics of projected forms, so diligently studied, consists not in the laws of form as such but in the laws that relate them to solid objects—the laws of projection and transformation?" To amplify what he meant by "the laws of projection and transformation," he wrote: "This way of considering size and shape points toward a conception of visual projected form which is very different from the traditional one. Perhaps a closed outline is not an independent entity as we have tended to think but some kind of variable. Perhaps we should conceive form not as a thing but as merely one of the variables of things. The projected shape of a perceived object would then be only one of its visual qualities among others such as the slant of its surfaces, its size, its color, its texture, and its distance, all of which can vary continuously along a scale or dimension. If we cease to think about forms as a set of geometrical entities and concentrate instead on the transitions between them, as we have learned to do for colors, our thinking about the visual process may be clarified."[9] In effect, without saying so in so many words, Gibson here calls for a consideration of visual forms from a topological point of view, a suggestion of tremendous importance, for topology is the mathematics of transformations, and as such is indispensable in any study of the transformational process. To illustrate very briefly how it differs from Euclidean geometry, the circle, square, rectangle, triangle, etc., so carefully distinguished the one from the other in Euclidean geometry, are topologically merely variations (homeomorphs) of a single figure, a simple closed curve, as are also the capital letters D and O. But the capital letters C, I, J, L, M, N, S, U, V, W, and Z are all topologically the same figure, a simple arc as is the "straight line" of common usage and the line segments of plane geometry. Basically, on the two-dimensional plane, the difference between a simple closed curve and a simple arc is that the simple arc does not create a "hole" in the plane: the ends of the line do not join. But the simple closed curve cuts the plane into two parts: The ends join to form a "hole" in the previously continuous plane. To return to Matisse and his scissors: His cutouts are formed of simple closed curves in that the completed cutout is precisely that, a cutout. Topology and Matisse thus combine to define form in drawing. The definition of *outline* and *form* in drawing—indeed topologically, in the visual field—thus strongly suggests that a careful examination of the phenomenon of linearity itself may prove highly instructive in respect to the "topology" of the literary language.

As the Impressionists were so fond of pointing out, the outline as conventionally used in painting and drawing does not exist in nature. What one sees in the visual world are "objective" or "subjective" contours and "virtual" lines, three different manifestations of one central phenomenon: Perception of form is the perception of discontinuities in gradients. In the words of the topologist, "En effet, le propre de toute forme, de toute morphogénèse, est de s'exprimer par une discontinuité des propriétés du milieu . . . [In effect, the characteristic of every form, every morphogenesis, is to reveal itself by a discontinuity in the properties of the environment]."[10] Of particular interest in the present context is a class of contours, variously designated as "subjective," "cognitive," or "anomalous," which are present to the perception despite the fact that no discontinuity is present to the senses: they are the product of cognitive processes rather than of retinal stimulation.[11] Essentially they are a three-dimensional version of the two-dimensional phenomenon known as "virtual" lines. For this reason it seems most effective to approach a discussion of subjective contours and their relevance to the concept of outline in writing by way of a discussion of the virtual line.

The most interesting manifestation of such a line, most interesting for the light it throws on the imagination, is the virtual line which results from the perception of three dots not in a straight line but equidistant from each other on a plane surface. Human perception spontaneously organizes this configuration into a triangle in the visual field by supplying lines to connect the three dots. As Gaetano Kanizsa says of such spontaneously formed lines, ". . . Although they are not actually seen, they are a real presence in our visual experience. They are far more compelling than other connecting lines that can be imagined. For example, the three dots could just as readily be points on a circle, but the curved connecting lines of the circle are more difficult to 'see' than the straight lines of the triangle."[12] The force of such virtual lines in the organization of perceived space is considerable and their role in the control of human behavior within perceived space is primary. A series of experiments reported by Piaget and Inhelder illustrates the point. The experiments focused upon imaged transformations performed upon perceptions of a wand, one end of which was fixed so that the wand could pivot. The children-subjects were asked to indicate by drawing or gesture the path which would be described by the free end of the wand should the wand be rotated from the vertical to the horizontal position. The most pervasive and consistent error throughout all the age groups tested (ages four through nine) was to designate the path of the virtual line, not the arc, which "connects" the end of the vertical wand as seen and its imaged position after an imagined rotation to the horizontal position. When, on the basis of this imagined rotation the subjects were asked to draw the obliques which would mark the position of the wand at 30° and 60°, the length of the obliques was underestimated in from 53 percent to 74 percent of the cases. The evidence indicates the existence in the subjects' imaginations of straight rather than curved connections, tip to tip, the existence of what Piaget and Inhelder called "frontiers" and, in addition, of a very strong reluctance on the part of the subjects to go beyond them in drawing the obliques.[13]

In certain figural contexts virtual lines transform to subjective contours by becoming a discontinuity in the gradient axis oriented at right angles to the virtual line. For example, as one stares at the center of a figure presenting but three dots and three small angles arranged in a certain fashion, the elements are perceived as two superimposed triangular surfaces upon a ground. Topologically, then, three points and three small angles spontaneously organize themselves into three surfaces: a ground, a lower triangle formed from the three angles and their connective virtual lines, and an upper triangle formed from the three dots and their connecting virtual lines. The illusion involves as well an apparent differentiation in the illumination of the three "surfaces": the "upper" or "nearer" triangle seems brigher than the "lower" where the "contour" of the "upper" crosses over it. The three

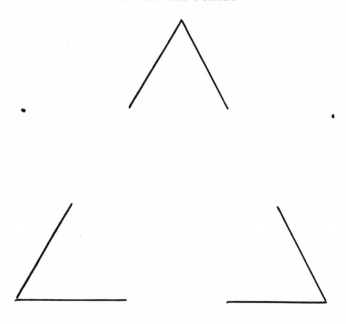

Virtual lines and subjective contours: When the two-dimensional configuration of three small angles and three dots is regarded fixedly at the center, it appears to be three-dimensional, composed of two superimposed triangular planes on a ground.

tips of the "lower" triangle are not only apparently much grayer than the "upper" one but even, surprisingly, slightly grayer than the ground. That all of this beyond the three dots and the three small angles is purely imaginary is quite obvious. In the words of R. L. Gregory, they are "cognitive fictions."[14] Nor are they limited to triangular or straight-line figures. Kanizsa and other researchers have demonstrated various other manifestations: circles, pear shapes, and curvilinear free-forms.[15] The phenomenon is one which has been known and exploited by graphic artists from prehistory to the present. The artists who painted Lascaux approximately 17,000 years ago commonly used it to achieve depth in the figures by "gapping" the outline. To form the contours of what in the visual world is the far leg of a horse, for example, the artist left a gap in the drawing where the outline of nearer portions of the figure cut across it. The eye is thus forced to supply a virtual line and a subjective contour to complete the image. Frequently other parts of the outline were also omitted with similar effects, effects of rounding, as, for example, at chin and chest of the second "Chinese" horse at Lascaux (see color plate). These effects are, of course, best perceived if one does not look directly at the outline portions in question. A comparable use of the phenomenon appears in an Aztec sun emblem design. Indeed the Central American artists of the pre-Columbian era were generally quite adept at the use of this device. A more direct dependence upon the subjective contour without the added complexity of virtual lines appears in a traditional Sufi meditation design, a design which is basically the same as the Aztec sun emblem without the gapping; however, it becomes more simplified and now appears composed of squares with "interlocking" corners which are in fact formed by subjective contours.

The topology of the imagination, then, insofar as the phenomenon of linearity is concerned, depends once again upon a fusion of transformable elements, a fusion of the same order as that observed in the drawing of the bison at Altamira, but occurring on a much more fundamental level. At Altamira, the artist had two ready-made forms at hand, the rock protuberance and a bison, and thus had merely to match supplied contour elements. In the case of virtual lines and subjective contours, the recept image furnishes neither gradient nor discontinuity. Instead it furnishes as little as a ground and a minimal disposition of discrete elements; the imagination furnishes all the rest: line, contour, form. The artistic consciousness of this fusion appears in an anecdote recounted by Brassaï: Picasso was skimming through Brassaï's volume *Graffiti* and came upon the chapter "The Birth of the Face," a grouping of photographs of faces done from two or three holes in a wall. Picasso studied the drawings with great interest and then commented: "I have often done faces like this myself. The people who scratch them out like this naturally gravitate to symbols. . . . Two holes—that's the symbol for the face, enough to evoke it without representing it. . . . But isn't it strange that it can be done through such simple means? Two holes; that's abstract enough if you consider the complexity of man. . . ."[16]

Such phenomena as virtual lines and subjective contours indicate that the origins of the phenomenon of linearity and the topology of the imagination are in that aspect of the human imagination which depends upon gaps and discontinuities, upon incompletion, in the receptible. As Hamada perceived, the essential movement in life is

Virtual lines and subjective contours: A Sufi meditation device (upper) in which subjective contours produce the illusion of interlocked squares and (below) a closely related figure, an Aztec sun emblem, with, in addition, virtual lines in the gapped outline. The Aztec sun emblem, from a flat stamp in the collection of the National Museum, Mexico City, is reproduced from Jorge Enciso, *Design Motifs of Ancient Mexico*, © 1953, courtesy of the publisher, Dover Publications, Inc.

that which is expressed with the word *unfinished*. In discussing the difference between his own work and that of Kawai Kanjiro, he said, "Kawai got so caught up that he almost hypnotized himself into thinking that he had completed everything. After all we cannot really complete anything in our lives—that is not a reality. But with myself . . . not complete, negating, unfinished [*sic*]. Perhaps the negative and positive are not different. If one says 'finished,' there is no life there anymore, but if one says 'unfinished,' life continues, movement goes on. I was going to write a piece to match Kawai's, but because my work is always unfinished, I still have not written it. That is, after all, the meaning of unfinished. When something is unfinished, it is finished."[17] Transformational perception at the level of virtual lines and subjective contours amply confirms his insight, for Hamada verbalizes what Picasso's comments exemplify: the human imagination of form begins with omission, discontinuity, or deficiency in the percept whether that percept be the motif—that which gives the archetropic impulse to the artist—or the art object—that which embodies it for the viewer. As it engages the imagination, the "unfinished" is both the essence of symbol and the essence of life.

But in reference to writing, the word *outline* commonly does not denote a discontinuity but rather usually is used to denote a linear phenomenon of quite a different order in that, as already noted, the word refers not so much to the definition and separation of forms as it does to the continuity in an orderly arrangement of sequential elements within a form. But as Joseph Joubert affirmed, "Si l'oeil n'était pas facile à séduire, les plaisirs que donne l'art de la peinture ne pourraient pas exister. Nous ne pourrions prendre ce qui est plan ni pour saillant ni pour enfoncé; le dessin même de Raphaël ne nous offrirait que des hachures et un griffonnage insignifiant. Il en est ainsi de l'art d'écrire: si le lecteur n'a pas une imagination qui ait le caractère de l'oeil, Virgile n'a pas de beautés [If the eye were not easily seduced, the pleasures which are furnished by the art of painting could not exist. We could not take what is flat either for projection or depression; the drawing even of Raphael would offer us only hachures and insignificant scribbles. It is thus with the art of writing: if the reader does not have an imagination with the qualities of the eye, Virgil has no beauty]."[18] The concept of linearity as continuity is the fundamental assumption of the Euclidean-Cartesian organization of space; the concept assumes a point-to-point sequence within a total span from beginning to end to form a line, a sequential movement of a line to form a surface, a sequential movement of a surface to form a three-dimensional object. The specific linear "direction" of the sequence corresponds to a direction in three-dimensional space which in terms of human vision or movement can be expressed by the word *forward*. One should note in this context the metaphor "line of sight." Psychologically and philosophically, as already suggested, it is expressed by the word *proposition*, and in poetics by the definition of a story as that which has a beginning, a middle, and an end, the Aristotelian story line. Consequently that which normally is called an outline in reference to writing may more properly be considered an "in-line." But, as suggestive as "in-line" may be, greater precision derives from the word *axis*: the outline in writing is an axis which derives its force from the fact that it is but one of a number of parallels which play a significant role in the geometry and topology of language. In the case of English in particular, of the Indo-European languages generally, and indeed of a predominant number of languages in the world, this axis is the "line" of syntax itself, that which is usually designated the subject-verb-object pattern. Obviously it is as well the time-space pattern of the verbal event, of the speaking, writing, hearing, or reading, in which the discrete units of the event (phonemes, morphemes, words, etc.) must be either enunciated, traced, or perceived sequentially in a given direction from a given point of origin in time-space. In this same sense, one may also speak of the parallel linear time-space pattern of the interiorized cognitive event, the "stream of consciousness," the pattern implicit in the metaphor as the vision of a stream which flows through time and space from source to mouth. The verbal event and cognitive sequences must "go" in the same direction since obviously one may not speak or write, hear or read or think a discourse without simultaneously experiencing duration, nor may one perform the event in reverse. Perhaps because of this fact of irreversible duration in the verbal event and the stream of consciousness the Western world at least has assumed a necessary parallel between these axes and the chronological past, present, and future, as well as the predicative pattern of thought itself, cause to effect.

But, as the phenomena of virtual lines and subjective contours illustrate, a line is in its very essence bimodal: in indicating continuity in one axis it necessarily and simultaneously indicates discontinuity in the transverse. Again Matisse's scissors are instructive: as the actioning of the scissors effects a continuous cut from one point to another along the contour of the emerging form, it simultaneously effects a discontinuity between contour-to-be and ground-to-be. The continuous cut thus in its very continuity simultaneously creates a centrifugal-centripetal opposition, the "outside" versus the "inside." Line, as Paul Klee has pointed out, is but the graphic manifestation of Matisse's scissors-cut: "When a linear form is combined with a plane form the

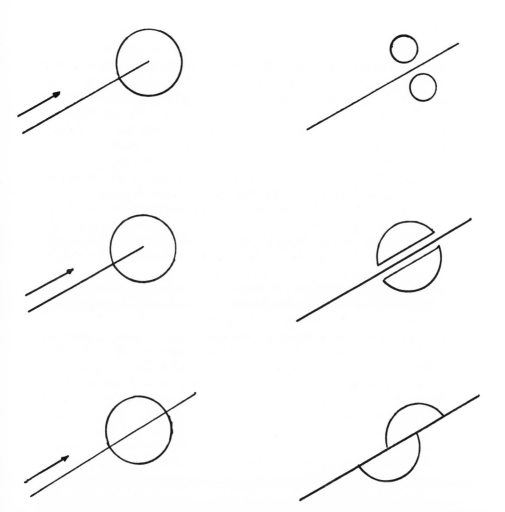

Paul Klee's dynamic line breaks one space into two individual spaces and displaces them laterally (upper), slices one space into two halves with no displacement (middle), or slices one space into two and displaces one or the other along the axis of thrust. Klee's diagram illustrates the bimodalism of a line. Reproduced from Paul Klee, *Das bildnerische Denken,* © 1956, courtesy of the publishers, Benno Schwabe & Co., Verlag, and of Lund Humphries Publishers, Ltd.

linear part takes on a decidedly active character and the plane a
passive character in contrast. If this is carried back to the first genesis
of form it leads to the phenomenon of cell division. . . . The active
part, the line, can accomplish two things by its impetus: it may divide
the form into two parts, or it may go still further and give rise to a
displacement [Bei der Kombination einer linearen Form mit einer
flächigen bekommt der lineare Teil einen ausgesprochen aktiven
Charakter und die Flächenform im Gegensatz dazu einen passiven
Charakter. Auf den Urvorgang der Formbildung, die Zeugung,
zurückgeführt, ergibt sich der Vorgang der Zellenteilung. . . . Der
aktive Teil, die Linie, vermag durch Angriff zweierlei: er gliedert die
betroffene Form in zwei Teile, oder er geht noch weiter und gibt
Anlass zu einer Verschiebung].[19] Matisse spoke of this same phenomenon when he described his paper cutting as "dessinant aux ciseaux
dans des feuilles de papier colorées à l'avance, d'un même geste pour
associer la ligne à la couleur, le contour à la surface [drawing with
scissors in sheets of colored paper, with but a single gesture needed to
associate the line to the color, the contour to the surface]."[20]

One finds this same linear bimodalism in, for example, several Aztec designs, each of which has as its basis a virtual line best described
as the "centerfold" should the figure be folded in half at right angles
to its longer axis. The longer axis then is more precisely described as a
discontinuous gradient, the discontinuity occurring at the point of
pattern reversal. Mathematically speaking, such figures exhibit
twofold symmetry in that there is a central axis in both orientations,
vertically and horizontally, but in formal terms the shorter axis, the
"base" line is in the continuous mode, cutting the plane from edge to
edge as in Paul Klee's illustration. The longer is in the discontinuous
mode. The totality is a holistic image of bimodalism. At least two
excellent examples of a compositional exploitation of this bimodalism
come from prehistory. The two bison in the "Nave" of Lascaux, depicted (see color plate) with overlapped hindquarters and symmetri-
cally arranged tails and hind legs, emphasize the discontinuous
modality in their vigorous charges in opposite directions in one of the
most animated compositions in all prehistoric art. The other example,
less moving aesthetically but more revealing schematically, is one particularly clear "tectiform" in a group of three on the left wall at Font-
de-Gaume, just after the Rubicon. According to Capitan, Breuil, and
Peyrony, the first men to study this cave systematically, the lines of this
tectiform are formed of carefully aligned dots, but a closer examination with more modern light and optical aids reveals the lines to be
virtual lines formed by a series of carefully aligned parallel strokes

Aztec designs exhibiting two fold symmetries based on linear bimodalism. In each instance, if the shorter axis through the center is viewed as a continuous line cutting the figure into two symmetrical halves, the longer axis becomes an axis of discontinuity with opposing thrusts originating at the transverse shorter axis. If the longer axis is viewed as the continuous line, the shorter one immediately shifts to the discontinuous mode. The designs, from flat stamps found in Mexico City, collection of the National Museum, are reproduced from Jorge Enciso, *Design Motifs of Ancient Mexico,* © 1953, courtesy of the publisher, Dover Publications, Inc.

transverse or nearly so to the axis of continuity. Of course, in either event, whether the lines are formed by dots or parallel strokes, the figure depends on the phenomenon of the virtual line, but the formation of a virtual line by the construction of transverse parallel lines, and in particular the careful alignment of the parallel strokes so that they all are precisely spaced and equal in length, reveals a deliberate exploitation of linear bimodalism by the prehistoric man who made the figure. The same awareness is the basis for the so-called "split" representations of animals characteristic, for example, of the totem-pole art of the Pacific Northwest, representations in which the three-dimensional form to be represented has been "split" down the back along the axis of symmetry and then "flattened" to achieve an opposi-

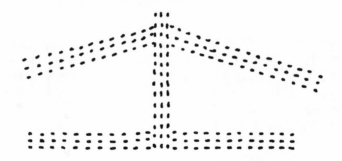

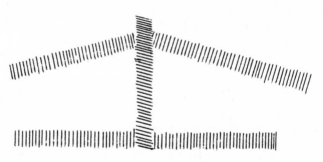

Tectiform near the Rubicon, Font-de-Gaume (base: 20 cm.) as observed by Capitan, Breuil, and Peyrony in 1909–10 (upper) and as observed by Mme Daubisse, current guardian of the cave, and the author and his assistant (below). The more modern observation reveals the prehistoric artist's conscious exploitation of linear bimodalism.

tion of features focused along the front axis of symmetry. As Claude Lévi-Strauss has pointed out, such art is fundamentally "a relationship of opposition" along the front axis. He elaborates the social or cultural significance of the phenomenon,[21] but in the present context the importance of such art is that it demonstrates once again the artist's awareness and exploitation of the discontinuous mode of a line.

The fact of linear bimodalism underscores the need for considerable caution when one turns from the one graphic mode to the other in calligraphy. In commenting upon the more explicit exploitations of the discontinuous in modern art, Roland Barthes concluded:

Tous ces artistes [Webern, Mondrian, Michel Butor] n'ont d'ailleurs nullement inventé le discontinu pour mieux en triompher: le discontinu est le statut fondamental de toute communication: il n'y a jamais de signes que discrets. Le problème esthétique est simplement de savoir comment mobiliser ce discontinu fatal, comment lui donner un souffle, un temps, une histoire. La rhétorique classique a donné sa réponse, magistrale pendant des siècles, en édifiant une esthétique de la *variation* (dont l'idée de "développement" n'est que le mythe grossier); mais il y a une autre rhétorique possible, celle de la *translation:* moderne, sans doute, puisqu'on ne la trouve que dans quelques oeuvres d'avant-garde; et cependant, ailleurs, combien ancienne: tout récit mythique, selon l'hypothèse de Claude Lévi-Strauss, n'est-il pas produit par une *mobilisation* d'unités récurrentes, de *séries* autonomes (diraient les musiciens), dont les déplacements, *infiniment possibles,* assurent à l'oeuvre la responsabilité de son choix, c'est-à-dire sa singularité, c'est-à-dire son sens? [In no way however did all these artists (Webern, Mondrian, Michel Butor) invent the discontinuous the better to triumph over it; the discontinuous is the fundamental law of all communication: there are never any but discreet signs. The aesthetic problem is simply to know how to mobilize this fatal discontinuity, how to give it a breath, a time, a history. Classical rhetoric gave its response, authoritative for centuries, building an aesthetics of *evolution* (of which the idea of "development" is but the rude myth); but there is another possible rhetoric, that of *translation* [in the physical sense]: modern, without doubt, because one finds it only in some avant-garde works, and, nevertheless, how ancient: is not all mythic recital, according to the hypothesis of Claude Lévi-Strauss, produced by means of a mustering of recurrent entities, an autonomous *series* (the musicians would say), the juggling of which, infinitely possible, assures the work its responsibility of choice, that is to say, its uniqueness, its sense?][22]

The insight is useful despite the fact that Barthes's view is rather limited: he sees the discontinuity in the juxtaposition of recurrent entities as an extension of the discontinuity, the gapping, between words in a sentence: The "line" which for him is marked out by the recurrences is still parallel to the line of the verbal event and the "thought." The point is manifest in the definition of *form* guiding him at this point: ". . . C'est par le retour régulier des unités et des associations d'unités que l'oeuvre apparaît construite, c'est-à-dire douée de sens; les linguistes appellent ces règles de combinaison des *formes*, et il y aurait grand intérêt à garder cet emploi rigoureux d'un mot trop usé: la forme, a-t-on dit, c'est ce qui permet à la contiguïté des unités de ne point apparaître comme un pur effet du hasard [It is through the regular return of units and associations of units that the work appears constructed, that is to say endowed with sense; linguists call these rules of combination *forms*, and there would be a great value in retaining this strict application of a word too widely used: form, it has been said, is that which permits the contiguity of units to appear in no way as pure happenstance]."[23] Thus literary form parallels syntactic form. But as suggested by a schematic representation of the linearity of William Faulkner's *The Bear* (five-part version), the story line, the Aristotelian beginning, middle, and end, may be transverse to the time-space line of the verbal event, resulting in a cognitive "configuration" in the axes of the totality similar to those of the Aztec patterns discussed earlier. In R. W. B. Lewis's diagram of the story line in *The Bear,* the solid lines represent sections of continuous narrative, the broken lines, temporal spans bridged by sudden leaps in the narrative sequence with no appreciable transition. The Roman numerals are the numbers of the five parts of the story, and the arrows indicate the direction of the verbal event in time and space. To this I have added the parenthetical letters A, B, C, and D, which mark the appearance of such recurrent entities as those of which Barthes speaks, in this instance returns to Ike McCaslin's age sixteen and the climactic episode in the ritualized hunt for the bear. From the diagram it is clear that the configuration of *The Bear* is based on what one may call a "virtual story line" which is the transverse of the verbal event so that the story exhibits a variant of the twofold symmetry in the Aztec designs: one axis running through points A, B, C, and D, the other along the gap in Part IV which carries the reader back from Ike's age twenty-one to age eleven or twelve. Of the story, Lewis says, "But while we are aware of strong currents carrying us forward and backward in *The Bear,* we must also acknowledge the corollary impression that time is motionless, and everything is occurring simultaneously."[24] As the diagram indicates, the stasis, the simultaneity in the midst of almost frantic action is a function of the bimodalism in the "linear" development of the story. A similar exploitation of bimodalism in the story line occurs in Robbe-Grillet's *La Jalousie* with the recurrent images of the smashed centipede on the wall in the dining room.

Faulkner's experiments with the topology of fiction, carried to even more complex patterns in such masterworks as *Absalom, Absalom!* and *Light in August,* explore the far opposite extreme of that which Roland Barthes describes in his discussion of the role of the French preterit in the formation of novelistic patterns of time and space. This tense, long since obsolete in everyday French, has generally been restricted to poetry and the novel. Indeed its very presence in a text is itself almost the indisputable sign of literary art, of "the unreal time of cosmogonies, myths, History and Novels." According to Barthes, "Its function is no longer that of a tense." Instead, by reducing the experiential to a single point in time, a single verb tense, it abstracts time and makes narration "a pure verbal act . . . directed towards a logical link with other acts, other processes, a general movement of the

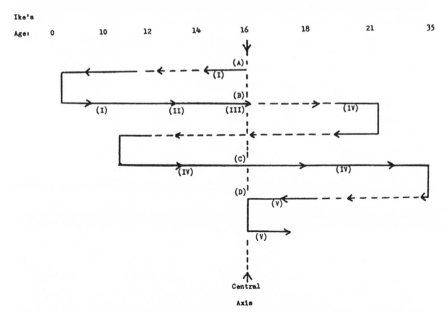

R. W. B. Lewis's plot diagram of William Faulkner's *The Bear* with the central axis through points A, B, C, and D supplied to reveal the twofold symmetry of the story based on a "virtual" story line which may be said to be "perpendicular" to the verbal event, the time-space sequence of the narration. Reproduced (with additions by the author) from R. W. B. Lewis, "The Hero in the New World: William Faulkner's *The Bear,*" *Kenyon Review* 13 (Autumn 1951): 641–60.

world: it aims at maintaining a hierarchy in the realm of facts." His logic leads Barthes from this "single point in time" to the assertion that "through the preterit, the verb implicitly belongs with a causal chain, it partakes of a set of related and orientated actions, it functions as the algebraic sign of an intention. Allowing as it does an ambiguity between temporality and causality, it calls for a sequence of events, that is, for an intelligible Narrative." Because "it presupposes a world which is constructed, elaborated, self-sufficient, reduced to significant lines," the preterit becomes the "operative sign whereby the narrator reduces the exploded reality to a slim and pure logos, without density, without volume, without spread, and whose sole function is to unite as rapidly as possible a cause and an end."[25]

Although, while here attempting to enunciate a general law for the literary language, Barthes tends to forget that not all languages enjoy such a special tense as the French preterit, the oversimplification which the fact of a single narrative tense entails permits a clear perception of the Cartesian basis for Barthes's analysis: The linearity implicit in the Aristotelian concept of story line here becomes explicit as Barthes attempts an extension toward analytical geometry. He values the preterit because it gives to what otherwise would be amorphous a logos-form through "significant lines," the lines of a cause and effect chain, in short of a fully articulated world— significant lines which are in effect the Cartesian coordinates. In his view of the geometry of literature the language within which literature exists is a bounding horizon with both limits and provides perspective: "[Language]," he asserts, "enfolds the whole of literary creation much as the earth, the sky and the line where they meet outline a familiar habitat for mankind. It is not so much a stock of materials as a horizon, which implies both a boundary and a perspective; in short, it is the comforting area of an ordered space." Language is, then, according to this view, the horizontal surface or plane the center of which is always the consciousness of the writer, as in perspective the center of the bounding circle of the horizon is always the eye of the observer. To this Barthes adds the writer's style which "has only a vertical dimension, it plunges into the close recollection of the person. . . ." Together, these two, language and style, function for Barthes as coordinates, the horizontal and the vertical axes, which order the writer's world: "A language is . . . a horizon, and style a vertical dimension, which together map out for the writer a Nature, since he does not choose either. The language functions negatively, as the initial limit of the possible, style is a Necessity which binds the writer's humor to his form of expression." Language and style thus become the Cartesian coordinates, the *x–y* axes, which in Barthes's analytical geometry of literature permits the definition of writing, of created literary form, as the equivalent of geometrical form in the Cartesian sense. One must not miss the mathematical import of the words *value, sign,* and *function* in the definition of form which he advanced in *Le Degré zéro de l'écriture:*

> Now every Form is also a Value, which is why there is room, between a language and a style, for another formal reality: writing. . . . A language and a style are data prior to all problematics of language, they are the natural product of Time and of the person as a biological entity; but the formal identity of the writer is truly established only outside the permanence of grammatical norms and stylistic constants, where the written continuum, first collected and enclosed within a perfectly innocent linguistic nature, at last becomes a total sign. . . . A language and a style are blind forces; a mode of writing is an act of historical solidarity. A language and a style are objects; a mode of writing is a function. . . .[26]

The indicated relationships among experiential time and space, history, and cognition which inform Barthes's geometry of literature are possible only in a context which assumes the same base vector for all these, that is, which assumes an essential parallelism in the directional "lines" of time-space, history, and the cognitive processes. But as the analysis of the phenomenon of linearity indicates, such an assumption is not necessarily the only assumption one can make. Indeed the evidence strongly suggests that it is a somewhat less valid assumption than others that can be made. The merging of painting and poetry in a calligraphy of artistic vision, the outlines of drawing, the non-Euclidean geometry of the visual field all lead to the same conclusion as that reached by René Thom: "En conclusion, il ne faudrait pas croire qu'une structure linéaire soit une nécessité pour transporter ou stocker l'information (plus exactement la signification). Bien que l'idée ne nous en soit pas familière, il n'est pas impossible qu'un langage, un *modèle sémantique* dont les éléments seraient des formes topologiques, ne puisse présenter, du point de vue de la déduction, des avantages sérieux sur le langage linéaire que nous pratiquons. En effet, les formes topologiques se prêtent par produit topologique, composition, etc. à une combinatoire infiniment plus riche que la simple juxtaposition de deux séquences linéaires [To conclude, it must not be thought that a linear structure is necessary for storing or transmitting information (or, more precisely, significance); it is possible that a language, a semantic model, consisting of topological forms could have considerable advantages, from the point of view of deduc-

tion, over the linear language that we use, although this idea is unfamiliar to us. Topological forms lend themselves to a much richer
range of combinations, using topological products, composition, and
so on, than the mere juxtaposition of two linear sequences]."[27] The
evidence suggests that the world of literature may not be Newtonian,
that the axes of the artistic vision may be other than the Cartesian
coordinates. Instead, the linearity and the geometry most significant
for a study of the literary language may be those toward which Proust
worked in his evasion of the Aristotelian imperatives, an evasion
which Beckett, also working toward the same goal, described as a
"non-logical statement of phenomena in the order and exactitude of
their perception, before they have been distorted into intelligibility in
order to be forced into a chain of cause and effect."[28]

Recognizable again, here now in Beckett's and Proust's aim, is that
precision in the prefiguring manifest in Matisse's cutouts and in the
basic truism in artistic vision: to see is to compose. A topological view
of the formation of the art object, instead of directing the verbal act
toward a logical linkage of cause and effect, reveals a synchrony in the
artistic vision and thus in literary form which precludes cause and
effect. In short, it reveals the phenomenon which came to occupy
Gertrude Stein's attention as a consequence of the attempt to compose *The Making of Americans:*

> When I was up against the difficulty of putting down the com-
> plete conception that I had of an individual, the complete rhythm
> of a personality that I had gradually acquired by listening seeing
> feeling and experience, I was faced by the trouble that I had ac-
> quired all this knowledge gradually but when I had it I had it
> completely at one time. Now that may never have been a trouble to
> you but it was a terrible trouble to me. And a great deal of *The
> Making of Americans* was a struggle to do this thing, to make a whole
> present of something that it had taken a great deal of time to find
> out, but it was a whole there then within me and as such it had to be
> said.
> That then and ever since has been a great deal of my work and it
> is that which has made me try so many ways to tell my story.[29]

The problem that she faced was how to tell a story which in the time
scheme of the imagination is "a whole present," a synchrony, but
which in the accumulation has a chronology. The telling necessarily
entails the time-space axis of the verbal event, and that which is to be
told has a history of acquisition and thus is in the experiential time-
space of past-present-future. But that which has been acquired and is
to be told, in and of itself merely *is*, is and constitutes a whole present,

a present which is complete, entire of itself. The problem is, then, the problem which lies behind Picasso's paintings of multiple perspective, and his solution points toward the necessary corrective in respect to writing. At the moment of artistic vision, the story is *outside* the Cartesian time-space and thus has no sequential continuity with it. Outline in writing, then, depends upon the discontinuity between the verbal-historical event and the literary form itself, the composition. Composition in writing becomes, as in drawing and the visual experience of the physical universe, the projection of that which is synchronous in time and centripetal in space. Again Gertrude Stein is instructive: "In beginning writing I wrote a book called *Three Lives* this was written in 1905. I wrote a negro story called *Melanctha*. In that there was a constant recurring and beginning there was a marked direction in the direction of being in the present although naturally I had been accustomed to past present and future, and why, because the composition forming around me was a prolonged present. A composition of a prolonged present is a natural composition in the world as it has been these thirty years it was more and more a prolonged present. I created then a prolonged present naturally. . . ."[30] Indeed her experience and experiments as a writer constitute a direct contradiction of a Cartesian geometry in the literary language. Toward the end of her career, that remarkable career of little success and great achievement, she said, "I found out that in the essence of narration is this problem of time. You have as a person writing, and all the really great narration has it, you have to denude yourself of time so that writing time does not exist. If time exists, your writing is ephemeral. You can have a historical time, but for you the time does not exist, and if you are writing about the present, the time element must cease to exist. . . . There should not be a sense of time, but an existence suspended in time."[31] "A marked direction in the direction of being in the present"—if one gives full value to the word *being*, one finds here the very essence of that centripetality which is form not only in our visual experience of the world but also in our representations of that experience in either painting or poetry.

A comment by Robert Frost, in the context of the topology of the literary form, has, then, a particular significance. He said, "Art should follow lines in nature, like the grain of an ax-handle. False art puts curves on things that haven't any curves."[32] For the poet, then, true art, one may assume, follows the curves of things which in nature have curves, follows, that is, the same curves which Matisse's scissors followed as the painter made his cutouts. For Frost the poem in its composition is contoured, a concept which Thomas Hardy insisted upon in talking about the shape of a novel: "Probably few of the general body denominated the reading public consider, in their hurried perusal of novel after novel, that, to a masterpiece in story there appertains a beauty of shape, no less than to a masterpiece in pictorial or plastic art, capable of giving to the trained mind an equal pleasure."[33] Hardy's choice of the word *shape* instead of the more usual *form* in such contexts is of considerable significance in view of his devotion to the intensive study of the paintings and sculptures he found displayed in museums and galleries, a study no less intense, apparently, than Hemingway's at the Palais du Luxembourg. *Form* is a more general word, equally at home in commentaries on either the verbal or the visual arts, and therefore more easily construed within an exclusively rhetorical frame of reference. But *shape* is somewhat less general: it still retains much of the force of the Anglo-Saxon *sceap*, "created thing (object)," and is thus heavily charged with the sense of those physical contours, mass, and volume which is the essence of a topological view of the literary art object.

5
Literary Form: The Topology of Metaphor

A frequently unappreciated but important fact about a painting is what Gertrude Stein referred to as the "reality of the oil painting as oil painting." In discussing Courbet and her reactions to his works, she noted that in his paintings he used the colors of the natural scene, the colors which anyone viewing the actual landscape would see, and then continued: "And what had that to do with anything, in fact did it not destroy a little of the reality of the oil painting. The paintings of Courbet were very real as oil paintings, they existed very really as oil painting, but did the colors that were the colors anybody could see trees and water-falls naturally were, did these colors add or did they detract from the reality of the oil painting as oil painting."[1] Her question focuses attention upon the fact that a painting or a drawing has its own objective existence within the receptible environment of the viewer: the painting is first of all an object, a form, which, like all other objects in the environment, manifests its presence by a discontinuity along its edges and a centripetal quality within the contours. This above all else distinguishes what is upon the canvas surface from all other aspects of the viewer's receptible environment: the painting does not borrow its reality, it is its own reality. The fact appears in Matisse's rebuke to a visitor to his studio, a woman who, pausing before one of his paintings, had protested, "But, surely, the arm of this woman is much too long." Matisse replied politely, "Madame, you are mistaken. This is not a woman, this is a picture."[2] In passing, it should be noted that, despite Gertrude Stein's misgivings in respect to

Courbet's paintings, the consciousness of the discontinuity still asserts the reality of painting as painting even when through the use of perspective and "realistic" colors the artist attempts to connect his painting with experiential diachrony. In the history of Western painting this consciousness guaranteed the continuity of synchrony from the medieval period through the Renaissance to the beginnings of Surrealism and Cubism. The insight is valuable when one turns to the study of literature, for one may equally well speak of the reality of a poem or novel as poem or novel, as having its own objective and formal presence within the reader's consciousness of the receptible environment. Or, as Northrop Frye put it in a comment which echoes Matisse's rebuke to his visitor, "To bring anything really to life in literature we can't be lifelike: we have to be literature-like."[3]

In a commentary addressed to the *Amherst Student* Robert Frost projected an image of the literary art object which vividly evokes once again Matisse's cutouts: "The background is hugeness and confusion shading away from where we stand into black and utter chaos; and against the background any small man-made figure of order and concentration. What pleasanter than that this should be so?"[4] The literary art object, the poem or novel, like a van Gogh form detached from the dizzy whirl and chaos, also has its contour manifest in a discontinuity which defines it and separates it from other forms. This is so obviously the case in the separation of the literary art object as form from the painting—the separation of the two stems of calligraphy—that it hardly needs commentary. Much greater significance attaches to the fact that it is also true of the separation of one verbal form (art object) from another and from the general ground constituted by language. One must remember at this point that *form* here refers not to *genre* but to the topological concept which underlies the linear phenomenon in painting or perception. The evidence so far adduced as to the nature of transformational perception in artistic creation, of the archetropic image, and of the topology of composition—that is to say the evidence of a fusion of images from two different orders, a consequent "surreality," and a synchrony in a discontinuous juxtaposition—suggests that the archetropic image, the "figure a poem makes" (to use Frost's phrase), and metaphor all are variant manifestations of the same phenomenon. A close examination of the metaphor, then, in its embodiment of transformational perception, should reveal the gradient involved in any given morphogenesis and the discontinuity which constitutes the contour of the literary form.

At least since Aristotle's discussion of the phenomenon, metaphor has been well known as the principal manifestation of "figurative" language, but equally well known, at least among poets, is the fact that "figurative" means something considerably more fundamental in the creative process than mere rhetorical decoration. Precisely how fundamental is implicit in the observation that metaphor occurred when, for example, man first looked at a stone or a stick and saw it not merely as stone or stick but as potential tool or weapon. Stone tool or what for Robert Frost is "the figure a poem makes": despite the intervening millenia, the transformational perception is the same, both begin in vision, archetropically, "in delight" and "end in wisdom": "It begins in delight," as Frost describes it, "it inclines to the impulse, it assumes direction with the first line laid down, it runs a course of lucky events, and ends in a clarification of life—not necessarily a great clarification, such as sects and cults are founded on, but in a momentary stay against confusion."[5]

The suggestion here, that metaphor is the poet's tool corresponding to the painter's line, is extended by Wallace Stevens's assertion that metaphor has its origins in the "ambiguity favorable to resemblance," in the perception that images from different categories of being lend themselves to a fusion. "The proliferation of resemblance extends an object," he declared: permits a fusion of the multiple into the one. Stevens's word *resemblance* emphasizes the correspondence of what I have called transformational form fragments in the two elements of the objective relation and thus identifies the metaphor as the verbal counterpart of the prehistoric artist's fusion of rocky protuberance and bison image into the art object at Altamira. The insight serves to distinguish the metaphor from the simile by opposing the synchrony of the metaphoric process to the diachrony of the simile. The metaphor reveals, as does the painter's transformational perception, another, an intensified reality. Stevens describes the revelation in the remainder of his comment: "In this ambiguity, the intensification of reality by resemblance increases realization and this increased realization is pleasurable. It is as if a man who lived indoors should go outdoors on a day of sympathetic weather. His realization of the weather would exceed that of a man who lives outdoors. It might, in fact, be intense enough to convert the real world about him into an imagined world. In short, a sense of reality keen enough to be in excess of the normal sense of reality creates a reality of its own. Here what matters is that the intensification of the sense of reality creates a resemblance: that reality of its own is a reality."[6]

The metaphoric process involves, then, the equivalent in the literary object of what Gertrude Stein called the "reality of the oil painting

as oil painting." It may consequently be supposed to involve a patterned synchronous superimposition. As Sparshott expresses it, "The
trick in metaphorical thinking is to superimpose two complex frames
of reference and play them off against each other, to avoid altogether
the ways in which one thing is damagingly unlike the other, but above
all to let the mind play round the fringes where it can catch glimpses
of remote and improbably likenesses in 'the light that never was on
sea or land.'"[7] The description is not altogether accurate, for it tends
to deemphasize the reality of the metaphor as metaphor; it nevertheless captures the principal movement: one "reality" is superimposed upon another. The result, however, is not just a glimpse by "the
light that never was on sea or land." Rather it is the creation of what in
the most basic sense one must call a surrealism, a word which in this
context needs some explication, for it is frequently popularly construed to mean "beyond the real," in a spatial metaphor with a horizontal orientation and consequent implications of the "fantastic" and
"irrational"—implications seemingly well warranted by the more
bizarre fantasies of such surrealist painters as Salvador Dali. But the
spatial metaphor in the word itself has instead a vertical orientation
imparted by the French preposition *sur,* the antonym of *sous,* "under."
As such, *sur* means "on" or "upon" in the various literal and
metaphorical configurations of one surface superjacent to another.
The word, then, as it will be used here, means simply the consequence
of the superimposition of one reality upon another with no preferen-
tial value given to either the one or the other. With the exception of
their relative positions in space, the only distinction intended between
the two is best described by the physicist's word *phase:* the different
physical states of the one composition with the necessary alterations in
mass, volume, and configuration as it undergoes its transformations
from the one state to the other. For example, a particular composition
of hydrogen and oxygen, H_2O, appears to the human perception in
three different phases: as a solid (ice), as a liquid (water), and as a gas
(steam). The line which defines the one, separating it from the other,
is visible in the separation between the ice and the water, between the
water and the steam. The discontinuity between contiguous phases is
the zone both of contact and of separation of the two surfaces.

The "surrealism" of metaphor thus leads back to the bimodalism of
a line and to a necessary implication in a comment by Sartre, who said,
"Les signes verbaux [d'un roman] ne sont pas, comme dans le cas des
mathématiques par exemple, des intermédiares entre les
significations pures et notre consciences: ils représentent la surface de
contact entre le monde imaginaire et nous [The verbal signs (of a

novel) are not, as in the case of mathematics for example, the inter-mediaries between pure signification and our consciousness: they represent the surface of contact between this imaginary world and us]."[8] Contact is contiguity, not continuity: one must always remember the separation, a separation which must be transcended as one moves from the one phase or form to the other. Precisely here is the pitfall in Sparshott's insistence that one must "avoid altogether the ways in which one thing is damagingly unlike the other," for such an avoidance focuses the attention too sharply upon an identity which is as inimical to metaphor as is similitude. As James Deese has noted, an insufficient separation is a major source of poor metaphors for it paradoxically highlights the damaging dissimilarities that one had hoped to avoid: "The literal and figurative concepts should not share too many important or salient features. It is uninformative to say that the lion is a tiger. It is even not very good to say that the tiger is the lion of India. We are bothered, even though there are close familial resemblances, because it is precisely those features in which lions and tigers differ that are brought to mind by the comparison. The literal and figurative concepts must have some features in common (by definition, given the analogies game), but they had better be neither too numerous or salient nor too obscure and dependent upon a kind of erudition."[9] As Stevens has noted, the approach to identity erases the separation and merges the two realities into a single entity: In short, it destroys the contours. "We are not dealing with identity," Stevens insists. "Both in nature and in metaphor identity is the vanishing-point of resemblance. . . . Nature is not mechanical to that extent for all its mornings and evenings, for all its inhabitants of China or India or Russia, for all its waves, or its leaves, or its hands. Its prodigy is not identity but resemblance and its universe of reproduction is not an assembly line but an incessant creation. Because this is so in nature, it is so in metaphor."[10]

Again, one may illustrate and clarify with an insight from painting. Max Ernst, in describing his experience of that image-fusion which he called the "new" technique of *frottage,* but which nevertheless is typified by the painted bison in Altamira, cites to his purpose a passage from André Breton's *Preface to the Max Ernst Exhibition* (May 1920): "It is the marvellous capacity to grasp two mutually distant realities without going beyond the field of our experience and to draw a spark from their juxtaposition; to bring within reach of our senses abstract forms capable of the same intensity and enhancement as any others. . . ."[11] The fact is worth emphasizing, once again, that the art object, painting or poem, is the consequence of an image fusion: of the percept of rock protuberance fused with the memory image of a bison. In physical terms the result in Altamira is a physical superposition of pigments in a bison like configuration upon the rock protuberance resulting in what is physically a separate layer (of pigments) in contact with the rock surface. The total configuration, protuberance plus pigment, has a reality of its own and is physically what was called the "image" in the Surrealist movement of the early twentieth century, first in French literature, then in painting before André Breton gave the concept that Freudian turn which invested it with an aura of irrationality and fantasy. The poet first, Guillaume Apollinaire to be precise, coined the word *surrealism* and applied it to the literary art object; another poet, Pierre Reverdy, gave that definition of the artist's image which Breton extended in his *Manifeste du surréalisme* to provide the theoretical basis for the painting of such Surrealists as Hans Arp, Max Ernst, Paul Delvaux, and of course Dali. Reverdy's definition of the surreal image in literature is that which is visually present in the reality of the oil paintings as oil painting:

> L'image est une création pure de l'esprit.
> Elle ne peut naître d'une comparaison mais du rapprochement de deux réalités plus ou moins éloignées.
> Plus les rapports des deux réalités rapprochées seront lointains et justes, plus l'image sera forte—plus elle aura de puissance émotive et de réalité poétique
> [The image is a pure creation of the mind.
> It cannot ensue from a comparison but from the bringing together of two realities which are more or less distant the one from the other.
> The more distant but appropriate are the relations of the two realities thus brought together, the stronger will be the image—the more emotive power and poetic reality it will have]. . . .[12]

Breton, in his more extreme position, placed one of the two "realities" in the Freudian subconscious, removing it thus beyond the realm of the rational, but others among the painters, notably Picasso, understood the word in Reverdy's terms, understood that the two realities are two separate forms from the receptible environment whose contiguity in the artist's imagination and consequent juxtaposition on the canvas result in a more intense reality, a surrealism. In at least two instances Picasso emphasized this point in words which recall the comments by Wallace Stevens: "I attempt to observe nature, always. I am intent on resemblance, a resemblance more profound, more real than the real, attaining the surreal. It was in this way that I thought of surrealism, but the word was used in an entirely different fashion. . . ."[13] In another instance, in response to a rather vitriolic attack by the critic Raymond Cogniat, who had called his art monstrous and inhuman, Picasso said, "This surprised me because on the contrary, I always try to observe nature. As you can see, I've put in this still-life a box of leeks, all right, I wanted my canvas to smell of leeks. I insist on likeness, a more profound likeness, more real than the real, achieving the surreal. This is the way I understood (conceived) surrealism but the word had been used quite differently."[14] Indeed, Breton himself eventually abandoned the extreme position which he exemplified in his appreciation of Dali's *paranoia* and redefined surrealism as quite simply transformational perception. He did so by redefining surrealism as a method inspired by ". . . the lesson of Piero de Cosimo and Leonardo da Vinci (losing one's self in the contemplation of a wad of spittle and an old wall until the eye organizes it into a second world; a world that can be revealed equally directly through the medium of painting. . .)."[15] The evidence thus identifies metaphor as the calligraphic unit in poetry which, in the necessary separation between its two "realities," most immediately manifests the discontinuity which is the sine qua non in the definition of the art object. The metaphoric process, then, is most literally the form-making process in literature.

The focus on discontinuity establishes a most significant link not only, as already noted, between the metaphor of the poet and the line of the painter, but further, between metaphor and line on the one hand and on the other one of the more important mathematical theories to be advanced in the modern era, the "catastrophe theory" formulated by the French mathematician René Thom and published in 1972. To understand the general importance of the theory and the particular connections among it, the metaphoric process, and the concept of form in literature which is advanced here, one must first understand that prior to the publication of Thom's theory, mathematics could deal only with continuous sequential phenomena, or, to state it in more visual terms, could deal only with real or assumed smooth gradients. Herein lay the major limitation of mathematics: models of change or process could be based only upon the concept of the differential with, consequently, an assumed continuity and predictability. Thus the discontinuous and divergent phenomena abounding for example in the biological and social sciences were beyond its reach: Such phenomena are the "catastrophes" with which René Thom deals. Although among mathematicians considerable and animated dispute surrounds the theory and its application,[16] its value, by no means inconsiderable, for description and analysis remains undiminished. And it is as a descriptive and analytic tool that it is most useful in the study of art: the connection is direct, immediately visible in the image of Matisse's scissors cutting through the colored paper. The shearing action of the two opposed blades of the scissors and the resultant cut in the paper constitute a counterpart to seismic action along an earthquake fault. In the mathematical sense, the one is no less catastrophic than the other.

In behavioristic terms, a catastrophe is the consequence, to use Thom's phrase, of a "bifurcation form," a situation typified by the simultaneous possibility for two or more responses. To illustrate, Thom invokes the Surrealism which is the focus of the present discussion: "En fait, on peut distinguer deux grands types de formes instables, qu'on peut relier par une chaîne continue d'intermédiaires; certaines formes sont *informes* parce qu'elles présentent une structure interne très compliquée; chaotiques, elles n'offrent à l'analyse que peu ou pas d'éléments identifiables, mais dont l'association en un même objet apparaît contradictoire ou hétéroclite (les chimères et autres monstres en fournissent des exemples types). Ces formes instables sont . . . des formes de *bifurcation;* leur point représentatif est situé sur un seuil entre deux ou plusieurs bassins d'attracteurs; à la vue de ces formes, l'esprit oscille indéfiniment entre les attracteurs adjacents sans parvenir à faire son choix. Il en résulte pour l'observateur un état de malaise ou d'angoisse; les peintres de l'école surréaliste ont bien connu ces effets qu'ils ont abondamment exploités [We can distinguish two major classes of unstable forms, each at an end of a continuous spectrum: first, forms that are nonforms by reason of their very complicated internal structure—chaotic and not amenable to analysis; and, second, those that consist of a number of identifiable objects but whose composition seems contradictory or unusual, for example, the chimera and other monsters. Unstable forms of this second type are . . . the bifurcation forms whose representative point lies on a threshold between two or more basins of attraction, and their appearance continually oscillates between the adjacent attractors. The effect is to upset or disquiet the observer—this is the technique known to and exploited by surrealist painters]."[17] Thom discerns seven elementary catastrophes, only one of which, the "cusp" catastrophe, will be discussed here because it involves only two basins of attraction and is, thus, in effect, a topological description of a simple copulative metaphor, a verbal form which is composed of two elements, two realities, or to use Thom's terms, two basins of attraction. To see the topological image clearly one must envision two adjacent basins, as for example a double kitchen sink—the two basins separated by a ridge or wall which both holds the two together and simultaneously separates them. The whole configuration, the two basins plus the common wall, is a total form, the "representative point" of which (freely speaking, the "representative point" is that point which marks the focus of the form's centripetality)—the "representative point" of which necessarily falls in the center, that is, upon the wall figuring the contiguity of the two basins.

To see more clearly the significance of the topological view of metaphor, we may note that the two possible modes of response—in Altamira, rock protuberance and bison—may be plotted as axes on a horizontal plane to produce a control surface for the lateral location of various possible response combinations along the scale from *rock* to *bison*. If one adds to this a vertical scale of valuation for the two modes, one may then plot for each point on the horizontal plane a corresponding valuation point above it, giving as a consequence the "behavior surface," corresponding to the control surface in its horizontal dimensions but differing considerably in that the behavior surface figures in its topography the various degrees of image fusion from the one reality to the other.[18] Such operations produce a pleated behavior surface, called a Riemann-Hugoniot surface, the pleat of which casts a shadow on the control surface in the form of a cusp. The overlap zone of the pleat (or the shadow area on the control surface) is the area of bimodality and synchronicity. The value of the Riemann-Hugoniot surface in the analysis of metaphor emerges more clearly when one notes that for the mathematician the "middle" surface, the reverse curve of the pleat, is to be ignored: This surface is the equivalent of a zero response in behavior—impossible if one assumes a normal physiology in the responding organism. Consequently the figure may be redrawn into a visual formulation of the various phenomena basic to the present study: First of all, in view of the fact that the overlap (figuring a hysteresis in the event) does not necessarily appear in all instances, the topological model is a model of Matisse's scissors cut, but, with the overlap, the model affords a mathematical demonstration of the theory of artistic vision presented here, for the overlap figures forth the distance between the "double take" and the archetrope itself.

Using the artist of Altamira as an example, we may now follow his experience on the Riemann-Hugoniot surface. The artist enters in experiential time to the point where the rock forms of the cave begin to impinge upon his perceptions, placing him thus, because of his potential for transformational perception, in a bifurcation form: Because his state is "negative," he perceives rock forms as rock forms and thus his progress is smooth and uneventful toward the lower

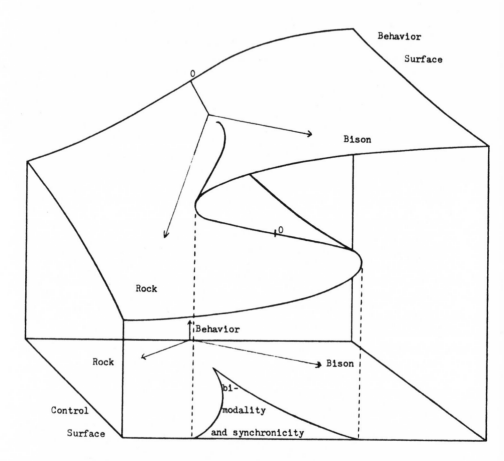

**The topological model (Riemann-Hugoniot surface) for the bifurcation
form rock protuberance vs. bison form at Altamira.**

front edge of the Riemann-Hugoniot surface. But simultaneously,
because his state is "capable," he contains the potentiality for transformations, experiences a strong tendency to see things as other than
they "are." The point where the line of his progress on the lower
surface intersects the shadow cast by the upper surface marks the
point where he perceives a certain rock protuberance and experiences the archetrope, an event figured on the behavior surface by a
penetration into the bimodal area under the lip of the upper surface.
A brief moment later occurs the "double take," figured in the model
by the arrival at the extreme right edge of the lower surface: the artist
"turns back" (a tropism) with focal attention now on the protuber-

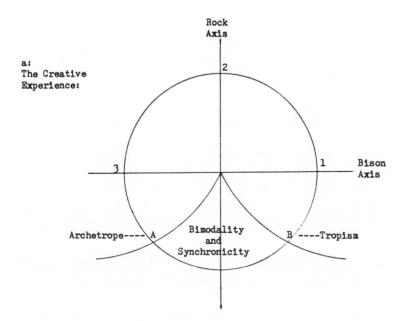

a:
The Creative
Experience:

Rock
Axis

2

3 ━━━━━━ 1 Bison
Axis

Archetrope----A Bimodality
and
Synchronicity

B/----Tropism

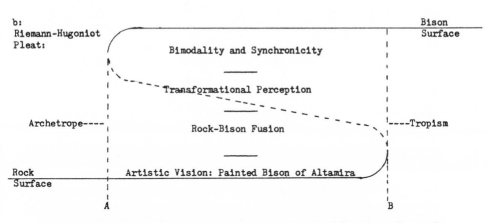

b:
Riemann-Hugoniot
Pleat:

Bison
Surface

Bimodality and Synchronicity

Transformational Perception

Archetrope----

Rock-Bison Fusion

----Tropism

Rock
Surface

Artistic Vision: Painted Bison of Altamira

A

B

Topological analysis of the creative experience in Altamira, the archetropic fusion of rock form and bison form to give rise to the art object. Advancing through arc 1-2-3, the artist confronts at A the rocky protuberance and experiences the archetrope; at point B he turns back with focal attention to a transformational perception and the vision which produced the painting now visible in the cave.

ance, fully committed to the realization of the protuberance
configuration as bison configuration, a tropism and a commitment
figured on the model by the jump from far right edge of the lower
surface to the far left edge of the upper surface.

The importance of this topological model in the definition of
metaphor should by now be amply clear. The metaphor is the most
fundamental archetropic image in the process of art-object construction. Its basic characteristic is a "resemblance," the essence of which is
a necessary separation between its two terms such that it operates
synchronously on two contiguous superposed planes, its two terms
functioning bimodally. The topological model thus helps reveal the
pitfall in such definitions as those which see metaphor as truncated
simile or as those, like Lévi-Strauss's, which see it as a statement of
equivalent ratios (A:B::C:D). As already noted, simile avoids the
discontinuity; in constructing his simile, the artist retraces his steps
and refuses to commit himself to the vision: in terms of the model, he
circles back, counterclockwise, to arrive at the bison-image by what is
in essence a differential, not a catastrophic process. As for the concept
of equivalent ratios, the very mathematics makes explicit the flaw
implicit in the theory of truncated simile: equivalent ratios are proper
to differentials and thus to continuity and diachrony. The difference
is crucial. A metaphor from Horatio's speech near the end of Act I,
scene I of *Hamlet* (line 150) will illustrate: "The cock that is the trumpet to the morn. . . ." The metaphoric relationship between cock and
trumpet is neither equivalence (cock:morning::trumpet:[soldier]),
similitude, nor identity, but congruence, a fact which appears when
the metaphor is placed upon the topological model, both words in the
bimodal and synchronous area, the trumpet superposed over the
cock. The procedure permits the perception that an appositional (or
metonymic) metaphor such as—reading downward from the one
plane to the other—"the clarion-cock" is the same thing. The perception is of the "nicety" which Wallace Stevens discerned as the difference between "imitation," his word for "simile," and resemblance: "An
imitation may be described as an identity manqué. It is artificial. It is
not fortuitous as a true metaphor is. If it is an imitation of something
in nature, it may even surpass identity and assume a praeter-nature.
It may very well escape the derogatory. If it is an imitation of something in metaphor, it is lifeless and that, finally, is what is wrong with
it. Resemblance in metaphor is an activity of the imagination; and in
metaphor the imagination is life."[19] The nicety, insofar as it involves
activity and life, is an important reminder of the movement inherent
in the artistic image: the superposition of the one image over the

other must not be understood in any passively restrictive sense. In his definition of metaphor Max Black spoke of the one term of a metaphor as a filter in the apprehension of the other.[20] The image he evokes is remarkably similar to the one projected here in view of the composite which results on the control surface of the topological model if, within the bimodal area, the two superposed images are allowed to fuse into one. But again the model reveals a crucial difference: the superposition conforms not the one to the other as would a filter—reducing the subject image to a passive role—but, as noted in chapter 1, conforms *each one* to the other. The mathematical model thus confirms the fact that transformational perception involves a mutual movement of the two images toward each other, requires a twofold deformation and reformation.

The mutual movement reemphasizes that "reality" of the art object as art object, oil painting or literature, which Gertrude Stein sought through the too natural colors of Courbet's paintings. Upon first seeing the works of Velázquez at the Prado she felt a confusion traceable again to a violation of the principle of surrealism as defined here: "The Velasquez bothered me as I say because like the Cazins of my youth they were too real and yet they were not real enough to be real and not unreal enough to be unreal."[21] Matisse illustrated the essence of the artist's imagination and the "reality" (surrealism) of the art object with an image whose physical configuration is surprisingly similar to the topological model of the metaphor, the image of a studio with three floors: "L'idéal serait d'avoir un atelier à trois étages. On ferait une première étude d'après le modèle, au premier étage. Du second on descenderait plus rarement. Au troisième, on aurait appris à se passer du modèle [The ideal would be to have a studio of three floors. One would make a preliminary study from the model on the ground floor. From the second one would descend more rarely. On the third, one will have learned to do without the model]."[22]

The topological model, then, makes manifest the fact that in a very real sense, all painting, all drawing is metaphor in that all art is the record of transformational perception and metaphor is but another term for the *trans-* of *transformation*. As Surrealist art demonstrated in a most explicit manner, the painter suggests such resemblances as easily as the writer. Nor need one confine himself to the Surrealist movement: one need but notice, for example, the manner in which van Gogh's rocks, as well as his trees and all other nonhuman forms, writhe in human torment. Nor is this "humanification" the consequence simply of the viewer's sympathy, a "reading into" the painting of the viewer's knowledge of van Gogh's torment, for van Gogh himself, quite early in his short career, clearly pointed to the process when he wrote to his brother, "I am drawing also a few landscapes; for instance, a nursery here on the Schenkweg. Theo, I am decidedly not a landscape painter; when I shall make landscapes *there will always be something of the figure in them*" [van Gogh's emphasis].[23] Indeed the metaphoric interplay of human and nonhuman form appears with its full vigor in another of his letters to Theo: "A row of pollarded willows sometimes resembles a procession of almshouse men. Young corn has something inexpressibly pure and tender about it which awakens the same emotion as the expression of a sleeping baby. The trodden grass at the roadside looks tired and dusty like the people of the slums. A few days ago, when it had been raining, I saw a group of white cabbages, standing frozen and benumbed, that reminded me of a group of women in their thin petticoats and old shawls which I had noticed early in the morning standing near a coffee stall."[24] The full extent of the unfettered metaphoric play appears to advantage in a juxtaposition of two anecdotes told about Picasso, both involving discussions of resemblances between inanimate objects and the human female form or vice versa. The first anecdote concerns what Picasso called "The Venus of the Gas Company"; in a conversation with André Warnod about the depiction of the female form, Picasso said:

> "Raphael's image of a woman is only a sign. A woman by Raphael is not a woman, it's a sign that in his spirit and ours represents a woman. If this woman is decorated with an aureole, and if she has a child on her knees, then she's a Virgin. All that's only a sign. We understand that this sign represents a woman because it can't represent a house or a tree. I'll show you something odd, à propos."

Warnod then recounts how Picasso left the room and soon returned with a statuette in iron, a statuette of a woman from some primitive culture, possibly Negro, but nevertheless very modern in its conception. After showing it briefly, Picasso then said:

> "What would you call it? I'd call it 'The Venus of the Gas Company.'"
>
> "Why?"
>
> "Because the object I'm showing you isn't a statuette. It's a simple part of my gas meter. You'd probably find the same in your kitchen."
>
> "I admit I was fooled."
>
> "Why fooled? This object could very well be the sign of a woman, and the lines and volumes are harmonious. It sufficed to discover them."[25]

The second anecdote is a conversation between Picasso and Brassaï about some of Brassaï's photographs which Picasso was examining, a series of close-ups of various portions of the female body which, Brassaï explained, were the result of his fascination with that aspect of the female body which gives it the appearance of some kind of vase or a musical instrument or a fruit—that aspect which is noticeably exploited in the art of the Cyclades Islands where the woman-shape is transposed into a sort of violin. He expressed, too, his surprise when he first noticed "how much the fruit of the coconut palm—the largest fruit there is—resembles the lower torso of a woman. . . ." Picasso was interested by Brassaï's results. "It was a good idea to do the female body in portions, this way. Details are always fascinating. . . ." He then turned to a study of some of Brassaï's photos in which nude female forms had been transformed into landscapes, photos in which ". . . one contour . . . outlines the body and, at the same time, sketches a relief of hills and valleys. . . . The eye passes directly from the sinuous line of the feminine body to the curving line of the valleys. Picasso remarks that, in some of the photos, the presence of 'gooseflesh' evokes the skin of an orange, the granulation of stone, or the network formed by waves when they are seen from a distance. One of the attractions of photography is the thought of mingling such similarities, such visual metaphors. We begin to talk about stones: sandstone, granite, marble. . . ."[26] One of Brassaï's photographs, of a female body as vase, is, it should be noted, a visual manifestation of the same metaphor upon which Keats built his "Ode on a Grecian Urn," the interplay between urn-shape and bride-shape: "Thou still unravish'd bride of quietness. . . ." That Keats, Brassaï and, in his ceramics, Picasso share the same metaphor justifies the extension to poetry of a remark by Matisse apropos of painting:

> . . . L'enrichissement inconscient de l'artiste est fait de tout ce qu'il voit et qu'il traduit picturalement sans y penser.
> Un acacia de Vésubie, son mouvement, sa grâce svelte, m'a peut-être amené à concevoir le corps d'une femme qui danse. . . .
> [. . . The artist's unconscious enrichment is built of all he sees which he translates pictorially without thinking.
> An acacia of Vésubie, its movement, its svelte grace, has perhaps led me to conceive the body of a dancing woman. . . .][27]

The insight afforded by the human vase is equally valid for sculpture. At least, such is Henry Moore's conviction: "All experience of space and world starts from physical sensation. This also explains the deformation of my figures. They are not at all distortions of the body's shape. I think, rather, that in the image of the human body one can also express something nonhuman—landscape, for instance—in exactly the same way as we live over again mountains and valleys in our bodily sensations."[28] In short, as visual metaphor is basic to painting, so the verbal metaphor may be considered the most basic and most ubiquitous manifestation of the transformational process in the literary imagination. Again, an anecdote about Picasso serves to illustrate: Once during a discussion of metaphor, he wrote the line, "Le cygne sur le lac fait le scorpion à sa manière [In his own fashion, the swan on the lake makes the scorpion]." In response to requests for clarification, he took up his pen again and on the back of an envelope sketched a swan floating in a glassy water which reflected in exact counterpart the long sickle-shaped neck of the bird. The result is, of course, in the configuration of swan plus reflection, the configuration of a scorpion.[29] The verbal metaphor is comprehensible only through the visual metaphor.

Picasso's swan-scorpion manifests the resemblance, the separation, and the reversibility (In his fashion, the scorpion on the sand makes the swan) of both the visual and the verbal metaphor. As verbal-visual totality, a calligraphic unit, it focuses attention upon what is perhaps the most important insight into metaphor provided by the topological model, in that it affords a necessary corrective to that concept of "figurative language" which is the basis for current structuralist hypotheses about the geometry of language and of literary form. I refer to the distinction made by Roman Jakobson between metaphor and metonymy. According to this view, derived from studies of aphasia since rendered obsolete by the work of Roger Sperry and others in neurophysiology, metaphor and metonymy reflect two fundamental linguistic aspects: Metaphor is based upon an aspect of similarity, metonymy upon an aspect of contiguity.[30] This distinction, much exploited by the semiologists and by semiological structuralists, provides two axes which then may be used, Cartesian fashion, to trace linguistic form. For example, echoing Lévi-Strauss and Roland Barthes, Guy Michaud recently wrote, "Selon [Jakobson], la métonymie, qui se fonde sur un rapport de contiguïté, donc syntagmatique—selon la chaîne parlée—, et la métaphore, qui se fonde sur un rapport de similarité, donc paradigmatique, correspondraient à deux types d'imagination foncièrement distinct, sinon opposés. On peut aller plus loin. Dire que la métaphore se situe sur un axe paradigmatique, c'est dire qu'elle met en relation deux codes ou systèmes de signification situés à des nivaux différents, alors que la métonymie maintient le discours à un seul niveau [According (to Jakobson), metonymy, which is based on a relationship in contiguity, thus syntagmatic—by virtue of the sequence of discourse—, and metaphor, which is based on a relationship of similarity, thus paradigmatic, would correspond two types of imagination fundamentally distinct, if not opposed. One can go even further. To say that metaphor is located on a paradigmatic axis is to say that it establishes a relationship between two codes or systems of signification located at different levels whereas metonymy maintains discourse at a single level]."[31] But as much as such a description of metaphor seems to accord with the topological model one should notice, as did Andrée Lyotard-May, that what Jakobson calls metaphor ("little house" for "hut" or "unmarried man" for "bachelor") are not metaphors at all, but synonyms, ". . . C'est-à-dire des unités qui appartiennent au même champ sémantique et qui ont un signifié analogue [. . . That is to say entities which belong to the same semantic category and which have an analogous signified]." As Lyotard-May points out, the observation is crucial, for Jakobson's definition of metaphor "apparaît très claire, mais il ne faudrait pas qu'il profite de l'homonymie qui la relie à la métaphore littéraire pour opérer un dangereux glissement de sens [would appear very clear, but he must not profit from the homonymy which links it to the literary metaphor to effect a dangerous sliding of sense]."[32] The topological model of a metaphor in conjunction with the instruction offered by the visual metaphors of painting permits the avoidance of such a sliding and consequently reinforces the perception that a metaphor, as a bifurcation form in Thom's terms, contains its own contiguity and thus is fundamentally metonymic.

The perception is of extreme importance in the discussion of metaphor and the role it plays in the topology of literature, for the composition of a metaphor, the contiguity of the two planes in a superposition with between them an essential discontinuity, makes it obvious, of course, that, as Bachelard noted, "metaphors are not simple idealizations which take off like rockets only to display their insignificance on bursting in the sky. . . ." Instead, the metaphor becomes the means by which the poet delineates the contours of the figure his poem makes. Something of this sort is at least suggested in the continuation of Bachelard's comment: ". . .On the contrary metaphors summon one another and are more coordinate than sensations, so much so that a poetic mind is purely and simply a syntax of metaphors. Each poet should then be represented by a *diagram* which would indicate the meaning and the symmetry of his metaphorical coordinations, exactly as the diagram of a flower fixes the meaning and the symmetries of its floral action."[33] The phrase "a syntax of metaphors" contains a concept of linearity and consequently, if all that has been said of the line has any validity, of a bimodalism: a continuity and in the transverse a discontinuity. At this point the discontinuity is the immediate concern: the continuity will be discussed in the next chapter. Thus the aspect of the floral "diagram" of particular interest at this point is the discontinuity which constitutes a contour and thus defines the "flower." To be even more precise, the concern is not with the totality of the creative imagination but only with that portion which is the individual art object in literature, a single literary work and the figure it makes. For if Bachelard's insight is true for the poet's mind in general it is even more so for the individual product of that mind, as indeed Bachelard indicates in his description of the manner in which the act of writing removes the writer from "reality": "Pour qui connaît la rêverie écrite, pour qui sait vivre, pleinement vivre, au courant de la plume, le réel est si loin! Ce qu'on avait à dire est si vite supplanté par ce qu'on se surprend à écrire qu'on sent bien que le langage écrit crée son propre univers. Un univers des phrases se place en ordre sur la page blanche, dans une cohérence d'images qui a des lois souvent bien diverses, mais qui garde toujours les grandes lois de l'imaginaire [For whoever knows that reverie called writing, for whoever knows how to live, fully live, as the pen flows on, the real is so distant! What one has to say is so quickly supplanted by what one finds oneself writing that one quite feels that the written language creates its own universe. A universe of sentences arranges itself in order on the blank sheet, in a coherence of images which has laws often quite diverse, but which always observes the great laws of the realm of the imagination]."[34]

The key word in this comment is *coherence,* its significance apparent in the fact that an acceptable simplified definition of form is "that which coheres" and of contour "the outer limit of coherence." In short, Bachelard describes for the act of writing that which Cézanne exemplified in his painting and taught by his example to Gertrude Stein and Ernest Hemingway. The text describes a writer who under the impulse of the archetropic experience has become, in Lu Chi's image "the hub," has become the organizing center of a cosmogenetic field which radiates in concentric circles outward from him to reach, ultimately the contour of the surreal world, the figure his writing creates. The literary creation of form is thus a coherent creation which repeats that universal creation described in the rabbinical text, "As an embryo grows from the navel, so God, in creating the world, began with the navel, and from there it spread in all directions." Or in

Paul Klee's words the self-selected point "sets itself in motion and an essential structure grows, based on figuration." For the poet or novelist the self-selected point is the originating, original metaphor, the *arché-trope*, which mates two realities to conceive a surreality. The evocation here of the process of procreation is deliberate: It is of course what lay behind James's choice of the word *germ* or *seed* for the origin of his novels. Hamada insisted on the same metaphor: " 'Create,' that word—so often we use it. People use the words 'to create' very readily, but I don't like to use them very often. The things that I do, my wares, are not made but born."[35] Again in Paul Klee's words, "The cosmogenetic moment is at hand. The establishment of a point in chaos lends this point a concentric character of the primordial. The order thus created radiates from it in all directions."[36] Stephen Spender and Robert Frost both indicate the same phenomenon in the case of poetry: the original metaphor, the cosmogenetic point, contains and thus constrains the poet to a "logic" which is the formulation of the entire poem. Spender described, for example, how a moment of transformational perception brought to him the metaphor "A language of flesh and roses" as a first line for a potential poem, a metaphor which presented calligraphically a complex vision at the moment of perception. He then commented, "Now the line [of poetry] . . . is a way of thinking imaginatively. If the line embodies some of the ideas which I have related . . . , these ideas must be further made clear in other lines. That is the terrifying challenge of poetry. Can I think out the logic of images?"[37] Speaking of the figure a poem makes, Robert Frost described the coherence as the consequence of a sort of predestination: "It has an outcome that though unforeseen was predestined from the first image of the original mood—and indeed from the very mood. It is but a trick poem and no poem at all if the best of it was thought of first and saved for the last. It finds its own name as it goes and discovers the best waiting for it in some final phrase. . . ."[38] In another context, he came back again to this question of predestination in the composition of poetry and, in doing so, he spoke, as did Spender, of a logic of images: ". . . You know, one of the funny things is that this *mood* you're writing in foretells the end product. See, it begins sort of that way and a way of talking that foretells the end product. There's a logic in that sort of thing."[39]

The word *logic* in such a context is evidently a logic of the poet's mythos and as such must not be confused with that logic which is, in Bruner's words, "the elegant rationality of science."[40] The reference is not to the logic of continuities and differentials but to the logic of resemblances and correspondences; the logic which Lévi-Strauss discerned in the savage mind, which Piaget and Inhelder discovered in what they called *schèmes,* which Matisse obeyed as he made his cutouts. Goethe referred to it when he somewhere said that it may be difficult for one accustomed to the exact sciences to realize that poetry is governed by a precision of the imagination no less intensive, a precision without which poetry would be impossible. The outline of the figure a poem makes emerges from it as in its precision of transformations it separates the real from the surreal worlds: recurrent metaphors in a transformational coherence constitute the verbal equivalent of virtual lines. Of Proust, Beckett said, "The Proustian world is expressed metaphorically by the artisan because it is apprehended metaphorically by the artist: the indirect and comparative expression of indirect and comparative perception. The rhetorical equivalent of the Proustian real is the chain-figure of the metaphor."[41] The same is true of all the surreal worlds of art within the realm of metaphor.

6

The Perception of Poetic Form

*I*n his admirable survey of structuralism, Jean Piaget wrote, "Let us not forget that, even in the domain of psychogenesis, genesis is never anything except . . . the transition from one structure to another, and while the second structure is explained in terms of this transition, the transition itself can only be understood in transformational terms if both of its termini are known."[1] Insofar, then, as metaphor manifests two termini in a transition, it as well reveals the gradient along which a transformation occurs. Such a revelation is of crucial importance, for, as the topological model for metaphor makes clear, it is along such gradients that one discerns the discontinuity which indicates contour. In her discussion of current trends in the analysis of metaphor, Josephine Miles complained that such metaphors for metaphor as vehicle, tenor, paradox, and tension are misleading because they obscure the significance of the destination. For her, the proper questions to be asked of the metaphor a poet uses are "Where is he going?" or "Where has he gone, and to what effect?" She continues, "*Vehicle* does mean a carrier, indeed so does the *-phor* in *metaphor,* like the *-fer* in *transfer;* but it is also the *meta,* the *trans,* that is important: Carried to where? To an alien land. This is foreign trade, as Aristotle makes clear in his list of odd uses in the Poetics."[2] Thus, to counteract those who value most the first of the two realities in the metaphor, the terminus of departure, she proposes a focus upon the "alien land," the other reality, the terminus of arrival. But as the topology of metaphor indicates, neither is more important than the other, a fact which makes possible the reversibility of a metaphor. The essential value instead attaches to the force, the archetropism, which deforms, then fuses the

125

two into the third entity, the surreality, to that force which Wallace
Stevens called the motive for metaphor. The central interest is, as
Picasso pointed out, neither in the one term nor the other of the
metaphor, but in the space between and the force which spans it, in
the "rapports de grand écart": "I start with a head and wind up with
an egg. Or even if I start with an egg and wind up with a head, I'm
always on the way between the two and I'm never happy with either
one or the other. What interests me is to set up what you might call the
rapports de grand écart—the most unexpected relationship possible between the things I want to speak about, because there is a certain
difficulty in establishing the relationships in just that way, and in that
difficulty there is an interest, and in that interest there's a certain
tension. . . ."[3] Before one misconstrues Picasso's word *rapport*, one
must notice that in discussing the role of *papier collé* in Cubist painting
he construed it as the "shock between," emphasizing thus the contact
of contiguity and the essential discontinuity: "The sheet of newspaper
was never used in order to make a newspaper. It was used to become a
bottle or something like that. It was never used literally but always as
an element displaced from its habitual meaning into another meaning
to produce a shock between the usual definition at the point of departure and its new definition at the point of arrival."[4] The essence of
metaphor in the artistic process is, as Picasso suggests, both that it
exists synchronously in two worlds *and* that it carries the audience
across a discontinuity from the one to the other in a specific trajectory.
What is trope for the reader was archetrope for the artist and becomes in turn archetrope for the reader. It follows, then, that for the
reader the archetropic experience of a coherence of metaphors is the
experience of the poetic form. To perceive the metaphor is to perceive the art object—is indeed to reexperience the poet's transformational perception, the image fusion and the consequent surreality,
figured in the topological model. But before such perception can
occur for the reader, several misconceptions, made manifest by the
topological model, must be exposed and put by.

It is important, then, that the discontinuity in metaphor never be
bridged in any explicit fashion. The "crossing" is a motion which
structures but is not itself in any sense a structure. To employ the
images projected in Stevens's poem "The Motive for Metaphor," the
motive exists in the seasons of transition, autumn and spring, "desir-
ing the exhilarations of changes." The transport would be negated if,
to speak metaphorically, one changed the nature of the going as the
modern Cartesians do in their insistence upon "the vital, arrogant,
fatal, dominant X." And for once the vital, arrogant, fatal, dominant

X comes to the aid of the poet, for the topological model for metaphor, the pleated Riemann-Hugoniot surface, product of mathematical theory, visually figures the essential point: it is impossible to explicate, to "unfold" the metaphor. Any attempt to do so alters the discontinuity between the two terms and, consequently, transforms the metaphor itself into something else. Nor is an unfolding in any way necessary for a critical evaluation of the art object: As Thom has pointed out for the mathematics of catastrophes in general, ". . . On peut identifier le type d'une catastrophe et son origine dynamique sans qu'on ait à connaître explicitement tous les paramètres internes dont dépend le système [the type and dynamical origin of a catastrophe can be described even when all the internal parameters describing the system are not explicitly known]."[5] Like the poet before him, then, the reader must either refuse completely the movement offered by the metaphor or experience the exultation attendant upon a submission to the transformational process. *Exultation* must in this context be understood in its root sense, derived from *ex-* and *salire,* "to jump out from." So understood, the word becomes, as in Emily Dickinson's definition of it, an admirable description for the experience of metaphor:

> Exultation is the going
> Of an inland soul to sea,
> Past the houses—past the headlands—
> Into deep Eternity—
>
> Bred as we, among the mountains,
> Can the sailor understand
> The divine intoxication
> Of the first league out from land?

To follow the "logic" of her metaphor: if a logician were to build a causeway or a bridge he would reduce exultation to pedestrianism.

Even more to the point, as Plato pointed out in the *Phaedrus,* the effort to rationalize and to intellectualize necessarily entangles the logician in ever-expanding problems of construction. In the dialogue, Phaedrus calls attention to the fact that he and Plato are walking near the spot where, according to the myth, Boreas carried off Orithyia. He then asks Plato if he believes such a story. Plato replies:

> The wise are doubtful, and I should not be singular if, like them, I too doubted. I might have a rational explanation that Orithyia was playing with Pharmacia, when a northern gust carried her over the neighbouring rocks; and this being the manner of her death, she

was said to have been carried away by Boreas. There is a discrepancy, however, about the locality; according to another version of the story she was taken from Areopagus, and not from this place. Now I quite acknowledge that these allegories are very nice, but he is not to be envied who has to invent them; much labour and ingenuity will be required of him; and when he has once begun, he must go on and rehabilitate Hippocentaurs and chimeras dire. Gorgons and winged steeds flow in apace, and numberless other inconceivable and portentous natures. And if he is sceptical about them, and would fain reduce them one after another to the rules of probability, this sort of crude philosophy will take up a great deal of time.[6]

Such warnings against efforts to rationalize or intellectualize the inner workings of metaphor would seem supporting arguments in favor of a submission to subjectivity, but such is not necessarily the case: essentially both must be avoided. That objectivity and subjectivity are necessarily the only alternatives in the discussion of metaphor is an illusion largely the consequence of the tension between the diachrony of discourse and the synchrony of the transformational perception embodied in the metaphor itself. The fact is implicit in that in a very real sense one neither writes nor reads, but experiences, a metaphor. By virtue of English syntax, the sentence "I write (or 'read') a metaphor" causes the word *metaphor* to submit to a predicative operation, places it into a propositional frame. The diachrony of the discourse and the verbal event encourages the thesis that the metaphor, objectified in and by the proposition, may, indeed must, be subjected to an objective (diachronic) study. But although the speaker of a propositional language necessarily refers himself to the metaphor or approaches it through the time-space of the proposition, he must not confuse this with the time-space of the metaphor itself: The one is *logos,* the other *mythos,* and the predicative pair *objectivity* and *subjectivity,* characteristic of the logos, cannot be transferred from the one to the other and, further, have no place within the contours of the mythos. Metaphor itself is neither subject of objectivity nor object of subjectivity: Like Archibald MacLeish's poem, it merely is.

The insight necessitates a most important distinction. The illusion has caused opponents of objectivity to assume that the only alternative is subjectivity, sometimes an almost militant subjectivity such as that evinced by Bachelard in his running battle with the psychoanalysts. Such a procedure merely continues the same obscurity which he opposes, for as admirable as may be Bachelard's abhorrence of psychoanalytical objectivity in literary criticism the alternative he chose, a sort of Jungianized subjectivity, is not a viable alternative.

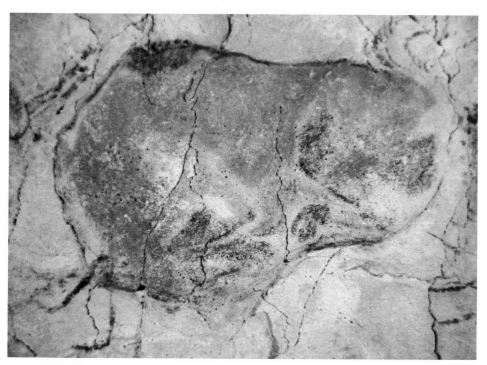

Polychrome bison, Altamira, Spain. Photo courtesy of the Spanish National Tourist Office.

The spotted horses, Pech-Merle, France. The placement of the spots along the exterior of the belly, forelegs, chest and head strongly suggests that to the prehistoric artist who placed the dots the head of the horse on the right is the head-shaped extension of the rock itself. Photo by Jean Vertut, courtesy of Jean Vertut.

Finger-painted mammoth, La Baume-Latrone, France. The figure appears in the midst of a panel of finger-painted doodles or "meanders." Photo by André Leroi-Gourhan reproduced courtesy of André Leroi-Gourhan and of Editions d'Art Lucien Mazenod, publishers of André Leroi-Gourhan, *Préhistoire de l'art occidental* (1965).

Section of a *Waka* scroll, calligraphy by Hon'ami Kōetsu on paper decorated by Tawaraya Sōtatsu. Original in the Hatakayama Collection, Tokyo. Reproduced from Yujiro Nakata, *The Art of Japanese Calligraphy* (1973) courtesy of John Weatherhill, Inc., publishers, and of The Hatakayama Collection, Tokyo.

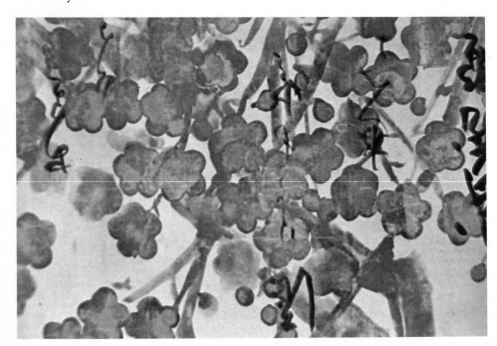

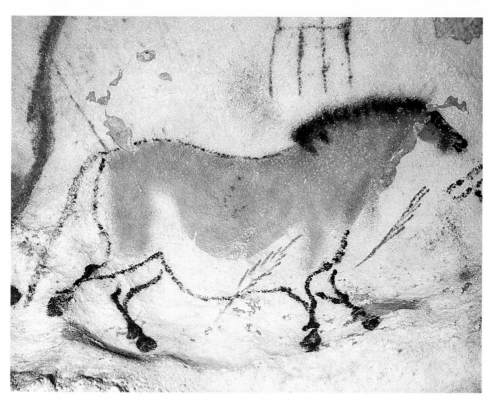

The second "Chinese" horse, Lascaux, France. Photo by Jean Vertut reproduced courtesy of Jean Vertut and of Editions d'Art Lucien Mazenod, publishers of André Leroi-Gourhan, *Préhistoire de l'art occidental* (1956).

The two charging bison, the Nave, Lascaux, France. Photo by Jean Vertut, courtesy of Jean Vertut.

Henri Matisse, *The Dancer.* **1949. Colored paper. Collection Robert Mother-well. Reproduced courtesy of Robert Motherwell.**

Henri Matisse, *Tabac Royal.* **1943. Oil on canvas, 63.5 × 81.3 cm. Private Collection. Reproduced courtesy of the owner.**

Instead, it is merely the verso of the coin he spurned. The distinction derived from this observation may be illustrated with a figure from a book Bachelard once marshaled to his support in his attack on objectivity: Jean Paulhan's *Les Fleurs de Tarbes,* a delightful little book whose denunciation of a sterile objectivity is sandwiched between two warnings, one at the beginning of the book, the other at the end—warnings in the form of notices, the second a revision of the first, posted at the gates of the public garden of Tarbes. The first reads:

> IL EST DÉFENDU
> D'ENTRER DANS LE JARDIN
> AVEC DES FLEURS À LA MAIN
> [IT IS FORBIDDEN
> TO CARRY FLOWERS
> INTO THE GARDEN]

According to Paulhan, this is the sign posted by the "objective" literary critic at the entrance to literature. In contrast, at the end of his book, Paulhan posts a new sign, the consequence of his own recommendation for the study of literature:

> IL EST DÉFENDU D'ENTRER
> DANS LE JARDIN PUBLIC
> SANS FLEURS À LA MAIN
> [IT IS FORBIDDEN TO ENTER
> THE PUBLIC GARDEN
> WITHOUT FLOWERS IN HAND][7]

It is, of course, true, as Bachelard indicates, that one goes to the public garden because of a love for flowers, and it would be somewhat silly to go there determined not to see them: ". . . La *critique littéraire* n'a pas pour fonction *de rationaliser la littérature.* Si elle veut être à la hauteur de l'imagination littéraire, elle doit étudier aussi bien l'expression *exubérante* que l'expression *retenue* [. . . The function of literary criticism is not to rationalize literature. If it wishes to rise to the heights of the literary imagination, it must study the exuberant expression as well as the restrained]."[8] But in attacking what he calls the non-sense of the cult of objectivity, he is, it must be feared, the perpetrator of another non-sense: the recto of the coin is inseparable from the verso. "The image can only be studied," he asserts, "through the image, by dreaming images as they gather in reverie. It is a nonsense to claim to study imagination objectively since one really receives the image only if he admires it."[9] But Bachelard forgets that if one enters the public garden with a huge bouquet from the private garden clutched before the eyes, it becomes somewhat difficult to see the flowers cultivated by the public gardener.

Both Paulhan and Bachelard wished to show the absurdity of a fear of flowers in a flower garden: the imagination must not be barred from the domain of the imagination. But the essential point is not that imagination must offer riposte to logic but that imagination must respond to imagination: the reader must enter the public garden not with objectivity, not with subjectivity, but with Negative Capability. The proper way to enter is suggested in a garden scene from Natsume Kinnosuke's novel *Kusa Makura,* the English title of which, *The Three-Cornered World,* derives from a passage introductory to the garden scene: ". . . An artist is a person who lives in the triangle which remains after the angle which we may call common sense has been removed from this four-cornered world."[10] The narrator of the story, a painter-poet, is resting at a rustic inn in the mountains where he has but recently made the acquaintance of a beautiful but enigmatic young woman. One evening, attracted by her voice singing in the garden, he leaves his room and approaches along the veranda. In the moonlight of the warm spring evening, he sees her silhouette near the hot-spring, moving among the flowering trees. But instead of entering the garden, he pauses to puzzle over the enigma presented by her presence at the inn and her behavior toward him. Suddenly, the shadow is gone and with it the spell which had originally drawn him toward the garden: "The shadow I had just seen, considered simply as a shadow and nothing more, was charged with poetry. So much so, that nobody who saw or heard it could possibly fail to appreciate the fact.—A hot-spring in a secluded village—the shadow of blossoms on a spring night—a voice singing softly in the moonlight—a figure flitting through the shadows—every one of them a subject to delight any artist. Yet for all that I had engaged in an investigation which was quite out of keeping with the situation, and had probed about pointlessly trying to find reasons for everything. I had been privileged to see the world of pure poetry, and had tried to apply to it the yardstick of logic."[11] Although the young man had not come with his own bouquet of flowers, had indeed committed the fault decried by Bachelard and Paulhan, he nevertheless points a caution against the alternative fault: "The shadow I had just seen, *considered simply as a shadow and nothing more,* was charged with poetry." The phrase I have italicized is charged with significance for poetry and the experience of metaphor: The silhouette he had seen was not the symbol of an enigmatic young woman in his experiences earlier in his stay; it was, within the garden experience, plainly and simply a shadow—nothing more, an element of the total composition within the contours of the garden. The young man's comment brings us back to Keats's Negative Capability: "when a man is capable of being in uncertainties, mysteries, doubts, without irritable reaching after fact and reason."

To shift from the analogy of the garden, the essence of the matter is again discernible in a consideration of the rock protuberances transformed into bison images by the prehistoric artist of Altamira. Today, no commentator in any of the literature on prehistoric art refers to these art objects in such a manner, as "rock protuberances transformed . . . ," etc. Instead when the intent is to refer not to the process but to the art object, the commentaries refer quite directly to "the painted bison of Altamira" or quite simply "the bison of Altamira." Why, then, one must ask, should the poet's reader persist in talking about the rock protuberances, the "real" world surface upon which the poet paints his surreal form? As Robert Graves pointed out in a book whose title—*The Common Asphodel*—brings us back to the garden image, the objectivist reader assumes that the poet starts with a prose summary, a down-to-earth concept, which he then translates into a poetic equivalent through the extravagances of metaphor and simile. For Graves, the assumption derives from two basic fallacies. The first is that the poet does not say in the poem what he means but rather something like what he means in a language which he has made prettier than the language he ordinarily uses when he talks about it to himself. The second fallacy, fundamental to the first, is that what the poet wishes to embody in poetry is not, in and of itself, very agreeable "so that he has to make a distinction between what is pretty and not pretty, poetical and not poetical." As a consequence, "it is almost impossible for a poet who really means what he says to make the literary critic believe that he does: the more he means what he says and the more earnest he is to make that clear, the more he will be thought to be concealing his meaning in clever evasions of 'obscurity.' "[12] Robert Frost agreed: "The freshness of a poem belongs absolutely to its not having been thought out and then set to verse as the verse in turn might be set to music. A poem is the emotion of having a thought while the reader waits a little anxiously for the success of dawn. The only discipline to begin with is the inner mood that at worst may give the poet a false start or two like the almost microscopic filament of cotton that goes before the blunt thread-end and must be picked up first by the eye of the needle. He must be entranced to the exact premonition. No mystery is meant."[13]

The reader, then, if he would follow the advice of Robert Frost and Robert Graves, indeed, if he would complete the pattern of calligraphy, must abandon the objectivist-subjectivist alternatives and instead become, like the artist himself, simply an objectifier if he is ever to perceive the full shape and dimension of literary form. Nor is this such a difficult or unnatural act as one might think. As Whorf pointed out, a major characteristic of our language, the presumed prosaic speech of routine discourse, is a metaphoric extension of physical properties to nonphysical concepts by means of "an almost inexhaustible list of metaphors that we hardly recognize as such, since they are virtually the only linguistic media available." This phenomenon is a manifestation of what Whorf called our linguistic scheme of "objectifying":

> . . . Imaginatively spatializing qualities and potentials that are quite non-spatial. . . . Noun-meaning (with us) proceeds from phsyical bodies to referents of far other sort. Since physical bodies and their outlines in PERCEIVED SPACE are denoted by size and shape terms and reckoned by cardinal numbers and plurals, these patterns of denotations and reckoning extend to the symbols of nonspatial meanings, and so suggest an IMAGINARY SPACE. . . . This has gone so far that we can hardly refer to the simplest nonspatial situation without constant resort to physical metaphors. I "grasp" the "thread" of another's arguments, but if its "level" is "over my head" my attention may "wander" and "lose touch" with the "drift" of it, so that when he "comes" to his "point" we differ "widely," our "views" being indeed so "far apart" that the "things" he says "appear" "much" too arbitrary, or even "a lot" of nonsense![14]

The phenomenon is visible in the very language of the objectivist who likes to "discern" "through" the symbols of the poem the "hidden" meanings "in" its various "levels." Again it must be emphasized, such metaphors are more than a manner of speaking. Instead, the evidence gathered by Solomon Asch and his team of investigators indicates that this phenomenon is basic not just to English, but to a sufficient number of languages to suggest that it is a universal cognitive phenomenon. These investigators studied the appearance in various languages of a number of such "buried" metaphors as those indicated by Whorf: classical Hebrew, classical Greek, Chinese, Thai, Hausa, and Burmese, with English as a control, all of which were found to have the same metaphors with the same duality (*straight, depth, sharp, hard,* as in "the sharp knife" or "his sharp wit," "a hard rock" or "a hard man"), terms simultaneously expressing both "physical" and "psychological" qualities. They "do not denote exclusively the 'raw materials' of experience; they are also the names of *concepts*," a fact somewhat obscured by the sensationalistic psychology according to which such terms are usually interpreted and which tends to exclude important "dynamic and physiognomic" properties inherent in them:

> The concepts in question have little in common with abstract logical operations. They are not generalizations of what is common to an array of different instances. Rather they are concrete cognitive operations in terms of which we naïvely comprehend events and similarities between them.
> The conclusion we have reached is that when we describe psychological events in the same terms we employ for the description of the forces of nature—of fire, sea, wind—we are referring to functional properties they share. . . . The dual terms . . . derive from this source, being shorthand names for functional relations and forces.[15]

But the very naturalness of such "buried" metaphors poses a particular problem in such contexts as the present one: How may the nature of metaphor ever be discerned if the metalanguage itself is also inherently, inescapably metaphorical? Or, in the words of Jacques Derrida, "How could we know what is meant by the temporalizing or spatializing of a sense or meaning, an ideal object, an intelligible tenor, without elucidating the meaning of 'space' and 'time'? But how can this be done without knowing already what a logos is, what a meaning-to-say which of itself spatio-temporalizes whatever it expresses? what logos is as metaphor?"[16] One is indeed faced with a dilemma without resolution so long as one remains within the logos, that is, tries to deal with metaphor as strictly a verbal phenomenon to be comprehended through a metalanguage which is also verbal. But when metaphor is perceived not as a linguistic but as a cognitive phenomenon, one may in effect evade the dilemma, for in the verbal-visual interplay one deals not so much with "metaphor" (verbal) in the metalanguage as with visuo-spatial models. Or to state it in another fashion: If poetry is the metalanguage for painting, painting is the metalanguage for poetry. To adapt Gertrude Stein's phrase, not only must the writer write with his eyes, the reader must also learn to read with his eyes. After citing Descartes, who said that the essence of theoretical science remains unchanged regardless of the object dealt with—as the sun's light is unchanged no matter what the variety of object illuminated—Ernst Cassirer concluded, "The same may be said of any symbolic form, of language, art, or myth, in that each of these is a particular way of seeing, and carries within itself its particular and proper source of light."[17] Henri Matisse, in another of his perceptive comments, added greater precision: ". . . L'artiste ou le poète possèdent une lumière intérieure qui transforme les objets pour en faire un monde nouveau, sensible, organisé, un monde vivant qui est en lui-même le signe infaillible de la divinité, du reflet de la divinité [. . . The artist or the poet possesses an interior light which transforms objects in order to make from them a new world, palpable, organized, a living world which is in itself the infallible sign of divinity, of the reflection of divinity]."[18] Instead of merely verbal phenomenon, metaphor is the manifestation of a particular relationship between the sensory being and his environment. With an appropriate adjustment in the word *subjectivity,* James Deese's comment is apropos: ". . . The mystery of the metaphor lies in the structure of human thinking and perceiving and their relation to the objective world. A good metaphor allows into the mind just those intersecting features between the literal and figurative concept that are the right ones—not the right ones in the objectivity of the world but the right ones in the subjectivity of human experience in that world."[19] In the visuo-spatial perception of form it is, of course, ultimately the shift in the gradient of illumination which reveals form; a shift in source or angle of illumination, as in the case of flickering light in a prehistoric cave, will alter the gradient and consequently accomplish a transformation. This is the effect of the interior light of, say, a Matisse. It is equally the effect of the interior light of a Frost, a Stevens, or any poet. The coherence of metaphors, then, in a particular work, all in marking the outline of the literary form, also reveals the angle of illumination which accomplishes the transformation.

It is, then, the "angle of illumination" which measures the motive for metaphor: The coherence of the metaphors and, consequently, the outline of the form emerge clearly only if, in keeping with Graves's and Frost's insistence and Picasso's example, the reader seeks out in the metaphor the specific *application* (in the physical and root sense of *ad-* plus *plicare,* "to fold over toward," "to pleat") by which it accomplishes the superposition of two "realities" to achieve a "surreality." To do this the reader must abandon traditional methods of classifying metaphor and insist on a most meticulous discrimination in the perception of the transformational process. To say that a metaphor accomplishes a transformation is to speak so generally as to deprive it of any possible significant role in a coherence of metaphors: *all* metaphors transform in the more general sense of that verb. The coherence of metaphors in a literary art object emerges only after the specific nature of the transformation has been established through a precise observation of the gradient involved in the transformation and of the exact nature of the transmutation which occurs as that gradient is traced from the one terminus to the other. As earlier comments have tended to suggest, psychologists are becoming more and more aware of such physical properties in metaphor as "concretizing," to use the term suggested by Werner and Kaplan.[20] One example, from Asch's study, has already been given: "a hard person," a metaphor in which flesh by metaphoric extension gains greater density—the verbal equivalent of those visual metaphors based upon the rock-person transformation as in Léger's *Nus dans la forêt.* To avoid confusion, however, one should, it seems to me, avoid the word *concretizing,* for it leads to the trap into which indeed Werner and Kaplan fall, the trap of the concrete-abstract oppositions in word classification.[21] In such a metaphor as "a hard person," the process which accomplishes the imaginative superposition of rock and flesh to produce the surreal "hard" person is better described as densification, a movement from a softer to a harder material. A more radical form of this type of metaphor would be "a flat, hard voice" which more clearly involves a true "concretization," or, to substitute a preferable word, a materialization, insofar as a voice in the receptible world has no substance: to term it "flat" and "hard" is to endow it in the surreal with the substance of rock or some other material as these are known to the senses. This is the process which gives objective presence to the "fragile beauty" of that wild rose bush beside the prison door in Hawthorne's *The Scarlet Letter.* The reverse is visible in Faulkner's metaphor "the sparrows . . . came . . . in random gusts" (in the first paragraph of *Absalom, Absalom!*): Sparrows, material in the receptible world, become gusts of wind in the "surreal"—a dematerialization which makes the sparrows the motive force driving inward the dust motes which will materialize the ghost of Thomas Sutpen.

As Whorf notes, "imaginatively spatializing qualities and potentials that are quite non-spatial" is a normal part of the linguistic scheme by which speakers of English objectify the nonmaterial or the abstract. But if one looks more closely at his examples, the word *spatializing* reveals itself as an all-inclusive term covering all or almost all the physical properties of objects, including those just discussed: densification, materialization, and dematerialization. Here again, greater precision is necessary to render the term *spatialization* of any use. The matter is important, for as James Deese has pointed out, "One of the most ubiquitous of the cognitive categories derives directly from our perceptual experience of space. An extraordinarily wide variety of interpretations placed upon abstract, symbolic, and even personal events requires the use of space as a model or metaphor. Explicit spatial imagery represents the obvious case. But there is also implicit application of spatial models and metaphors. These are not quite so obvious, and perhaps they are more important because they are more pervasive."[22] Deese refers here to such phrases as "a high intensity light," "you are nearly right," "low grade ore," "far out music," "close friend," and "distant relative," the sort of phrase which abounds, for example in even the most innocent-seeming of Henry James's prose. The opening phrases of *The Aspern Papers* furnish an excellent illustration: "I had taken Mrs. Prest into my confidence; in truth without her I should have made but little advance, for the fruitful idea in the whole business dropped from her friendly lips. It was she who invented the short cut, who severed the Gordian knot. It is not supposed to be the nature of women to rise as a general thing to the largest and most liberal view. . . ." In the context of the imaginative process of spatialization, the very first clause, "I had taken Mrs. Prest into my confidence . . . ," one which ordinarily would occasion no particular notice, excites a more than casual interest: precisely what is the force of the preposition *into?* and what then is the consequence for the verb *had taken* and the noun *confidence?* In short, what is the totality of the calligraphic unit? Certainly the phrases "little advance" and "dropped from" are clearly in a spatial frame of reference which metaphorically materializes *idea* and perhaps transfigures it to a fruit of some sort to drop, like Newton's apple, from the "friendly lips." The combination gives both horizontal and vertical dimensions, expanded in the phrase "to rise . . . to the largest and most liberal view" to give a very physical sweep to the word *liberal.* James's self-consciousness in this process appears in the second sentence in the pun accomplished with "short cut," the success of which depends precisely upon its "figurative" meaning in terms of physical space and its "literal" meaning in terms of a stroke with a sword. Thus in even so short a span, the material-spatial coherence of the metaphors manifests itself and thus invests with enhanced materiality and spatiality the initial phrase "I had taken Mrs. Prest into my confidence. . . ." The phrase is part of a material-spatial gradient which extends from the "confidence" of discourse to a material-spatial confidence one can be "taken into." It thus accomplishes what for Conrad was the writer's task—"by the power of the written word to make you hear, to make you feel—it is, before all, to make you see"— and the truth in Max Black's contention that verbal metaphors are not restricted to nouns and verbs but may be accomplished with any part of speech.[23] Spatialization as an imaginative process reaches what seems to me its greatest evocative force not in metaphors of "exteriorized" spatiality such as those dealt with by Deese, surface measures, dimensions, and dispositions but in metaphors of "interiorized" spatiality, metaphors which, in verbal counterpart to Henry Moore's sculptures, endow with an internal spatiality in the surreal world that which is either impenetrably solid in the receptible, or which has, in a preliminary metaphoric transformation, been materialized. For example, in Fitzgerald's *Tender Is the Night* we are told how the cool waters of the Mediterranean "ran into the corners of [Rosemary's] body." Hawthorne takes us to the "interior of a heart," an organ which indeed does have an interior space, but by no means as much as Hawthorne needs to work out the drama which he stages there. James takes his readers to the interior of Isabel Archer's mind and tells them "Her imagination was by habit ridiculously active; when the door was not open it jumped out of the window. She was not accustomed to keep it behind bolts. . . ." An insight into how spacious such interior realms may be appears in the extension of the opening phrase of *The Aspern Papers*, an extension which constitutes the first eight chapters: The narrator, after taking Mrs. Prest into his confidence, acts upon her suggestion that he gain entry into the confidence of the Misses Bordereau by becoming a lodger in their palazzo: In his simultaneous penetration of confidence and palazzo, confidence becomes as spacious as the palazzo. It is not, of course, the purpose here to give an exhaustive list of all the transformational possibilites; the aim instead is to isolate a phenomenon and to suggest a method. The essential point to be derived from this discussion is then that the specific nature of the transformational process in any metaphor is readily discernible to those with eyes to see and the courage to heed the poet-painter.

As a first approximation in a definition of structuralism, Jean Piaget wrote, ". . . We may say that a structure is a system of transformations. Inasmuch as it is a system and not a mere collection of elements and their properties, these transformations involve laws: the structure is preserved or enriched by the interplay of its transformation laws, which never yield results external to the system nor employ elements that are external to it. In short, the notion of structure is comprised of three key ideas: the idea of wholeness, the idea of transformation, and the idea of self-regulation."[24] What Piaget neglects to say here but does say by implication throughout his entire study is that these three key ideas are necessarily interdependent. The comment is directly applicable to the present discussion, for the coherence of metaphors in an individual literary work is *compositional:* as system, it reveals not only the outline of the literary art object but simultaneously, in its archetropism, the centripetality of the form. The motive for metaphor carries not only the poet but the reader as well to the structural center of the poetic form. Morphogenesis is repeated as a consequence of that self-regulation which Henry Moore called the "individual form vision" of the self at the center of the surreal world: ". . . Everyone has a sort of individual form vision. In all the greatest artists the seed of this form vision has been present even in their early work, and to some extent their work has been a gradual unfolding of this rhythm throughout. In their later work it becomes more concentrated, that's all. It's something the artist can't control—it's his make-up."[25]

At this point in the discussion, a comment by Matisse lends a corrective precision to a comment by Bachelard. In speaking of the fact that a painter can make a few variations on a form seem like the endless multiplicity of nature, Matisse said:

> Ma conviction sur ces choses s'est formée lorsque j'ai eu constaté que par exemple dans les feuilles d'un arbre,—dans le figuier particulièrement,—la grande différence de formes qui existe entre elles n'empêche pas leur réunion à un caractère commun. Les feuilles de figuier dans toutes les fantaisies de leurs formes restent bien des feuilles de figuier. J'ai fait la même remarque dans les autres produits de la terre: fruits, légumes, etc. . . .
> Il existe donc une vérité essentielle à dégager du spectacle des objets à représenter. C'est la seule vérité qui importe.
> [My conviction on these things was formed when I had ascertained that for example in the case of the leaves of a tree—particularly the fig tree—the great difference in form which exists among them does not prevent their assimilation into a common character. Fig leaves in all the vagaries of their forms nevertheless remain fig leaves. I have made the same observation in the case of the other products of the earth: fruits, vegetables, etc. . . .
> There exists then an essential truth to be disengaged from the spectacle of objects to be represented. It is the only truth which counts.][26]

In speaking of the transformational process in such an image as "Et la chambre est autour d'eux comme un ventre [And the room is about them like a stomach]" in Ribemont-Dessaignes's *Ecce Homo,* Bachelard found that the basis of the image is an "isomorphism": "Les grandes images qui disent les profondeurs humaines, les profondeurs que l'homme sent en lui-même, dans les choses ou dans l'univers, sont des images isomorphes. C'est pourquoi elles sont si naturellement les métaphores les unes des autres. Cette correspondance peut paraître bien mal désignée par le mot *isomorphie,* puisqu'elle se fait dans l'instant même où les images *isomorphes* perdent leur forme. Mais cette perte de forme tient encore à la forme, elle explique la forme [The great images which express the human depths, the depths which man senses in himself, in things or in the universe, are isomorphic images. That is why they are so naturally metaphors the ones of the others. This correspondence may seem poorly designated by the word *isomorphism* in that it appears in the very instant when the *isomorphic* images lose their form. But this loss of form is still an aspect of form, it explains form]."[27] The particular image in question is, of course, a simile, not a metaphor. Consequently it does not accomplish the fusion of "real" and "real" on the surreal plane: it merely suggests the possibility and then recoils, does not actually transform. The fact reveals that Bachelard applies the word *isomorphism* to the wrong aspect of the transformational process. *The* room (definite) in the image and *a* stomach (indefinite) are not truly isomorphic, do not have the same configuration. To be sure, functionally both contain—it is this which misled Bachelard—but the one has right-angled corners and four plane surfaces, is box-shaped, whereas the other is rounded, somewhat lima-bean shaped. The image presents, then, in the movement *room* to *stomach,* an instance of transfiguration (in general, the first terminus, the room, retains all of its "real" world qualities, except for its shape, its *figura,* which changes as the motive for metaphor impels it toward the "surreal" world). But as demonstrated in the discussion of memory images, within the surreal world the stomach shape superimposed upon the room shape is a typification of *stomach* as Matisse's fig leaf is a typification of all the vagaries of fig leaf forms. Both *stomach* and *fig leaf* are Bachelard's and Matisse's labels for what Piaget and Inhelder called *schèmes:* the room *as stomach shape* becomes isomorphic as are the stomachs constituting the *schème,* as any one fig leaf is isomorphic in the *schème fig leaf.* A closer analysis, then, of Bachelard's example permits the perception that, in discussions of art, isomorphism is more properly considered a characteristic of the surreal plane. Here, within the contours of the art object, it is one of the laws of the self-regulation of the structure, a law of simultaneity in subsumption—that is, of synchronicity. It is the law in art which constitutes the basis of the artistic symbol, its operation succinctly suggested in a comment which Allan Paivio quotes approvingly from Rand: "Synchronic objects lead to synchronous sensations and these in turn to synchronous ideas."[28] But this anticipates matters.

To return to the isomorphism itself: it would be a mistake to assume that it is restricted to the process of typifying such things as fig leaves or other classes of forms. It is as well that which insures the holism within the outlines marked by the syntax of metaphors and, further, that which imparts coherence to the metaphors themselves. The law of isomorphism permits a definition of the literary work as a composition comprising a multiplicity of metaphors (calligraphic units) disposed along the temporal-spatial axis of the verbal event. In pure literature, as one reads, one confronts successively the various coherent metaphors whose isomorphism does not fully appear until the reader reaches the end of the work and "glances back," as it were. For those who would savor literature to the fullest, the law of isomorphism, then, is what makes imperative that second reading upon which so many from such distant camps as Bachelardian phenomenology and Barthesian structuralism have in rare agreement insisted. The backward glance should be more deliberate than just a glance, it should achieve a "backward vision," to adopt Henry James's phrase, a vision best realized in a rereading, for without this vision the literary art object remains but a series of events, an entity scattered along the length of the verbal event like Proust's woman, "a being scattered in space and time [who] is no longer a woman but a series of events on which we can throw no light, a series of problems that cannot be solved, a sea that, like Xerxes, we thrash with rods in an absurd desire to punish it for having engulfed our treasure."[29] When we reread a poem or a novel, its metaphors interact across the linear sequence of the first reading: each occurs in the context of the entire work. In Bachelard's words "Seule *la deuxième lecture* peut donner à l'image-force ses véritables récurrences. . . . Il n'y a *littérature* qu'en deuxième lecture [Only *the second reading* can give to the image-force its true recurrences. . . . *Literature* exists only with the second reading]."[30] The consequence is, as Roland Barthes has noted, to shift the time-space pattern of the literary work from chronology to the synchrony of a mythos: " . . . Rereading draws the text out of its internal chronology ("this happens *before* or *after* that") and recaptures a mythic time (without *before* or *after*); it contests the claim which would have us believe that the first reading is a primary, naïve, phenomenal reading which we will only, afterwards, have to 'explicate,' to intellectualize."[31] To build an analogy from a procedure employed by Willem de Kooning, it is as if one walked along a corridor, picking up successively various drawings of fig leaves, each on a sheet of tracing paper, gathering them into a bundle, examining each one carefully: at the end of the corridor, one knocks the bundle into alignment and perceives a form, the figure a poem makes, on and through the last sheet gathered. If one were to turn the stack over, he would of course see the same form, perceived this time on and through the first sheet gathered. And if he were to flip rapidly through the stack, he would then see how each successive drawing in its variation from the others within the outline of the totality contributes to the totality, takes its place in the isomorphism. The analogy is that which Robert Frost expressed when he spoke of "a gathering metaphor to throw [a poem] into shape and order," that which "is the height of poetry, the height of all thinking, the height of all poetic thinking. . . ."[32] The law of isomorphism, then, is the manifestation in literature of that unity in multiplicity which Henry Adams sought in history, that "principle" which Coleridge discerned as necessary consequence of "the high spiritual instinct of the human being impelling us to seek unity by harmonious adjustment: . . . the principle, that *all* the parts of an organized whole must be assimilated to the more *important* and *essential* parts. . . . The composition of a poem is among the imitative arts; and that imitation, as opposed to copying, consists either in the interfusion of the SAME throughout the radically DIFFERENT, or of the different throughout a base radically the same."[33] *"The interfusion of the SAME throughout the radically DIFFERENT, or of the different throughout a base radically the same"*: the *or* does not separate two mutually exclusive possibilities—instead it links alternative ways of saying the same thing. The interfusion is of *all* the parts with the more important and essential on the basis of a sameness to produce an organized whole.

A close adherence to this law gives sharply defined form to the art object and evidence, as Bachelard noted, of the genius of the artist, for a consequence of it is what Bachelard called "une *monotonie géniale*."[34] The work is a monotony because it is isomorphic, essentially the same thing throughout; it is *géniale* because the monotony is hidden behind artful variations or is revealed in artful links among the various. Both the monotony and the genius appear to advantage through a comparison of how the law operates in painting and in poetry. Much has been written in the literature of art criticism about the harmonies which the painter achieves with his colors, the rhythms of his shapes and masses, the interplay of his values, but behind these surface manifestations lurks the isomorphism which is their *raison d'être*. Almost at the beginning of his career van Gogh wrote:

> More and more I feel that the drawing of the figure is a good thing that indirectly has a good influence on the drawing of landscape. If one draws a willow as if it were a living being, and it really is so after all, then the surroundings follow in due course if one has only concentrated all one's attention on that same tree, and does not give up until one has brought some life into it. As I told de Bock . . . if we do not draw the figure or draw trees as if they were figures, we are people without backbone, or with a weak one. He had to agree with me.[35]

The isomorphism of a willow and its surroundings is the natural consequence of the transformational process in the visual metaphor of willow-human. The operation of the law is even better exemplified in van Gogh's solution to a compositional problem during the painting of *The Potato-Eaters,* his first major work. While painting the figures, he encountered a rather serious problem with his colors: "As for the flesh colours, I know quite well that considered superficially they seem what is called flesh colour. At first in the picture I tried to paint them so with yellow ochre, red ochre, and white. But that was ever so much too light and was decidedly wrong. What was to be done? All the heads were finished, and even finished with great care, but I repainted them straightway, unmercifully, and the colour in which they are painted now is like *the colour of a good dusty potato, unpeeled.*"[36] The problem was, as van Gogh's emphasis indicates, that with ordinary or "school" flesh-tones the humans in the painting were too human, were not "potato" enough: the metaphor did not emerge clearly—the isomorphism was flawed. A glance at the final version will show how this one amendment in color mends the form of the whole: Now the "potato" unity of potatoes, cups, faces, and lamp—the lighted area of the painting—permits all these scattered entities to interfuse in a total space, a low, dark, heavy, *earthy* space which for these "humans" is the isomorph of the underground "potato space" in which potatoes exist: the metaphor, human-potato, is complete—a metaphor which appears in the double-entendre of the English version of the title: *The Potato-Eaters.*

As one would expect from the evidence, a poet similarly mends a similar flaw in his poem. Stephen Spender provides the illustration in a detailed description of how he met and solved a problem of metaphor in the poem "Seascape, *In Memoriam M.A.S.,*" first published in *Poems of Dedication* (1947). The troubled passage, in its first published form, reads as follows:

> There are some days the happy ocean lies
> Like an unfingered harp, below the land.
> Afternoon gilds all the silent wires
> Into a burning music of the eyes.
>
> On mirroring paths between those fine-strung fires
> The shore, laden with roses, horses, spires,
> Wanders in water, imaged above ribbed sand.

The occasion for the poem was Spender's perception, as he looked down at the sea from a high headland, of the image of the opposite

headland reflected in the water through the ribbed effect caused by
the waves, this while he heard the sound of music coming from the
town on the opposite headland. In the writing the wave-harp-musical
staff metaphor posed the problem: "In the next twenty versions of the
poem I felt my way towards the clarification of the seen picture, the
music and the inner feeling. In the first version . . . , there is the
phrase in the second and third lines

The waves
Like wires burn with the sun's copper glow.

This phrase fuses the image of the sea with the idea of music, and it is
therefore a key-phrase, because the theme of the poem is the fusion
of the land with the sea."[37] The cause of the dissatisfaction with this
phrase was precisely Spender's awareness on the one hand of the
difference between metaphor and simile and the need on the other of
retaining the formal coherence of parallel wave crests, strings of a
harp, and lines of a musical staff while fusing them all on the same
transubstantive gradient, while merging, that is, water, metal, and
sound on the same level of materiality. The fact emerges in the various revisions in the order in which they were written. In the first
revision, Spender rejected the original simile, "The waves like wires,"
and achieved a direct imaginative movement which retains the *figura*,
the parallelism, in a transmutation of water to metal:

1.   The waves are wires
Burning as with the secret song of fires.

But the revision drifts, in the word "burning," toward the gradient of
sound (cf. "music") and moves into another simile which points toward another gradient entirely, vivification (personification), in "the
secret song of fires." The poet does, of course, want to objectify music,
but the original vision requires that it be done on the gradient of
materiality-transubstantiation. This imperative leads to the second
revision:

2. The day burns in the trembling wires
With a vast music golden in the eyes.

The intruding gradient is suppressed, but remnants evocative of
another linger on in the verb "burns" and the two prepositions "in"
and "with," and it becomes clear that the sound of the burning is
intruding upon the poet's image. The third revision, in the substitu-

tion of "glows" for "burns," moves the image back toward the transmutative "sun's copper glow" of the original:

> 3. The day glows on its trembling wires
>   Singing a golden music in the eyes.

The first line is thus restored to the same gradient as "golden music," but the word "singing" continues the intrusion of the personification. The next three versions show Spender's struggles to remove the conflict between "singing" and "golden":

> 4. The day glows on its burning wires
>   Like waves of music golden to the eyes.

> 5. Afternoon burns upon its wires
>   Lines of music dazzling the eyes

> 6. Afternoon gilds its tingling wires
>   To a visual silent music of the eyes

It should be noted that, after publishing the "final" version in this sequence, "Afternoon gilds all the silent wires / Into a burning music of the eyes . . . ," after his analysis of the problem and the illustration of the solution, Spender again revised slightly in the second published version in *Collected Poems* (1955):

> There are some days the happy ocean lies
> Like an unfingered harp, below the land.
> Afternoon gilds all the silent wires
> Into a burning music for the eyes.
> On mirrors flashing between fine-strung fires
> The shore, heaped up with roses, horses, spires,
> Wanders on water, walking above ribbed sand.

In the two published versions, more strongly in the second than in the first, the interfusion which achieves the isomorphism moves smoothly through the simile "like an unfingered harp" into the metaphoric transmutations "silent wires," "burning music," "fine-strung fires," and "ribbed sand." The problem here, of course, was in keeping the various metaphors isomorphic with the archetropic image of a harp superimposed upon the sea, the harp's strings aligned with the crests of the sea's waves; the string-crests brightly reflecting the sunlight, the whole constituting, as musical staff, a visualization-materialization of the heard music. Spender's struggles with these two lines give some indication of the nature and the extent of the sustained effort neces-

sary for the accomplishment of form in literature. A further indication appears in Faulkner's account of how *The Sound and the Fury*
began. During one of his seminars at the University of Virginia, a
student asked, "You had said previously that *The Sound and the Fury*
came from the impression of a little girl up in a tree, and I wondered
how you built it from that, and whether you just, as you said, let the
story develop itself?" To this Faulkner replied:

> Well, impression is the wrong word. It's more an image, a very
> moving image to me was of the children. 'Course, we didn't know at
> that time that one was an idiot, but they were three boys, one was a
> girl and the girl was the only one that was brave enough to climb
> that tree to look in the forbidden window to see what was going on.
> And that's what the book—and it took the rest of the four hundred
> pages to explain why she was brave enough to climb the tree to look
> in the window. It was an image, a picture to me, a very moving one,
> which was symbolized by the muddy bottom of her drawers as her
> brothers looked up into the apple tree that she had climbed to look
> in the window. And the symbolism of the muddy bottom of the
> drawers became the lost Caddy, which had caused one brother to
> commit suicide and the other brother had misused her money that
> she'd send back to the child, the daughter.[38]

The interfusion of metaphor, discourse, and calligraphic unit in an
isomorphism, embryonic in Faulkner's image-symbol, justifies the
view that poetry like painting not only has it origins in a single visuo-
spatial image but also, in its finished state, figures forth a single image,
the isomorphic image. Reference has already been made to James's
The Aspern Papers and the spatial transformations fundamental to it.
One should notice how the progression through the verbal event
figures the narrator's progression through the *palazzo* occupied by the
Misses Bordereau, from the most public to the most private apart-
ments, a progression figuring in turn the narrator's growing "intimacy" (from Latin *intimus,* superlative of *intus,* "within") and his
progress in his effort to penetrate the secret hidden in Miss Juliana's
memories of Jeffrey Aspern. As Mrs. Prest, the woman he had taken
into his confidence, suggested, the way to intimacy is to become an
"inmate" [in the first published version; revised to "intimate" in the
New York Edition]: "Simply ask them to take you in on the footing of
a lodger." One should notice how these various parallels merge (as
they may in non-Euclidean geometry) to focus upon the image of the
narrator in Miss Juliana's private apartment, unbidden, unwelcome,
secretly, late at night with lamp in hand, standing before the secretary.
The double meaning in the word *secretary* (item of furniture or person

entrusted with secrets) reiterates the calligraphy of "had taken . . . into [one's] confidence." In doing so it measures the full extent of the interior space of the story and of the word *confidence*. It consequently may be said to be the focus of the *novella's* centripetality. The phenomenon may also be observed in Hawthorne's *The Scarlet Letter* which has an *opening* chapter entitled "The Prison Door" and as *closing* chapter one which concludes with a view of the fated lovers' tombstone. The entire intervening narrative is subsumed under the movement from prison door to tombstone, the one the isomorph of the other, through a central chapter entitled "The Interior of a Heart."

The isomorphism of prison door and tombstone appears in their very complementarity, the fact that the one opens, the other closes, for here is exemplified an axiom inherent in the law of isomorphism figured in the sheaf of fig-leaf drawings on tracing paper: the recto necessarily has the same form as the verso. This principle governs, for example, Henry James's sense of "what groups together" in his choice of conclusion for *The Portrait of a Lady*. In a notebook entry, James wrote, "The obvious criticism of course will be that it is not finished— that I have not seen the heroine to the end of her situation—that I have left her *en l'air.*—This is both true and false. The *whole* of anything is never told; you can only take what groups together. What I have done has that unity—it groups together. It is complete in itself— and the rest may be taken up or not, later."[39] The unity, the grouping together, derives again from the fact that Isabel Archer's "portrait" is "framed" as it were by two images: her entry at the beginning of the novel into the garden at Gardencourt from the door of the house "in the perfect middle of a splendid summer afternoon" and her departure from the garden through the same door "through the darkness" at the end of the novel. The two images are complementaries, and to add or subtract anything would be to destroy the complementarity and thus the isomorphism. The principle involved here was stated by Matisse who, in explaining how he broke from the influence of Seurat, declared:

Dans un tableau post-impressionniste, le sujet est mis en relief par une série de plans contrastants qui demeurent toujours secondaires. Pour moi, le sujet d'un tableau et le fond de ce tableau ont la même valeur, ou, pour le dire plus clairement, aucun point n'est plus important qu'un autre, seule compte la composition, le patron général. Le tableau est fait de la combinaison de surfaces différemment colorées, combinaison qui a pour résultat de créer une expression. . . . Un tableau est la coordination de rythmes contrôlés, et c'est ainsi que l'on peut transformer une surface qui apparaît rouge-vert-bleu-noir en une autre qui apparaît blanc-bleu-rouge-vert; c'est le même tableau, la même sensation présentée différemment, mais les rythmes ont changé.

[In a post impressionist painting, the subject is set in relief by a series of contrasting planes which always remain secondary. For me, the subject of a painting and its background have the same value, or, to say it more clearly, no single point is more important than another, only the composition, the "superintendent," counts. The painting is made from the combination of differently colored surfaces, a combination resulting in the creation of an expression. Just as in a musical harmony each note is a part of the whole, so too I wished that each color have a contributing value. A picture is the coordination of controlled rhythms, and thus it is that one may transform a surface which appears red-green-blue-black into another which appears white-blue-red-green; it is the same painting, the same sensation presented differently, but the rhythms have changed.][40]

Both sensations are sensations of blue, but the second color-harmony, white-blue-red-green, is of course the reverse and the complementary of the first. The second painting is the isomorph of the first as the last garden image of *The Portrait of a Lady* is the isomorph of the first image or as the tombstone image at the close of *The Scarlet Letter* is the isomorph of the opening prison door image.

7
Logos and *Mythos*

Pursuing the insights into artistic creation afforded by the phenomenon of transformational perception, we have discovered that in that calligraphy called poetry the metaphor is the most immediate manifestation of that synchronous archetropic fusion discerned in transformational perception, the fusion of two images from "reality" to form a third, a surreal image. These perceptions and a subsequent one, that a poem is an isomorphism, a coherence of metaphors, raise a most pertinent question about the language in which the work of literature is written. What warrant do I, a speaker of English, have that the book of poems I am about to read—poems by a fellow speaker of English—is written in the same language as I and the poet speak, is written in accordance with the same syntactic and lexical rules as those of the English I speak?

To be sure, when the eye falls upon the first printed marks on the first page of the text, it encounters what seem to be familiar words, the words, the phrases, the sentences of ordinary discourse in the "real" world. But such a seeming must be measured against the artist's insistence that he creates a new language for his work. Henry Miller, for example, declared, "[The artist] creates . . . a reality in which he can live out his unconscious desires, wishes, dreams. The poem is the dream made flesh, in a two-fold sense: as work of art, and as life, which is a work of art. . . . He scorns the ordinary alphabet, which yields at most only a grammar of thought, and adopts the symbol, the metaphor, the ideograph. *He writes Chinese.* He creates an impossible world out of an incomprehensible language, a lie that enchants and enslaves men."[1]

"He writes Chinese"—Miller's image evokes the calligraphy basic to this study. But from Miller's emphasis one must understand that he means much more than the merely ideographic. He means as well that his poetic language is as far removed from the ordinary language of discourse as Chinese is from English, a point emphasized by the Chinese poet Lu Chi in the distinction he made between the Chinese of ordinary discourse and the Chinese of the poet, for, according to Lu Chi, the poet, "immersed in phrases painfully consenting . . . like darting fish . . . dragged from the depths of an unplumbed pool," creates a "fine diction omitted [unknown] through a hundred ages. . . ."[2] Even more, another statement by Miller leads to the isomorphism in the calligraphy which is also basic to this study. He wrote, "I do not believe in words, no matter if strung together by the most skillful man: I believe in language, which is something beyond words, something which words give only an inadequate illusion of. Words do not exist separately, except in the minds of scholars, etymologists, philologists, etc. Words divorced from language are dead things, and yield no secrets. A man is revealed in his style, the language he has created for himself."[3] If one insists upon the logic inherent in the combination of Miller's comments, one may conclude, then, that one of his works of literature does not consist of words fashioned into phrases, sentences, paragraphs, and chapters. Instead, one of his works is a whole or holistic utterance, in effect, a single calligraphic sign one book long. The concept is one Guy Michaud reached as a consequence of his study of the literary language of French poets:

Il s'agit donc pour le poète d'introduire au sein de l'ordre linguistique "des modules de désordre organisé" afin de reconstruire, au sein du désordre même, un nouveau type d'organisation, qui brave toute probabilité en même temps que toute équiprobabilité (c'est-à-dire du hasard), un nouveau système linguistique qui trouve en lui-même ses propres lois, et dont l'originalité sera définie à la fois par son caractère hautement improbable et par sa haute teneur en signification. Ainsi, au lieu d'être plus ou moins attendu, chaque mot d'un poème est "neuf, incantatoire," et ceci parce qu'il s'insère dans un vers—et celui-ci dans un poème—qui lui-même constitue un véritable mot neuf et total, un "signe pur général," dit encore Mallarmé. En d'autres termes, au lieu de procéder du mot à la phrase et au discours, le poète procède à l'inverse: il part de l'ensemble. . . . [It is a question, then, of the poet's introduction of "modules of organized disorder" into the heart of the linguistic order for the purpose of reconstituting at the very heart of disorder, a new type of organization which simultaneously sets at defiance all probability and all equiprobability (that is to say, of chance), a new linguistic system which finds in itself its own laws and whose originality will be defined at the same time by its highly improbable character and by its high degree of signification. Thus instead of being more or less expected, each word of a poem is "new, incantatory," and this because it is inserted in a line—and this latter in a poem—which itself constitutes a veritable new and total word, a "sign, pure, general," again said Mallarmé. In other words, instead of going from the word to the sentence to the discourse, the poet goes in the opposite direction: he starts from the whole. . . .][4]

Such comments strongly suggest that one should search for the formal significance of the literary language, the "structure," as Jean Paulhan phrased it, "with a certain original property," not in the rules of that language which reader and poet share before the act of creation occurs, but rather in the observable differences. They also serve to emphasize that the differences one seeks are not those which in common phraseology are subsumed under the heading of "poetic language," such superficialities as meter, rhyme, obsolete linguistic forms, and distorted syntax. Coleridge declared, "I write in meter, because I am about to use a language different from that of prose."[5] Meter and other phenomena of the same level are not themselves of the different language: they are concomitants, perhaps, but they are not constituents. Instead the essential differences, the differences in constituents, are at a much more fundamental level in that, as Michaud points out, they involve the question of structure, that which is inherent in form. Thus once again, the principle illustrated by the topological model of the transformational process affords a valuable insight. Indeed, one may go back even further to Henri Matisse's cutouts and the discontinuity which reveals form: An essential element in the complexity of such forms is the element of contrast. If the line indicative of the contour of a form is bimodal, continuous in one axis, discontinuous in the other, there is as well another level implicit in the phenomenon of bimodalism, a level dependent upon the principle of contrast, of positive versus negative. Continuity is perceivable only against a contrasting discontinuity. The centripetality of a form is perceivable only in contrast to the centrifugal quality of the adjacent areas, centrifugal in relation to the centripetality of the one form because these adjacent areas belong to other forms with their own centripetalities. The truism in Matisse's sheet of colored paper, the total sheet before the artist even prefigured the form to be cut, let us assume the *Nue bleue,* is that even the color blue does not exist until a contrasting color is at least envisioned: in and of itself the universe of uniform blue which is the as yet untouched sheet of paper, offers not even the possibility of form. For Matisse, the possibility emerged with the vision of a true or near complementary, to render the blue perceivable as blue. At this point it is important to realize that as the blue nude is cut out from the sheet of paper the artist makes two forms, not one: one is the form which, when transferred to a complementary ground, became *Nue bleue,* the other is the form, the sheet of blue with the hole in it, which remained after the cutting—the not-blue nude revealed by the surrounding blue. Matisse's exploitation of both the positive and negative in the single work appears to advantage in the cutout *La Danseuse* (see color plate) in which the "positive" pirouetting free-form of the dancer's movement, is simultaneously the "negative" ground for the dancer's profile—Matisse's version of the well-known Peter-Paul goblet illusion. The principle is basic for form not only in two dimensions but also in three, as a comment by Henry Moore aptly discloses: "This is what the sculptor must do. He must strive continually to think of, and use, form in its full spatial completeness. He gets the solid shape, as it were, inside his head—he thinks of it, whatever its size, as if he were holding it completely enclosed in the hollow of his hand. He mentally visualises a complex form from all round itself: he knows while he looks at one side what the other side is like; he identifies himself with its centre of gravity, its mass, its weight; he realizes its volume as the space that the shape displaces in the air."[6] The experience revealed by this comment is one of the most breathtaking in all the multitudinous experiences of form. That three-dimensional form is perceptible as the shaped space enveloping it in the same manner as a ship's hull below the waterline is perceptible as the shape of the displacement in the water, indeed that space is a mold for physical form, transforms the entire receptible environment in much the same manner as the Peter-Paul goblet illusion transforms the two-dimensional plane. Something of the electrifying effect of the experience appears in James Lord's account of Giacometti's first encounter with it. The artist, while at work upon Lord's portrait, was talking with his model about Giacometti's bust of Diego, the artist's brother, and demonstrating his comments by pointing to features of the bust. After a while, Diego removed the bust and Giacometti turned back to the easel: "He began to paint once more, but after a few minutes he turned round to where the bust had been, as though to re-examine it, and exclaimed, 'Oh, it's gone! I thought it was still there, but it's gone!' Although I reminded him that Diego had taken it away, he said, 'Yes, but I thought it was there. I looked and suddenly I saw emptiness. I *saw* the emptiness. It's the first time in my life that that's happened to me.' "[7] Such experiences in the artist's view of the world constitute an exemplification of that Taoist view of space reflected, according to Kakuzo Okakura, in traditional Japanese architecture, especially tea-room architecture, in a vacancy perceptible not so much in the sparseness of the furnishings as it is in the sense of fragility in the walls and screens. This view of space is based upon Laotse's favorite metaphor, that of the Vacuum. "He claimed that only in vacuum lay the truly essential. The reality of a room, for instance, was to be found in the vacant space enclosed by the roof and walls, not in the roof and walls themselves. The usefulness of a water pitcher dwelt in the emptiness where water might be put, not in the form of the pitcher or the material of which it was made. Vacuum is all potent because all containing. In vacuum alone motion becomes possible."[8] True art is possible not so much when the artist masters the physical properties of that which he would represent as when he masters the vacuum which is that subject as molded by the enveloping space. Only then may he move to the center, become, as Lu Chi put it, the hub, and create his art, for only then may the artist freely respond to what Wallace Stevens called the motive for metaphor.

As Matisse's cutouts and Henry Moore's sculptures suggest, this principle is fundamental not just to Japanese art or the Taoist view of the universe but to all art, fundamental to all form and to all representations of form: a basic technique learned early in drawing classes is that the representation of complex forms is greatly simplified if one draws not the form but the space surrounding it. The complex perspectives, for example, of a chair's legs and cross-braces are easily mastered if one draws instead the shapes of the spaces cut out by the legs and cross-braces. This is the technique which led Piet Mondrian to such paintings as *Appletree in Bloom* and *Trees in Bloom* where the branches and trunks of the trees are reduced to lines marking the bounds of the enclosed spaces. Mondrian's transmutation of branches and tree trunks into outlines brings us back once again to the line and its bimodalism and thus to an emphasis upon the complementarity of the positive and the negative. The one is neither more nor less dominant than the other; instead the two are synchronous modalities of a single entity. Picasso in his own fashion expresses the concept in a comment about Cézanne's apples, thus bringing us back again to what Gertrude Stein and Hemingway learned from their study of Cézanne: "If one occupies oneself with what is full: that is, the object as positive form, the space around it is reduced to almost nothing. If one occupies oneself primarily with the space that surrounds the object, the object is reduced to almost nothing. What interests us most—what is outside or what is inside a form? When you look at Cézanne's apples, you see that he hasn't really painted apples, as such. What he did was to paint terribly well the weight of space on that circular form."[9]

The interdependence of the positive-negative modalities in painting is highly significant for a study of the literary language, for it tends to render explicit what is implicit in Coleridge's statement that he wrote in meter because he was "about to use a language different from that of prose": If by *prose* one understands the language of ordinary discourse in the "real" world, the logos, his "different language," the mythos, becomes "positive" perceivable only in contrast to the negative. The statement suggests again what is already indicated by references to Thom's "catastrophe theory" that the language of any literary art object is a linguistic shape whose form is modeled by the displacement it effects in the surrounding linguistic medium. The suggestion is, thus, of a fact self-evident in the work of those writers whose overt efforts have been directed toward the creation of an unmistakably separate literary language, such writers as Gertrude Stein, e. e. cummings, the James Joyce of *Finnegans Wake*. In discussing the language which the literary artist seems to share with his fellow inheritors of a particular linguistic tradition, Gertrude Stein called attention to the choice exercised by the writer as he works, the choice from elements already meaningful in the logos which he shares with his potential reader; she then continued, "there is inside it [the seemingly shared language] a separation, a separation from what is chosen to what is that from which it has been chosen."[10] The comment makes the writer's choice an equivalent of Matisse's scissors effecting a cutting-out, a separation of the writer's language from the previously undifferentiated linguistic field, this latter the equivalent of Matisse's sheet of blue paper prior to the cutting. The perception of this vital separation led Gertrude Stein to a view of the writer's language remarkably close to the view of sculptured form or form-to-be-sculptured expressed by Henry Moore: "In the early civilizations when any one was to be a creator a writer or a painter and he belonged to his own civilization and could not know another he inevitably in order to know another had made for him it was one of the things that inevitably existed a language which as an ordinary member of his civilization did not exist for him. That is really really truly the reason why they always had a special language to write which was not the language that was spoken, now it is generally considered that this was because of the necessity of religion and mystery but actually the writer could not write unless he had the two civilizations coming together the one he was and the other that was there outside him and

creation is the opposition of one of them to the other."[11] The thesis
may be questionable insofar as ethnology or cultural anthropology is
concerned, but as far as art and art history are concerned its validity is
beyond question, as Stein's own version of English literary history
illustrates. In talking of the impact of the Norman invasion upon
English literature, she traced the glories of Chaucer's art to the presence of Norman French words in the midst of the previously uniform
Anglo-Saxon. There were, to be sure, a number of factors which
contributed to the making of a Chaucer, "but and that must not be
forgotten," she wrote, "words were in that daily island life [of En-
gland] which had not been there before and these words although
they did not make for confusion did make for separation. This separation," she continued, "is important in making literature, because
there are so many ways for one to feel oneself and every new way
helps, and a separation way may help a great deal, indeed it may, it
may, it may help very much. And this did."[12]

The value of the Norman French among the Anglo-Saxon words is
the value of Matisse's consciousness of a complementary as he faced
the sheet of blue paper preparatory to creating the form entitled *Nue
bleue.* The two together point toward a larger value which the reader's
consciousness of contrast brings to the literary language, a value suggested by the reason which Matisse advanced for his voyage to Tahiti.
In an interview with Tériade he said of this excursion, "En art, ce qui
importe surtout, ce sont les rapports entre les choses. La recherche de
la possession de la lumière et de l'espace dans lesquels je vivais me
donnait le désir de me rencontrer avec un espace et une lumière
différents qui permettraient de saisir plus profondément cet espace et
cette lumière dans lesquels justement je vivais, ne fût-ce que pour
prendre conscience de ces derniers [In art what counts above all are
the rapports among things. The search for the possession of the light
and space within which I lived gave me the desire to make the acquaintance of a different space, a different light, which would permit
a more profound grasp of this space, this light in which I was living,
were it only to become aware of these latter]."[13] The fact that the artist
is better equipped to render the familiar in his art by "knowing,"
becoming aware of, the unfamiliar constitutes the value of expatriation for the artist, for expatriation is one of the many ways by which
he may become aware of the negative which validates his choice of the
positive. The insight is equally important for the reading of the literary language, as Merleau-Ponty has pointed out: "Expressive speech
does not simply choose a sign for an already defined signification, as
one goes to look for a hammer in order to drive a nail or for a claw to

pull it out. It gropes around a significative intention which is not guided by any text, and which is precisely in the process of writing the text. If we want to do justice to expressive speech, we must evoke some of the other expressions which might have taken its place and were rejected, and we must feel the way in which they might have touched and shaken the chain of language in another manner and the extent to which this particular expression was really the only possible one if that signification was to come into the world. In short, we must consider speech before it is spoken, the background of silence which does not cease to surround it and without which it would say nothing."[14] A consciousness on the reader's part of alternatives, a consciousness of all the linguistic possibilities which were explicitly or implicitly rejected by the artist brings a heightened awareness of the positive content in the literary language before him. To illustrate briefly, we may look back at the opening phrase of James's *The Aspern Papers,* "I had taken Mrs. Prest into my confidence. . . ." If one substitutes a few of the alternative ways of expressing a confiding relationship, one achieves a heightened awareness of the force of James's phrasing, a phrasing which places the relationship in a particular paradigm, the "had-taken-into" paradigm, much more physically spatial than, let us say, "I had trusted Mrs. Prest. . . ." The perception of the choice immediately gives particularity to the chosen. A wedge has been inserted and a separation begun. Gertrude Stein discovered this fact as the consequence of a translation she was asked to do, for the task of translation directly involves the reader in the process of choice and the weighing of alternatives: "A young French poet had begun to write, and I was asked to translate his poems, and there I made a rather startling discovery that other people's words are quite different from one's own, and that they can not be the result of your internal troubles as a writer. They have a totally different sense than when they are your own words. This solved for me the problem of Shakespeare's sonnets, which are so unlike any of his other work."[15] In short, she discovered what is implicit in Coleridge's statement that he wrote in meter because he was about to use another language.

To illustrate the nature of this other language, Paul Valéry evoked the concept of complex numbers. He wrote, ". . . There is a language of poetry in which words are no longer the words of free and practical use. They are no longer brought together by the same laws of attraction; they are charged with two values, acting simultaneously and of equal importance: their sound and their instantaneous psychological effect. They remind us, then, of those complex numbers of the geometers."[16] Complex numbers, it will be remembered, are expressed in the formula $a + bi$, where a is a real and bi an imaginary number. The relationship between a and bi is plotted in the same manner as the relationship between the Cartesian x and y: a is a horizontal axis corresponding to the Cartesian x axis, and bi is a vertical axis corresponding to the Cartesian y axis. Consequently, one way of describing the complex number system is as a system of imaginary numbers comprising a different plane from that of the real numbers in the Cartesian system. In Valéry's image, then, the sounds of the poet's language are "real," as are the real numbers a in the geometrical formula, but the "instantaneous psychological effect" is unreal or imaginary, analogous to the bi in the formula, the two together serving to remove the poet's language to another plane, a plane called in this study the surreal plane, where the words are governed by laws of attraction different from those (the syntax) of the "real" language. Thus the image which Valéry projects is remarkably close to the topography already discerned in the analysis of metaphor and of transformational perception. It justifies an extension of the poet's insistence upon a separation between the literary language and the surrounding linguistic medium to the conclusion that the topological model of a cusp catastrophe figures not only metaphor and transformational perception but the literary language itself, whose vocables are rooted in the logos but whose signification is formulated in the mythos. The correspondence among these three in turn serves to clarify the relationship between the literary language and that of ordinary discourse: on both sides of the separation one has vocables which have a "real" existence in the language of discourse. But the superposition of the chosen upon the lexicon from which the choice is made produces once again an area of bimodalism and synchronicity, an area where the vocables figure simultaneously in two modes.

As noted toward the end of Chapter 4, René Thom speculated on the possibility of a language consisting of topological forms: ". . . Il ne faudrait pas croire qu'une structure linéaire soit une nécessité pour transporter ou stocker l'information (plus exactement la signification). Bien que l'idée ne nous en soit pas familière, il n'est pas impossible qu'un langage, un modèle sémantique dont les éléments seraient des formes topologiques, ne puisse présenter, du point de vue de la déduction, des avantages sérieux sur le langage linéaire que nous pratiquons. En effet, les formes topologiques se prêtent par produit topologique, composition, etc. à une combinatoire infiniment plus riche que la simple juxtaposition de deux séquences linéaires [. . . It must not be thought that a linear structure is necessary for storing or transmitting information (or, more precisely, significance); it is possible that a language, a semantic model, consisting of topological forms could have considerable advantages, from the point of view of deduction, over the linear language that we use, although this idea is unfamiliar to us. Topological forms lend themselves to a much richer range of combinations, using topological products, composition, and so on, than the mere juxtaposition of two linear sequences]."[17] Although Thom had in mind a substantially different application for his speculation, it is nevertheless true that the evidence supports an application in the present instance. In a very essential way the literary language, itself a form which may be described and analyzed topologically, is a structure consisting of metaphors, themselves topological forms. Or, another way of stating the insight is to say that the literary form of English, let us say, or of any language which as *graphē* is not overtly figural as is Chinese, is nevertheless a true calligraphy in which the writer supplies through the coherence of his metaphors the figural mode which in Chinese is overtly present in the ideograph.

Behind such a concept, both as justification for and explanation of the conclusion, is a considerable body of evidence derived from the remarkable series of experiments in neurophysiology carried out by Roger W. Sperry and his team at the California Institute of Technology, a series of experiments which has revolutionized man's thinking about his thinking. The story of Sperry's achievements begins in the early 1950s with his work with Ronald E. Myers at the University of Chicago. In the course of their studies, Sperry and Myers discovered that when the corpus callosum of a cat, that is, the bundle of nerve fibers joining the two hemispheres of the cat's brain, was cut, each hemisphere functioned independently of the other as if it were a separate brain. After moving to the California Institute of Technology, Sperry and a team composed of Michael S. Gazzaniga, P. J. Vogel, and Joseph E. Bogen began in 1961 a series of investigations into the implications of this discovery insofar as the human brain was concerned, investigations which would lead in 1982 to a Nobel Prize for Sperry. As subjects for their study, they secured the cooperation of several epileptic patients who had undergone the surgical procedure known as commissurotomy (the surgical cutting of the corpus callosum and other commissures connecting the two hemispheres). The operation had been performed to help control the epileptic seizures and thus to prolong the lives of the patients. Surprisingly enough in view of the rather drastic nature of the operation, the patients manifested overtly little or no change in behavior after the operation. Sperry and his team undertook in a series of studies to discover what had happened in the cognitive processes as a consequence of the procedure. Their results established the general nature of the functional asymmetry of the human brain, an asymmetry long recognized but never before so fully understood.[18]

Although much remains to be done and many puzzling conflicts and contradictions in the evidence remain to be resolved, the principal pattern of the asymmetry as it bears upon the language functions and upon that aspect of the human imagination, the visuo-spatial image, central to the present discussion, is now well established. Sperry and his team brought strong bolstering evidence to those who held that the previously accepted view, the view that the left hemisphere is "dominant," and right "minor," needed considerable revision. The theory of a dominant left hemisphere grew out of the accumulation of evidence in the late nineteenth century concerning the consequences of cerebral traumas. First noted was the fact that a stroke or other damage in certain areas of the left hemisphere was the cause of aphasia, a total or partial loss of the ability to use or understand language. Subsequent research in the late nineteenth century and the first half of the twentieth revealed that left hemisphere damage also produced losses in the abstract-symbolic processes of mathematics and, as one would suspect, in conceptualizing insofar as it is an ability to reason abstractly. That is to say, damage in the left hemisphere deprived the victim of one or more of the various "higher" functions: conceptualization, mathematics, language. It was upon this evidence that Roman Jakobson built his theories about the metaphor and the literary language.

As far as the right hemisphere was concerned, it was not until data on the handedness of victims were included that late in the nineteenth century right-hemisphere control of left side perception and movement was noted. Prior to the inclusion of these data, because the majority of traumas to the right hemisphere produced no appreciable handicap in the so-called higher functions, the right hemisphere acquired status as the "mute" or the "minor" hemisphere. But as the data on handedness accumulated, an occasional bit of contradictory evidence was reported in cases of right-hemisphere trauma: from time to time such traumas in a left-handed person produced aphasia. The modern discoveries have permitted at least a partial resolution of the contradictions and some insight into the relationship between handedness and the distribution of functions in the brain. They have demonstrated as well that although to some extent the right hemisphere of a right-handed person is "mute," it is by no means "minor": its functions are every bit as important in the total cognitive functioning of the human being as are those of the left hemisphere. In the discussion which follows, one must bear in mind that reference is always to normally right-handed monolinguals, unless otherwise specifically stated. For left-handed persons, bilinguals, and polyglots the question of hemisphere specialization becomes considerably more complex, involving, among other matters, the age of the person in question, the degree of second-language fluency, and as well the fact that many who call themselves left-handed are not truly so though they may prefer to use the left hand for writing and other tasks which a right-handed person normally performs with the right.

In the language function, the hemispheres seem to differ sharply in expressive abilities. The left hemisphere is highly verbal: Centered here are the word memory, the grammatical and syntactic abilities which permit the propositions and predications of discourse. In conjunction with these skills, a semantic or conceptual decoding of written words and the ability to analyze phonetically seem to give to the left hemisphere an unquestioned superiority in the language functions. But without the aid of the right hemisphere, it does have language problems. Of significance for this study is one not easily perceived. This is a deficiency in visuo-spatial orientation in language and consequently a degree of pure verbalization without visuo-spatial referents, a verbalization which should be compared with that which characterizes the speech of the congenitally blind.

As Jean Piaget has noted, students of the phenomenon of language tend frequently to forget that the development of representational skills and of thought are closely connected not only with language but with a more general semiotic function which, indeed, manifests itself prior to language and continues through life in parallel with language in such forms as mimicry, symbolic play, and mental imaging. The most obvious evidence for this is, of course, that which is afforded by deaf-mute children where the deaf-mutism is not the consequence of some brain damage. Such children play make-believe, invent symbolic games as do normal children, and master a language of gestures which, formalized, is carried through adulthood. Although the development of logical structures is to some extent slowed, studies of the analytical-logical operations of deaf-mute children indicate that it is in no way as seriously affected as it is in the case of children blind from birth: "In the case of blind children, language, which is quite normal, only slowly makes up for gaps in their sensori-motor schemata, whereas the deaf-mute child's deprivation of language does not interfere with the development of operational structures. . . ."[19] Similar studies of blind subjects indicate that the senses of touch and hearing in no real way compensate for the lack of sight in the performance of various cognitive operations. For example, blind subjects are severely handicapped in tests which require the abstraction of common features from a series of sets presented either aurally or haptically, a handicap, that is, in the perception of the resemblances on which metaphor presumably is based.[20]

The difficulties experienced by the blind in such manipulations correspond with the significantly poorer performance of blind subjects on purely mathematical, that is, purely abstract-symbolic tasks. As Edmund Rubin has noted, a possible explanation for the disparity in performance levels between the blind and sighted subjects on the mathematical tests appears in the claim of the sighted controls that they had visualized numerical patterns as an aid to solutions. Further evidence came from one of the adventitiously blind subjects who was of the opinion that his manner of forming concepts had changed since the occurrence of his blindness: ". . . He described the change as being mainly a decreased reliance on visual imagery." Rubin's study concludes with a corroboration of Worchel, who "found a high correlation between age at onset of blindness and test scores on a tactual recognition task. Performance on such a task was aided by visual imagery so he concluded that the longer a person is deprived of vision, the less he depends on visual imagery. In other words, richness and vividness of imagery may require periodic stimulation."[21] Such studies add detailed substantiation to the generally recognized fact that the thought processes and conceptualization of the congenitally blind are different from those of the sighted person. The extent of the difference is apparent in the case of sixty-six blind patients who regained their sight after surgical removal of congenital cataracts. The fact that these newly sighted persons had need of extensive learning and instruction before they could perceive even simple forms indicates that the congenitally blind conceptualize in a manner significantly different from that of the sighted.[22] The world is quite literally a different place for them despite the fact that they speak, overtly at least, the same language as the sighted. The essence of the matter is, of course, in the fact that the congenitally blind person is deprived of the interplay between the verbal patterns of the language and the patterns formed by the visuo-spatial images of right-hemispheric consciousness.[23]

In the average adult, the right hemisphere is characterized by a sharply diminished verbal activity, especially a greatly impaired expressive capability, the characteristics of which are best observed in the case of left hemispherectomy (surgical removal of the hemisphere). The neurosurgeon Aaron Smith describes the expressive capability of one left hemispherectomy patient in the following terms:

> Although all language functions were profoundly impaired, speech was not abolished, and ability to follow simple verbal commands revealed some comprehension of speech. In [the patient's] attempts to answer questions immediately after surgery, he could produce isolated words, but after struggling to organize a meaningful reply, he uttered expletives and short emotional nonpropositional phrases, but could not communicate an idea in speech. Speech slowly improved, and though still severely impaired a year after surgery, his ability to communicate in short spoken sentences had increased significantly.[24]

Further, the right hemisphere apparently has little or no verbal memory, a loss particularly noteworthy in the case of words denoting abstract concepts. But as at least one study has suggested, the loss may well be the consequence of an inhibitory effect operating in the adult through some postulated "metacontrol" system which continues to reserve to the left hemisphere the linguistic functions which, after trauma, that hemisphere is no longer capable of performing.[25] According to this view, the adult right hemisphere has a much larger expressive potential and could take over the full language function, could the inhibiting mechanism be located and suppressed. Strong evidence in support of the hypothesis comes from the fact that in young children the right hemisphere does indeed take over the language function in cases of left hemispherectomy or left hemisphere trauma. Such a takeover occurs, with varying degrees of facility, up to the age of ten or twelve years. Further evidence for a greatly expanded linguistic capability in the adult right hemisphere comes from various studies of bilinguals and polyglots, one of which, carried out by Martin L. Albert and Loraine K. Obler of the Veterans Administration Hospital, Boston, led to the suggestion that:

> . . . It would no longer be correct to accept the traditional dogma that the left hemisphere is necessarily dominant for language in right-handers. This doctrine was obtained from many years of study in monolinguals and it probably remains correct for most monolinguals. Evidence from studies of bilingualism, however, suggests that the brain is a plastic, dynamic organ which continues to change throughout life as environmental (e.g., educational) stimuli impinge upon it. The right hemisphere may have as much capacity to acquire language in adulthood as it does in childhood. It may even be dominant for one of the languages of the bilingual.[26]

If the capacity of the adult right hemisphere for expressive language remains to some extent a matter of conjecture, there is no question about its superiority over the left in the formation of visuo-spatial images. This capability is the major specialization of the right hemisphere, a specialization most sharply manifested in tests based on nonverbal stimuli. In contrast, a deficiency in the image-forming capability renders the left hemisphere markedly inept in the perception of perspective and in space-time orientations. Indeed the left hemisphere is quite inept, even with the model before it, in drawing even simple geometric shapes, despite the fact that it controls the right hand of a normally right-handed person. The right hemisphere is the converse: It excels in visual orientations in space and time, and compensates for its apparent lack of verbal memory with a remarkably efficient image memory. In direct contrast to the left hemisphere, it can reproduce easily, even if somewhat awkwardly through the left hand, not just simple but also fairly complex line drawings of such three-dimensional objects as houses, cubes, wagons. This specialization in visuo-spatial transformations carries over into the interpretation of tactile stimuli as well. For example, the left hemisphere, when presented the tactile stimulus of a three-dimensional object placed in the right hand behind or under a screen, has difficulty in matching it with a two-dimensional "fold-out" drawing of the object presented to the left hemisphere in the corresponding visual field, an exercise posing no difficulty for the right hemisphere, which readily matches the three-dimensional object in the left hand with the corresponding two-dimensional drawing presented visually in its visual field.[27]

The sharp differentiation in specialization between the two hemispheres leads to the conclusion that the normal individual possesses the capacity for two distinctly different cognitive modes: left-hemispheric, characteristically a sequential, analytic mode manifest, for example, in logic chains of cause and effect in abstract-symbolic (mathematical) or verbal-propositional representations, and right-hemispheric, characteristically a patterned, figural mode which Bogen prefers to designate as appositional:

> Various kinds of evidence, especially from hemispherectomy, have made it clear that one hemisphere is sufficient to sustain a personality or mind. We may then conclude that the individual with two intact hemispheres has the capacity for two distinct minds. This conclusion finds its experimental proof in the split-brain animal whose two hemispheres can be trained to perceive, consider, and act independently. In the human, where *propositional* thought is typically lateralized to one hemisphere, the other hemisphere evidently

specializes in a different mode of thought, which may be called appositional.[28]

Although the word *appositional* may adequately express the nature of the right-hemispheric language capability of right-handed and many left-handed monolinguals, the word does not adequately reflect the overall mode of functioning. Characteristically the right hemisphere apprehends holistically in concrete, visuo-spatial images and its "generalizations" are made analogically, whereas left-hemispheric apprehension is analytic and its concepts are constructed on the abstract-symbolic level.

A bimodal consciousness dictates a new model for human cognition in which perceptions, insofar as they involve sensory stimuli, are processed simultaneously in two different modes: the stimuli are presented through both the right and left hemispheres to be processed in respectively the left and right visual cortexes, there to be integrated into the cognitive mode appropriate to the hemisphere. Insofar as they involve visuo-spatial transformations, perceptions are processed predominantly in the right hemisphere, a fact which justifies Doreen Kimura's conclusion that ". . . the right hemisphere plays a dominant role in man's perception of his environment."[29] The right hemispheric imagination, insofar as it is a holistic, visuo-spatial activity, and left hemispheric conception, insofar as it is a verbal and abstract-symbolic activity, must, in an idealized model of the human psyche, be conceived of as continuing to process in parallel modes the information thus received.

Fundamental to this processing is the fact, already suggested, that the human brain has two memory systems, not one: a linguistic or verbal memory in the left hemisphere and an image memory in the right. That the two can be functionally independent appears from the fact that damage to the right hemisphere or its removal can impair memory for nonverbal material without interfering with verbal memory. Conversely damage to or removal of the left hemisphere severely impairs or completely suppresses the verbal memory while leaving the image memory intact. Studies of normal persons involving the presentation of materials selectively to either hemisphere through either the right or left visual field lead to the same conclusion.[30]

The concept of two separate memory systems is to some extent, however, misleading when one speaks of the normal person engaged in the routine tasks of day-to-day living where materials are not presented selectively to one or the other half of the brain. In the normal situation one should probably speak not of two systems but of one bimodal system, a point which Gordon H. Bower has made. After rejecting the efforts of the behaviorists to reduce imagery effects to verbal processes, he comments, "The alternative is to postulate two memory modalities, imagery and verbal, with very rich interconnections. . . . The interconnections permit us to describe pictures, to describe our imagery, to have words evoking imagery, and so forth."[31] The two memory modalities, of course, reflect or parallel the two functional modalities of the human psyche; the verbal memory operates sequentially, as perforce it must, because words must occur, both in the formulation and in the recall, as separate and discrete entities in a temporal sequence either as list or as proposition. A verbal proposition cannot be so integrated that its various words occur simultaneously: even Lewis Carroll's portmanteau words, words such as *brillig, slithy, mimsy,* or *frumious,* which achieve a certain degree of telescoping, exhibit sequentiality in the syllables which evoke first one word then the other. The image memory is, on the contrary, holistic. Recognition tests, for example, reveal a clear superiority of the image memory over the verbal, because several elements can be readily integrated into one image as, for example, in a metaphor and thus made available for simultaneous recall and processing.[32] Much, of course, remains to be done to achieve a fairly complete clarification of the precise roles played by the two modes in the total functioning of the human psyche, but enough is already known to encourage the conclusion that

> . . . creativity, which is often considered the highest form of thinking, presumably involves an extraordinary degree of interplay of imaginal and verbal processes. Through its high memory capacity and freedom from sequential constraints, imagery contributes richness of content and flexibility in the processing of that content, so that diverse bits of information could be quickly compared and evaluated relative to a particular problem. These imagistic attributes may underlie the intuitive leaps of imagination that often characterize creative thinking. . . . They may also explain why concrete visual models play such an important role in the process of discovery. . . . On the other hand, verbal processes give logical direction to the stream of thought, preventing unconstrained leaps of imagination from lapsing into daydreaming.[33]

The conjunction of the conclusions derived from the study of the calligraphy of painters and poets with the evidence derived from the research of Sperry and others in neurophysiology points to the further conclusion that the essential difference between the artist and the nonartist is that the artist's specialized mode of thinking is imaginal, a mode in which the right-hemispheric modality predominates and that the artist is skilled in combinations, amalgamations, generalizations in images.

One may further conclude, then, that despite hemispheric dominance in linguistic behavior, any given language will exhibit at least traces of that mode which is the opposite of the dominant mode, that more generally communication through language is achieved in consequence of an interplay between the two modes. Again, the neurophysiologist furnishes clinical evidence which supports the conclusion suggested here in reference to the literary language. Gazzaniga, for example, found sufficient grounds to say of English-speaking subjects that "imaging processes surely must play a very important and critical role in our overall cognitive behaviour," a role which "prominently" features the right hemisphere: "These results suggest that when concrete, highly imagable words are used in a sentence, an image is developed and actively processed in the right hemisphere during the communication process."[34] A study by the British psychologists Stuart J. Dimond and J. Graham Beaumont adds a further precision to the nature of the interplay between the hemispheres. In word-association tests of the right and left hemispheres they found that the left hemisphere made associations which were "significantly more common," associations which presumably may be accurately characterized as quite prosaic, whereas the right hemisphere produced "less common" responses. The difference between the two sets of responses was sufficient to warrant the conclusion that the right hemisphere is, linguistically, the creative hemisphere: "We take the finding of greater variability and ingenuity in the right hemisphere to indicate the greater participation of the right hemisphere in the creative aspects of thought, attributing to it in this respect a specialized role. This role is seen as concerned with the more inventive, exploratory and improvisatory aspects of mental activity."[35]

The role of hemisphere specialization in linguistic bimodalism was observed by Clementina Kuhlman in the course of her studies of the linguistic attainments of children with a high or a low image-forming ability. She found first of all that children with high imagery excelled over the others in the association of arbitrary verbal labels and pictures, a process akin to that by which the Trobriand Islander names the various phases of yam development, a separate name for each phase with no concept of a generic connection among the various phases.[36] The process is the same as that upon which Chinese ideograms are based. Conversely, the child with low imagery excelled in tasks that required the abstraction of a concept from the observation of a shared attribute in a series of pictures, a task which involves an exercise in linear continuity. Kuhlman was led to comment, "A functional attribute or a complexly patterned perceptual attribute is frequently criterial for the meaning-categories, and hence for the correct use of language." The child who continues to rely upon visuo-spatial perceptual indices is handicapped in the attainment of abstract conceptual meanings; conversely the child who shifts almost exclusively to the newly acquired conceptual categories and the abstract-symbolic language which goes with them does so at the cost of the imagery role in language, which "decays with disuse."[37] Further support for Kuhlman's conclusions and the present application of them comes from tests of the capability for logical symbol discovery in the deaf. If as noted earlier the blind are severely handicapped in the perception of common features from a series of sets or in the transfer of a principle in problem solving from one sensory mode to another, the English-speaking deaf child is specifically handicapped in the perception of cause-and-effect chains and in the verbal formulations of abstract cause-effect principles.[38] To oversimplify somewhat in order to reveal what for the present purpose is the essential significance: The linguistic handicap of the blind child is such that he is deprived of the synchronous, discontinuous imagery mode in language and the linguistic handicap of the deaf child is such that he is deprived of the diachronic, sequential mode. Insofar as the English of ordinary discourse is concerned, Kuhlman's evidence points to an evolution in the interplay between the two modes in the language capability which is toward a greater and greater dependence upon the abstract-symbolic rather than the figural and visuo-spatial, a conclusion with which Bruner, who quotes Kuhlman extensively, concurs and for which Allan Paivio in his own studies adduces substantial confirmation.[39] The evidence afforded by the present study thus adds a further dimension: the literary language upon which the poets insist, the separate language which Miller called Chinese, with its own laws of attraction, may fruitfully be considered a complement with a high right-hemispheric modality to the predominantly left-hemispheric abstract-analytic conceptualization of ordinary discourse. The essential attractive force among the elements of the literary language is no longer the syntax of ordinary discourse, the syntax of left-hemispheric propositions but instead is the *morphē*, the right-hemispheric visuo-spatial image, upon which the isomorphism of the literary language is based.

A bimodalism in language is dependent upon a separation at least analogous to the separation insisted upon by the poets, the separation figured by Valéry in his image of complex numbers and modeled here after the discontinuity of the topological form of the cusp catastrophe. To this extent, then, the hypothesis adds a corrective to an otherwise perceptive comment by Roland Barthes. Building from his concept of language and a writer's style as the Cartesian coordinates of writing, Barthes concluded, "A language is . . . on the hither side of literature. Style is almost beyond it: imagery, delivery, vocabulary spring from the body and the past of the writer and gradually become the very reflexes of his art. Thus under the name of style a self-sufficient language is evolved which has its roots only in the depths of the author's personal and secret mythology, that sub-nature of expression where the first coition of words and things takes place, where once and for all the great verbal themes of his existence come to be installed. Whatever its sophistication, style has always something crude about it: it is a form with no clear destination, the product of a thrust, not an intention, and, as it were, a vertical and lonely dimension of thought."[40] The evidence afforded by the calligraphic approach and the supporting evidence from mathematics and neurophysiology suggest instead that the "self-sufficient language" of the poet is a form with a clear destination, a destination attained as consequence of the thrust which carries the poet from the "real" to the "surreal" language. The thrust is precisely the same as for the metaphor, and thus a comment by Paul Ricoeur apropos of the metaphor is equally apropos of the literary language. The comment grew out of Ricoeur's discussion of metaphor as a discovery of novel properties of things, that process which I have called the archetropic experience: "But to speak of properties *of things* (or *of objects*) [in the meaning of metaphors] which were not yet meant is to concede that the novel meaning is not *drawn from* anywhere, in language at least (property is a thing-implication, not a word-implication). And to say that a novel metaphor is *not drawn at all,* is to recognize it for what it is, that is, a momentaneous creation of language, a semantic innovation which has no status in language, as already established, neither as designation nor as connotation."[41] The full significance of Ricoeur's insight becomes clear when one keeps in mind the poet's insistance that the single "sign, pure, general" which is the poem is a metaphor. For example, Robert Frost declared, ". . . There are many other things I have found myself saying about poetry, but the chiefest of these is that it is metaphor, saying one thing and meaning another, saying one thing in terms of another, the pleasure of ulteriority. Poetry is simply made of metaphor. . . . Every poem is a new metaphor inside or it is nothing."[42] The extension of Ricoeur's insight from a single metaphor to the level of the literary language itself points toward a central distinction between the literary and the "real" language. The form which Barthes regretfully concluded has "no clear destination" is instead its own destination: the art object is object for both artist and reader. Of necessity then the literary language, like the metaphor and transformational perception, is for the reader essentially synchronous despite the seeming diachrony of the syntax and the sequence of the vocables carried over from the "real." It was the consciousness of this synchrony which caused Henry Miller to reject words as such and which permitted Mallarmé and Guy Michaud to speak of the entire poem as a totality, a "signe pur général."

In a particularly revealing passage reported by Louis Aragon, Matisse discussed the difference between the tree of his surreal world and a tree of the "reality" shared with all others who look at trees in the receptible environment. When it is a matter of drawing the tree, "il n'est pas question de dessiner un arbre que je vois. J'ai devant moi un objet qui exerce sur mon esprit une action, pas seulement comme arbre, mais aussi par rapport à toute sorte d'autres sentiments. . . . Je ne me débarrasserais pas de mon émotion en copiant l'arbre avec exactitude, ou en dessinant les feuilles une à une *dans le langage courant.* . . . Mais après m'être identifié en lui, il me faut créer un objet qui ressemble á l'arbre. Le signe de l'arbre [it is not a question of drawing a tree which I see. Before me I have an object which sets my spirit to work, not only as tree but also in relation with all kinds of other sentiments. . . . I would not discharge myself of my emotion by copying the tree exactly or in drawing the leaves one by one *in the common language.* . . . But after having identified myself in it, I must create an object which resembles the tree. The sign of the tree]." He went on then to indicate that Claude Lorrain and Poussin, for example, each had his own way of drawing the leaves of a tree; they each had their personal language ("Ils avaient leur langage personnel"), a personal language with, however, a curious property: its result is such that the viewer is led to believe the tree has been drawn leaf by leaf whereas in actuality the artist has so manipulated the sign *leaf* as to induce in the viewer the belief that, although in actuality seeing only fifty or so leaf-versions, he sees two thousand leaves.[43] The passage is full of import for the identification of a crucial aspect of the literary language. For if *trunk, branch,* and *leaf* are the three signs with which the ideogram *tree* is written, apart from the trunk which is singular (i.e., by the "law" of isomorphism only one is absolutely necessary for the ideogram), the signs must be repeated in a variety of "words" all of which nevertheless remain versions of either the sign *branch* or of the sign *leaf,* diagrammatic synonyms, as it were. Sufficient versions must be given to designate a multiplicity, but the versions must all be within the limits of the generic sign: the isomorphism which governs the images of a work governs as well the language and is again the source of the linguistic synchrony distinguishing the "positive" literary language from the "negative" of ordinary discourse. The variety is such that the isomorphism is obscured to the extent that a reader is lulled into the belief that he reads his own language, but even as he succumbs to his belief, the isomorphism is at work leading him deeper into a linguistic centripetality focused upon the archetropic image, "the gathering metaphor," at the cosmogenetic point. Quite literally and paradoxically the reader does not learn to read a particular poem or novel until after he has read it—another reason for the indispensable second reading.

Thus the vocables which the literary artist uses have their meanings in the logos and, simultaneously, their participation in the form of the mythos. The interplay between the two gives significance to the art object. That the vocables *are* words of the logos encourages the attempt to read through the meanings to intention, but that they are constituents of a form provides an impulse in the opposite direction, an impulse to which it is absolutely necessary to succumb if the significance is ever to be perceived. For the unwary reader of a literary work, the very familiarity of the vocables causes him to run a continual risk, that of falling into a "logical" reading, a risk quite similar to that which the English-speaking person runs when, in attempting to speak French, he uses the French loan-words of English with the French pronunciation but with the English meanings (formidable, *formidable*), a procedure which, as anyone knows who has made the experiment, produces consequences ranging from the satisfactory through the hilarious and the disconcerting to the disastrous. Instead it is much safer to seek what William Fifield found in the later work of Joan Miró, "the yield of not-think," a phrase not so far out of context as one might believe. Fifield used the phrase as a summation after noting Miró's opinion of efforts to explain the creative process: "I think the explanations of the creative process until now have been very superficial. The artists don't really go into it; the art critics start with preconceived ideas. If you have a preconception, any notion of where you are going, you will never get anywhere."[44] If one falls victim to the seeming familiarity of the vocables in the mythos, one necessarily falls victim to a preconception: The vocables become specifically the words of the logos, and the opportunity to see the holistic form of the mythos slips away unperceived. In distinguishing her "cubistic" writing from the writing of the nineteenth-century English writers, Gertrude Stein said, "They thought about what they were thinking and if you think about what you are thinking you are bound to think about it in phrases, because if you think about what you are thinking you are not thinking about a whole thing. If you are explaining, the same is true, you cannot explain a whole thing because if it is a whole thing it does not need explaining, it merely needs stating."[45] The objection is substantially the same as that voiced by Nietzsche in his definition of literary decadence: "How is *decadence* in *literature* characterized? By the fact that in it life no longer animates the whole. Words become predominant and leap right out of the sentence to which they belong, the sentences themselves trespass beyond their bounds, and obscure the sense of the whole page, and the page in its turn gains vigour at the cost of the whole,—the whole is no longer a whole."[46]

We thus arrive once again at a point touched upon earlier from another angle of vision, the fallacy in Etienne Gilson's equation of *explanation* and *language* in his assertion that "it is as impossible to paint by means of words as it is to speak by means of painting." As noted there and here confirmed, a poem does not "explain" a painting, it represents: explanation is of the logos, representation is of the mythos. The possibility of what Gilson calls impossible is manifest in the hundreds of Japanese scrolls of combined paintings and poems, the poems both representations of the paintings and beautiful examples in their own rights of the figural-conceptual interplay in which they figure. Among the finest examples of such work are the poetry scrolls produced in the early Edo period by Sōtatsu Tawaraya, who made the designs, and Kōetsu Hon'ami, who selected and wrote the poems. Such art approaches what one might call a Total Art because the poems which represent the drawings were frequently composed by some poet other than Kōetsu: Kōetsu "recomposed" them—drew them—in a calligraphy whose physical form is suited both to the poem and the painting, the relationship between the poet and Kōetsu, between Kōetsu and the painter, thus becoming somewhat similar in a two-pronged way (what I have called the calligraphic way) to that between, say, Beethoven and Rubinstein—composer and concert musician.

More to the immediate purpose, however, is the fact that the distinction between logos and mythos necessitates a complete revision of the argument that painting, by virtue of its lines and colors, is uniquely equipped to treat of forms which exist simultaneously in space, but that poetry is uniquely equipped for, indeed is properly concerned with, actions, sequences in time. The corrective appears in a delightful play upon the dual meaning of *succeed* in a comment by Gertrude Stein addressed to precisely the point under discussion:

> Anybody really anybody can realize this thing and realizing this thing can realize that narrative up to the present time has been not a succession of paragraphing but a continuing of paragraphing, a quite different thing.
> ... So now we really do know what sentences and paragraphs are and they have to do everything in narrative writing the way narrative has been written. Because as narrative has mostly been written it is dependent upon things succeeding upon a thing having a beginning and a middle and an ending.
> Now these are two things do not forget that they are not one thing. Succeeding one thing succeeding another thing is succeeding and having a beginning a middle and an ending is entirely another thing.[47]

The characteristic feature of the savage mind, so Lévi-Strauss concluded, is its holistic grasp of the world, its apprehension of the receptible environment "like that afforded of a room by mirrors fixed on opposite walls, which reflect each other (as well as objects in the intervening space) although without being strictly parallel."[48] The apprehension of the world is as a simultaneity of multiple superimposed images, no one of which is exactly the duplicate of any other, but which nevertheless groups with the others by virtue of invariable visuo-spatial properties. The evidence permits the assertion that this capability is not limited to the savage mind. The artist has long known such an apprehension of the world and, since the earliest epoch of prehistory, has continually projected it in his art, both painting and poetry.

8

Words and Signs

*T*he narrator of Beckett's "Text for Nothing: 8," all in describing his own text, states as well a truism about the language of literature in general: "It's an unbroken flow of words and tears. With no pause for reflection. But I speak softer, every year a little softer. Perhaps. Slower too, every year a little slower. Perhaps. It is hard for me to judge. If so the pauses would be longer, between the words, the sentences, the syllables, the tears, I confuse them, words and tears, my words are my tears, my eyes my mouth. And I should hear, at every little pause, if it's the silence I say when I say that only the words break it. But nothing of the kind, that's not how it is, it's for ever the same murmur, flowing unbroken, like a single endless word and therefore meaningless, for it's the end gives the meaning to words."[1] Wallace Stevens pointed to the same phenomenon in a much more succinct fashion when he wrote; "A poet's words are of things that do not exist without the words."[2] In essence both of these artists insist that, despite the meanings assigned in the dictionary entries, the poet's insertion of his chosen words in a form gives meanings (or one may prefer to say "significations") which obtain only as long as the words remain constituents of that form. The significance of both comments becomes much clearer when one studies carefully the cubist painter's use of words in the painting, especially the use of words versus broken letters and fragmented words in, for example, one of Picasso's *Ma Jolie* versions (1913).

In this painting appears the table full of objects beloved of the cubist painter: the table itself as an underlying form; on it or across the space, depthwise above it, a violin; on it as well a bottle, a clarinet,

Pablo Picasso, Spanish, 1881–1973, *Ma Jolie*, 1914; oil on canvas, 61.36. Indianapolis Museum of Art, Estate of Mrs. James W. Fesler. Photo by the Indianapolis Museum of Art.

and plates, cups, and glasses. There are also two parallel rows of letters: In the upper left corner, slanting upward toward the right on an angled sheet of paper (echo of the "MENU" typical of such cubist paintings), we find the letters *MAJOLIE:* at the bottom of the painting, we find the letters *Jour* on the linear representation of a folded newspaper (echo of the "JOURNAL" also typical of such cubist paintings). But the *J* extends above the edge of the newspaper form, the *o* is broken at the bottom by a thumb which grasps the lower edge of the folded paper, and the *r* is decapitated so that only the stem remains. Thus in the cubist "perspective" we have the point of view of a newspaper reader at one side of a table, the JOURNAL falling into fragments; across the table, in the position of the companion, the fully formed "carte" or "menu" *MAJOLIE,* the two forming a tête-à-tête linked by the violin and the bottle. When one notices that, by virtue of the decapitated *r* whose stem may be seen as an *I*, the deformed *journal* may be a *jouissance* in process of becoming, the range of significance is complete, a range which designated to Gertrude Stein when she saw the painting the fact that Picasso's departed mistress Fernande had been replaced by someone else. The interplay between the visual form of a menu and the verbal forms perceivable in *MA-JOLIE* (Ma Jolie), between the visual form of a newspaper and the various possible verbal forms one may develop from *Jour*— or *Joui*— establishes the range of significance in the painting. The full width of the range is underscored by the bottle of Bass with its discursively conformed word-label and shape *(logos)* intermediary between the other two word-shape formations *(mythos)*.

The key to the interplay is in Picasso's defense against what he called the "grab bag" approach to "reading" a painting. In his denunciation of such paintings as Jackson Pollock's, he said, "Whatever the source of the emotion that drives me to create, I want to give it a form which has some connection with the visible world, even if it is only to wage war on that world. Otherwise a painting is just an old grab bag for everyone to reach into and pull out what he himself has put in. I want my paintings to be able to defend themselves, to resist the invader, just as though there were razor blades on all surfaces so no one could touch them without cutting his hands. A painting isn't a market basket or a woman's handbag, full of combs, hairpins, lipstick, old love letters, and the keys to the garage." His defense against such readings is his use of what he called "attributes" in the painting:

> In those polyhedric Cubist portraits I did in tones of white and gray and ocher, beginning around 1909, there were references to natural forms, but in the early stages there were practically none. I painted them in afterwards. I call them 'attributes.' At that period I was doing painting for its own sake. It was really pure painting, and the composition was done as a composition. It was only toward the end of a portrait that I brought in the attributes. At a certain moment I simply put in three or four black touches and what was around those touches became a vest.
>
> I suppose I use that word 'attribute' in the way a writer might use it rather than a painter; that is, as one speaks of a sentence with a subject, verb, and attribute. But the verb and the subject are the whole painting, really. The attributes were the few points of reference designed to bring one back to visual reality, recognizable to any one. And they were put in, also, to hide the pure painting behind them. . . .
>
> . . . You know my Cubist portrait of Kahnweiler? . . . In its original form it looked to me as though it were about to go up in smoke. But when I paint smoke, I want you to be able to drive a nail into it. So I

added the attributes—a suggestion of eyes, the wave of the hair, an ear lobe, the clasped hands—and now you can.[3]

In the *Ma Jolie* version under discussion, the concept inherent in the words "ma jolie" (my pretty one) provides an attribute to govern the visual form of a menu; vice versa, the visual form is an attribute for the words. The attributive interplay holds the other row of letters to a parallel attributive interplay: from a deformed-deforming journal-like day-to-day pattern (menu for daily living) to a newly forming *jouissance*, a full-bodied, voluptuous pleasure *(ma jolie)* signaled as well in the bottle of Bass and the violin. Thus, all together, the painting constitutes a visual-verbal form of the purely verbal metaphor "What a dish!" Insofar as the words and letters are concerned, then, this painting makes manifest what Jean-Paul Sartre discerned in the language of literature. Using the vocabulary of the semiologist, he said, "En gros nous pouvons dire que les mots, pour le lecteur d'un roman, gardent ce rôle de signe. . . . Mais le savoir imageant tend bien trop fort vers une intuition . . .; il use alors du signe comme d'un dessin [In general, we can say that words, for the reader of a novel, retain this role as sign. . . . But the imaging consciousness tends too strongly toward an intuition. . .; it uses, then, the sign as design]."[4] The painting is thus an excellent formulation of that visual-verbal convergence which in the last chapter was discerned as the essential factor distinguishing the literary language, the mythos, from the language of discourse, the logos.

In *The Making of a Poem* Stephen Spender recorded an instance of archetropic experience which, when conjoined with the resulting poem affords a rare and remarkable view of the same attributive interplay, figural-verbal and vice versa at work in the poet's moment of creation. In his discussion of how poems are made, Spender comments upon the poet's effort to make even the verbal event itself isomorphic with the rest, so that the very dispositional pattern of the language interfuses with the images to constitute a total form. To illustrate his point he recounts that on his way to the hospital to visit his wife and their newly born son, Michael, he was suddenly struck by two things; the percept image of a cross on a church and the thought of how the whole history of the world "prepared" for the child's arrival, prepared not only the good but the bad as well:

Then I thought of the child as like a pinpoint of present existence, the moment incarnate, in whom the whole past, and all possible futures *cross*. This word *cross* somehow suggested the whole situation to me of a child born into the world and also of the form of a

poem about his situation. When the word *cross* appeared in the
poem, the idea of the past should give place to the idea of the
future and it should be apparent that the *cross* in which present and
future meet is the secret of an individual human existence. And
here again, the unspoken secret which lies beyond the poem, the
moral significance of other meanings of the word *cross* begins to
glow with its virtue that should never be said and yet should shine
through every image in the poem.[5]

What he speaks of here is not the sort of picture making by textual
arrangement on the page which characterized either the "shaped
poems" of the seventeenth-century English metaphysical George
Herbert or the *calligrammes* of Apollinaire, although, to be sure, the
best of such experiments with linear form in words underscores that
which Spender sought, a dispositional pattern which makes the discourse itself contributory to the figure the poem makes. In Spender's
case the archetropic image was not realized as art object, did not find
objective form, until after the death of his son along with four other
young airmen during a raid in World War II. The poem reads as
follows:

Air Raid across the Bay at Plymouth

I

Above the whispering sea
And waiting rocks of black coast,
Across the bay, the searchlight beams
Swing and swing back across the sky.

Their ends fuse in a cone of light
Held for a bright instant up
Until they break away again
Smashing that image like a cup.

II

Delicate aluminum girders
Project phantom aerial masts
Swaying crane and derrick
Above the sea's just lifting deck.

III

Triangles, parallels, parallelograms,
Experiment with hypotheses

On the blackboard sky,
Seeking that X
Where the enemy is met.
Two beams cross
To chalk his cross.

IV

A sound, sounding ragged, unseen
Is chased by Excaliburs of light.
A thud. An instant when the whole night gleams.
Gold sequins shake out of a black-silk screen.

V

Jacob ladders slant
Up to the god of war
Who, from his heaven-high car,
Unloads upon a star
A destroying star.

Round the coast, the waves
Chuckle between rocks.
In the fields the corn
Sways, with metallic clicks.
Man hammers nails in Man,
High on his crucifix.

(Collected Poems, 1928–1953)

Examining the poem "archetropically," one discovers it is based
upon a series of transfigurations by which the searchlight beams, in
the "real" world insubstantial rays of light, become successively in the
surreal world a "cone of light" of sufficient materiality to be smashed
like a cup; "delicate aluminum girders" projecting the masts, crane,
and derrick of a ship's superstructure; chalked geometrical figures on
a blackboard; sword blades; and finally ladders. In short, the poem
confronts the reader with a succession of metaphors, of images comprising an archetropic coherence in the transfigurative searchlight
beams presented in a succession of different materialities, each materiality with its own *figura*. The coherence justifies the hypothesis that
the form presented directly to the reader is a transfiguration of the
essential form.

As a purely visual phenomenon, the calligraphy presents blocks of
lines on a contrasting ground arranged to present an overall symmetry, containing, however, a slight but significant asymmetry. The
symmetry is figured in the five sections of the poem, the first and the

last composed of two internal stanzas, the second, third, and fourth of one group each, thus:

$$\text{II} - \text{I} - \text{I} - \text{I} - \text{II}$$

This pattern is centripetal upon the third section, whose Roman numeral (III) and form again reinforce the pattern of symmetry, the number figuring the fact that the section is composed of seven lines centripetal upon the line "Seeking that X." The entire poem then is in the transfigurative mode focused upon a section devoted to mathematical figuring, a section focused upon an X, itself a symmetrical figure. The middle section with its three lines on either side of the central line is thus a miniature version of the overall symmetry of the total poem. But there is a transfiguration: the two stanzas of Section V do not exactly balance the two corresponding stanzas of Section I. Instead they figure an asymmetry both within the section and in contrast to the corresponding section: Section V is longer than Section I by three lines, and internally the second stanza of Section V is longer than the first. The fact justifies a refinement of the hypothesis: The figural asymmetry constitutes a transfiguration of the symmetrical X.

A reexamination of the images of the poem reveals an extensive list of transfigurations of X both as a visual and a verbal phenomenon. As a visual phenomenon, that is, as the intersection of two straight lines at various angles and with varying points of intersection, the transfigurations are visible in the crossed beams of light; a ship's masts, derrick, and crane; the crossed chalk lines of the mathematical x on a blackboard; the cross-hairs of gunsights (implied but still very present at the center of the poem); a sword blade and hilt; the fuselage and wings of an airplane, and finally of course the cross of the Crucifixion. As a verbal phenomenon, they are present as word (the repeated *cross* in the last two lines of Section III), as syllable (both as the *-cross* of *across* and the *ex-* or *experience*), as syllable-symbol (the *Ex-* of *Excalibur* which transfiguratively is the X of *X-caliber,* for antiaircraft guns of unknown caliber), as letter (either the x of English or the *chi* of Greek, as in *Christos*), and as word-letter (the last vocable of the poem, *crucifix,* which in its range from *crux* to x sums up the calligraphy of the poem.

These visual-verbal transfigurations converge as do the searchlight beams to form a larger transfiguration as a consequence of the symmetry of the last section. Imaginally the last section moves from the figure of Jacob ladders to a crucifix; through the biblical allusions, the signs move from Jacob's dream to the Crucifixion. The combination, the calligraphy, in conjunction with the entire poem moves from the Crucifixion of Christ, the Son, to the death in a cruciform airplane of

Spender's son, whose name, Michael, is that of the militant archangel, Milton's wielder of a flaming sword, an Excalibur of light. But the crucifixion of Spender's Son and his fellow bomber crewmen is, transfiguratively, memorialized in a poem depicting the deaths of German bomber crewmen over Plymouth. The calligraphic reading thus permits a participation in a very moving personal experience of another Transfiguration. Jacob went out from Beer-sheba toward Haran. At nightfall, near a place called Luz, he arranged some stones for his pillow and lay down to sleep. He dreamed,

> . . . and, behold, a ladder set up on the earth, and the top of it reached to heaven: and, behold, the angels of God ascending and descending on it. And, behold, the Lord stood above it, and said,
> "I am the Lord God of Abraham thy father, and the God of Isaac: the land whereon thou liest, to thee will I give it, and to thy seed; and thy seed shall be as the dust of the earth, and thou shalt spread abroad to the west, and to the east, and to the north, and to the south: and in thee and in thy seed shall all the families of the earth be blessed. . . ."

In sharp counterthrust to this, in an almost unbearable, otherwise inexpressible x-ing out of this, Spender, waking, went out toward a place called Plymouth, and beheld:

> Jacob ladders slant
> Up to the god of war
> Who, from his heaven-high car,
> Unloads upon a star
> A destroying star.

Jacob, as a consequence of his dream, set up his pillow-stone as a pillar, consecrated it, and vowed: "If God will be with me, and will keep me in this way that I go, and will give me bread to eat, and raiment to put on, so that I come again to my father's house in peace; then shall the Lord be my God: and this stone, which I have set for a pillar, shall be God's house: and of all that thou shalt give me I will surely given the tenth unto thee." Spender, as a consequence of his waking nightmare, composed a cruciform poem, a crucifix "In Memoriam: M.A.S."—a Christian cross (whose stem is asymmetrical in the symmetry) derived from the cruciform airplanes (British and German), a cross fixed to embody the anguish of the several sons thereon crucified, several sons, who, like that other Son, surely cried out at the moment of the nailing: "My God, my God, why hast thou forsaken me?"

In short one must be fully conscious of the manner in which the diagrammatic cross, the intersection of two straight lines, like the figural menu or newspaper in Picasso's painting, controls the range of lexical meanings from the logos, ruling out such incongruent meanings as "peevish" or "irritable." But if form is necessary for significance in the cubism of the mythos, the formative values within the range of lexical meanings in the logos must at least be suggested "attributes" to retain a consciousness of present contour behind the re-presentation in the surreal form if the calligraphy is to remain properly balanced. In the course of her experiments with words "of equal value," Gertrude Stein soon discovered that formal value (as opposed to merely "value") inescapably involves an interplay with lexical meanings in the logos: "While during that middle period I had these two things that were working back to the compositional idea, the idea of portraiture and the idea of the recreation of the word. I took individual words and thought about them until I got their weight and volume complete and put them next to another word, and at this same time I found out very soon that there is no such thing as putting them together without sense. It is impossible to put them together without sense. I made innumerable efforts to make words write without sense and found it impossible. Any human being putting down words had to make sense out of them."[6] Individual words may have "equal values" in isolation, but in the juxtaposition of two or more words as in the juxtaposition of two or more forms in a painting there must necessarily be modulations in value else there will be no formation. Uniformity in value produces the amorphous, returns us to Matisse's uncut sheet of blue.

Eric H. Lenneberg posed for himself the question "What is meant by knowing a language?" and concluded, "In order to understand the nature of language, it is first of all necessary to rid ourselves of the notion that its most important components are simple labels or 'names.' Language is relational in every aspect and at every term. Hence to teach someone to speak is essentially *to invite him to relate aspects of the environment in such and such a way.* The language community induces the child to treat what is before him in quantitative, qualitative, comparative terms; induces him to say something that relates an object to its use, or to the speaker, or to the listener, or to another object. In order for such an invitation to relate to be succcessful, the subject must have a natural inclination to deal with his environment in certain ways."[7] The conclusion is quite germane in respect to the central question of this study. The literary art object, like the painting or the sculpture, objectifies, formalizes the artist's "natural inclination," here termed archetrope, and derives from that technique defined in Chapter 3 as "the precision which creates movement." Instructed by the topological model of a metaphor, we are carried by the word *precision* (Latin *prae*, "before" + *caedere*, "to cut"), back to Matisse's scissors, the sensation of flight in the artist's interior space, and the artistic vision which preceded the actual cutting: Metaphor is but another name for the archetropism of the transformational process—the artist's natural inclination: *natural* because it is human, as the heliotropism of the heliotrope is natural because it is heliotrope. The art object, once created, thus created, induces in the reader a corresponding "natural inclination" to relate in a particular way the lexicon of his logos to the form and space of the mythos, to perceive corresponding values. And once the invitation to relate has been accepted, the reader finds he has arrived at the elemental insofar as the literary language is concerned: The metaphor as verbalism is inseparable from the metaphor as vision, as form. In Matisse's cutout *Nue bleue*, the cutout form is *essentially* inseparable from the blue which is cut out: One faces the irreducible in the calligraphy.

Wilhelm von Humboldt said in respect to language, "Man lives with his objects chiefly—in fact, since his feeling and acting depend on his perceptions, one may say exclusively—as language presents them to him. By the same process whereby he spins language out of his own being, he ensnares himself in it; and each language draws a magic circle round the people to which it belongs, a circle from which there is no escape save by stepping out of it into another."[8] This is not necessarily true as far as the artist is concerned, for in the creation the vision shapes the language. As far as the reader is concerned it is quite true, but one must understand that the difference between the first and the second reading of a poem, for example, is precisely the escape of which Humboldt speaks, the stepping from the one magic circle to the other and even more: a *naturalization*—a happily apt word from Wallace Stevens—within the new magic circle. Speaking from the poet's point of view, Stevens extends the experience of metaphor to a transformation in the poet's very nature: "The way a poet feels when he is writing, or after he has written, a poem that completely accomplishes his purpose is evidence of the personal nature of his activity. To describe it by exaggerating it, he shares the transformation, not to say apotheosis, accomplished by the poem." So too does the reader share the transformation, the apotheosis, for in the very process of reading, under the shaping impact of the poet's words, the reader moves to the center, becomes the organizing center of the morphogenetic field which thenceforth radiates in widening concentric circles outward to the contours of what has now become the reader's surreal world. In Stevens's words, "We are interested in this transformation primarily on the part of the poet. Yet it is a thing that communicates itself to the reader. Anyone who has read a long poem day after day as, for example, *The Faerie Queene*, knows how the poem comes to possess the reader and how it naturalizes him in its own imagination and liberates him there."[9] The word *naturalizes* must be understood here in its most basic sense, as "to endow with a natural inclination," that natural inclination central to Lenneberg's comment. For without this essential inclination the vocables of the text will steadfastly resist the transformation, will remain naught but the shapeless lexicon of the logos without defining, definitive values, and form will be no better than that of a dictionary, the alpha to omega of words of equal values. As Robert Frost said, "Form in language is such a disjected lot of old broken pieces it seems almost as non-existent as the spirit till the two embrace in the sky."[10] The mythos, then, and the significance of the signs coherent in the form of the mythos are—is, since the two are one—"incredibly," again in Stevens's words, "the outcome of figures of speech or, what is the same thing, the outcome of the operation of one imagination on another through the instrumentality of the figures. To identify poetry and metaphor or metamorphosis is merely to abbreviate the last remark."[11] The observation does much to clarify the old argument over the "meaning" of the art object and whether or not art "communicates" a "meaning," for inherent in the observation, in view of Stevens's previous comment about naturalization, is a shift in emphasis in the word *communicate*, a shift to the region where *communicate* merges with *commune*, and *meaning* becomes *being:* a poem does not mean—it is. Thus it is not the communicable but the communal to which Valéry refers when he says, "It is the reading of the poem that is the poem," or to which Joseph Joubert referred when he said, "One finds poetry nowhere if there is no poetry within." Picasso was more precise with the verb *lives:* "The picture lives only through the man who is looking at it." He thus emphasized the same vital quality which Gertrude Stein insisted upon in her "being in the present." In another remark he amplified his point:

> . . . We must enable the viewer to paint the nude himself with his eye.
> You know, it's just like being a peddler. You want two breasts? Well, here you are—two breasts. . . .
> We must see to it that the man looking at the picture has at hand everything he needs to paint a nude. If you really give him every-

thing he needs—and the best—he'll put everything where it belongs, with his own eyes. Each person will make for himself the kind
of nude he wants, with the nude that I will have made for him.[12]

Because of the communal aspect in the experience of the mythos
the definition of a poetic sign becomes something more than
definition, for *definition* (Latin: *de-*, "from" + *finire*, "to set a limit to,"
"bound") means merely to provide an outline in what is essentially a
two-dimensional plane. Because the reader has replaced the artist at
the organizing center of the morphogenetic field, the significations of
the signs become centripetal and three-dimensional; they are not
within outlines (defined), they are contoured and exist as that which is
within the contour in the unity of form and space. The sign in the
mythos is isomorphic with the mythos, and its form-space is the form-
space of the mythos within the enveloping and centrifugal logos. The
artist's view of form as that which is within the mold of the surrounding and enveloping space—the view discussed in the preceding chapter—aids in a differentiation between the poetic sign, the sign of the
mythos with its form and value, and the prosaic word, the word of
purely lexical definition within the logos. The artist's view emphasizes
the *inwardness* of the form in space and gives added force to the prefix
in- when one speaks of the incarnate word. Both words and signs are
polysemous: but in their polysemy the words of the logos tend to be
centrifugal; the signs of the mythos become centripetal, their multiple
dimensions contained within the displacement they cause in the enveloping medium. It is to this aspect of the poetic style that
Wordsworth referred in a comment which Thomas de Quincey treasured:

> His [Wordsworth's] remark was by far the weightiest thing we
> ever heard on the subject of style; and it was this: that it is in the
> highest degree unphilosophic to call language or diction "the *dress*
> of thoughts". . . . He would call it the *"incarnation* of thoughts."
> Never in one word was so profound a truth conveyed. . . . And the
> truth is apparent on consideration: for, if language were merely a
> dress, then you could separate the two; you could lay the thoughts
> on the left hand, the language on the right. But, generally speak-
> ing, you can no more deal thus with poetic thoughts than you can
> with soul and body. The union is too subtle, the intertexture too
> ineffable,—each co-existing not merely *with* the other but each *in*
> and *through* the other.[13]

It is this aspect of the artistic creation which is figured in Picasso's *Ma
Jolie* and Spender's "Air Raid across the Bay at Plymouth."

An example from William Empson's "ambiguities" will serve to illustrate the difference in emphasis. To illustrate a genitive relationship commonly appearing in Shakespeare's literary language,
Empson quotes from *Othello:*

> That I did love the Moor to live with him,
> My downright violence and storm of Fortunes
> May trumpet to the world.
>
> (1.3.247–49)

As Empson notes, the phrase "violence and storm of Fortunes" requires a shift in meaning in the preposition *of* as one goes from
"violence of Fortunes" to "storm of Fortunes."[14] But simultaneous
with the "ambiguity" of the preposition is the fact that the total phrase
has another dimension in a newly created sense for the word *violence,*
which in this mythos may signify not just vehemence but also the state
of being violated: The loss of Desdemona's virginity is one proof of
her "fortunate" love for the Moor. In essence one has in such an
instance a compounding in the etymology of the word, a shift in the
"history" which in effect imparts a new history isomorphic with all else
within the form. The process is the same as that observed by Murray
Krieger in John Donne's "A Valediction Forbidding Mourning":

> Dull sublunary lovers' love,
> Whose soul is sense, cannot admit
> Absence, because it doth remove
> Those things that elemented it.

Krieger comments, "Here, with a pun on 'absence' that covers a winking etymology, 'sense' is forced upon us as the root of 'ab*sence*' in letter
as well as concept. We are taught what 'absence' really is: a word with a
soul of 'sense,' with 'sense' the thing 'that elemented it' and thus the
thing that 'cannot admit' it since 'absence' involves—in word and concept, in word *as* concept—the deprivation, indeed the elimination of
'sense.'"[15] In this case, the etymology is "winking," but it is much less
so, is indeed a terrible and terrifying sense in Carson McCullers's
novel *The Heart Is a Lonely Hunter* when the two adolescents Mick Kelly
and Harry Minowitz experience physical love together. As they walk
disconsolately back from the scene of their adventure they accuse
themselves of "adultery," a charge which is totally incomprehensible
and thus totally absurd in the light of the logos but which makes a
terrible kind of sense in the fact that through their intercourse they
have lost their virginity and become adults in a world of lonely hunter
hearts. The one word, then, in the very shifting of its etymology to a

parallel with such words as *drudge, drudgery* or *slave, slavery,* manifests dimension in the whole episode in a span from childish absurdity to adult terror. Something similar occurs in Hawthorne's *The Scarlet Letter,* in which several "wearers of petticoat and farthingale" discuss the various means by which Hester Prynne might cover with various articles of clothing the shameful emblem she is forced to wear on the bosom of her gown. The discussion follows hard on the heels of the word *invest,* thus emphasizing the etymology of the word: to enclose in clothing, *in-* plus *vestire.* The textual movement, then, invests the word *inhabitant,* used to designate these "wearers of petticoat and farthingale," with a new significance and a new etymology in addition to the lexical meaning. The word now spans from one who lives within a community to one who is enveloped in a habit (*costume* as well as *custom*), inhabitants who discuss Hester's punishment as a "costumary" not a customary one. Empson notes a similar spanning in the case of the verb *tears* in Marvell's elegy for the death of the Lord Hastings. The particular passage reads:

> The gods themselves cannot their Joy conceal
> But draw their Veils, and their pure Beams reveal:
> Only they drooping Hymeneus note,
> Who for sad *Purple,* tears his Saffron coat,
> And trails his Torches through the Starry Hall
> Reversed, at his Darling's Funeral.

Empson analyzes the situation as one in which the verb *tears* (to rend, rip) gains a new meaning, "to moisten with tears," and thus becomes through a double-meaning truly ambiguous.[16] But it would be more accurate to see these two meanings not as ambiguous but as isomorphous, for an alternate analysis would see the two meanings as a new range of significance, from "rend" or "rip" to "moistening with tears." One has in effect a new verb which subsumes both the sobbing and the racking.

Such examples illustrate what Siegfried Sassoon has pointed out, that the poetic language does not depend upon overt departures from the logos, such as those by Gertrude Stein or James Joyce, to mark its nature as mythos. As rich as such devices may be, the history of literature amply proves they are not indispensable. Instead, "In good poetry the most ordinary words can somehow acquire a local magic of their own, a sort of glow-worm independence of common usage." To illustrate what he meant he likened the poet's use of words to the finding of seashells on a dry beach. Out of the water, dried and dusty in the sand, the shells appear lifeless and colorless. But if one takes them home and puts them in a bowl of water they suddenly "revive to floral freshness and delicate aqueous colour": "Thus it can be with words. In the dry element of the dictionary they are merely printed sounds capable of serving our linguistic purposes. But when transfused by the other element of poetry they 'suffer a sea-change into something rich and strange.' And the water—or whatever my simile chooses to call it—which transforms them is emotion."[17] The manner in which the "transfusion" is accomplished almost forces one to shift to the word *infusion* to emphasize the fact that merely by virtue of their insertion into a form the words of the lexicon acquire significance. Two examples chosen from passages which Empson cited to other purposes will illustrate: The first, from Pope's *Unfortunate Lady*, is similar to what already has been demonstrated with *tears* in Marvell's elegy:

> How loved, how honoured once, avails thee not,
> To whom related, or by whom begot;
> A heap of dust is all remains of thee;
> 'Tis all thou art, and all the proud shall be.

A doubled dimension appears in *remains,* which may be read as either noun or verb and should be read as both simultaneously in an expanded range of significance which then more fully informs the fourth line, a process reinforced by the thrice repeated *all.* Such words, as these turn inward upon themselves, seem to expand, to extend their dimensions to embrace surrounding words, to "inform" them. Another example comes to hand in Shakespeare's Sonnet xiii:

> Who lets so fair a house fall to decay,
> Which husbandry in honour might uphold
> Against the stormy gusts of winter's day
> And barren rage of death's eternal cold?
>   O none but unthrifts, dear my love you know,
>   You had a father, let your son say so.

Here *dear* functions in a polysemous, "polytactic" fashion, as appositive to *unthrifts* in the semantic field of *expensive* or *costly,* as adjective to *love* thus linking back to *honour* in an honorable love, and as adverb to the verb *know* in a semantic field allied to that of *costly* but also verging to the senses of *grievous, dire, fell. Dear* thus expands in its significance to subsume the entire sonnet. In doing so the one "word" achieves significance: focuses, serves as organizing center to, ultimately *is* the poem.

For multiple dimensions, then, the word *ambiguity* is ill-chosen—as indeed other commentators have noted—for it images the reader in a state of vacillation somewhere in the center of various meanings, like an ill-informed traveler at a crossroads or a chess player hesitating between two possible "readings" of his opponent's move. In true ambiguity the reader, like the chess player, must either hesitate forever and thus forfeit the game or in choosing one course, forgo the other. Such is the lesson of the two types of ambiguous sentences beloved of the structural linguists: In the case of "Flying planes can be dangerous," the syntactic ambiguity forces the reader to vacillate forever between the two possible intentions. In the case of "They are eating apples," the choice of the one definitively excludes the other. But not so with the sort of polysemy with which we are dealing. The phenomenon is a matter of the *dimensions* of the word-become-sign and consequently both of simultaneity in the multiplicity, as in ambiguity, *and also* of centripetality in the multiplicity, that is, of isomorphism. Because the various meanings are totally compatible, the loss of some produces an effect quite the contrary of the effect in ambiguity where, if an incompatible element is lost, linear continuity and consequently clarity results. In the case of such polysemy and polytaxis as concerns us the loss of some does not impair the coherence and cohesion of the remainder but does distort the total form, effecting as a consequence a "lopsidedness" in the poem as perceived. Nor is this a matter of levels of meaning in the usual sense of that phrase, a sense which imparts a kind of vertical dimension, a "cross-sectioning," to the process of reading. Again, the polysemy and polytaxis of which we speak involves the total dimensionality of the sign and thus of the calligraphy.

One may illustrate such a total dimensionality with the Attic shape of Keats's famous "Ode on a Grecian Urn," an Attic shape which confines or contains the polysemy of the vocables *beauty* and *truth* with which Keats constructed that enigmatic aphorism "Beauty is truth, truth beauty." As words in the logos these vocables are assuredly amorphous enough to cause anyone to throw up his hands, as they did T. S. Eliot, amorphous enough to sustain the long-lived debate which has attended them almost from the moment of their appearance in the urn's message to mankind. To be sure, a calligraphic reading of the Ode probably will not resolve the debate, but it will add significant data which will at least refocus the debate by placing these vocables in a figural context, a centripetality. Insofar as such a placement provides contours, it as well, then, tends to define.

First of all, a reader of the Ode must notice that paradoxically the urn's message is "spoken" by a "silent form" which in the basic metaphoric development from the "still unravish'd bride" of the first line to the "silent form" of the last stanza figures, and in figuring contains, the often remarked polysemy of the word *still* which, insofar as it includes *silent*, encompasses then the central attribute of the "speaker." In its polysemy, the signification of *still* ranges over most, if not all, of the lexical denotations current in Keats's time: the silence of "unheard melodies," the calm of a "Cold Pastoral," the motionlessness of "marble men and maidens," and the yet, the ever of "still unravish'd." But the centripetality of the polysemy does not become manifest until one notices how the figural in the poem focuses the polysemy in a form. The semantic movement of *still* from the first to the last stanza does not become fully significant until one couples it with the visual metaphor, achieves the surreal image consequent to the superimposition of the form of a living, human bride "still unravish'd," "warm and still to be enjoy'd" upon the "silent form" of an urn. That is to say, one must see what Picasso and Brassaï saw, the woman-shape in the vase-shape: the in-curve of lip to neck of the urn corresponding to the in-curve from breasts to waist of the bride, the out-swelling to the full diameter of the urn and the out-swelling from waist to hips of the bride, and the taper from diameter to pedestal of the urn and the long, smooth taper from hips to thighs to feet of the bride. The archetropic fusion of the two into the form-space of torso-urn brings a heightened sense of the interiority of the Attic shape, the sheer volumetric capacity of the bride for pregnancy, the urn for ashes, and the poem for the significance of *still*, a heightened sense, that is, of what one may call the Beauty-truth of the bride and the Truth-beauty of the urn:

ODE ON A GRECIAN URN

I

Thou still unravish'd bride of quietness,
    Thou foster-child of silence and slow time,
Sylvan historian, who canst thus express
    A flowery tale more sweetly than our rhyme:
What leaf-fring'd legend haunts about thy shape
    Of deities or mortals, or of both,
        In Tempe or the dales of Arcady?
    What men or gods are these? What maidens loth?
What mad pursuit? What struggle to escape?
        What pipes and timbrels? What wild ecstasy?

II

Heard melodies are sweet, but those unheard
   Are sweeter; therefore, ye soft pipes, play on;
Not to the sensual ear, but, more endear'd,
   Pipe to the spirit ditties of no tone:
Fair youth, beneath the trees, thou canst not leave
   Thy song, nor ever can those trees be bare;
     Bold Lover, never, never canst thou kiss,
Though winning near the goal—yet, do not grieve;
   She cannot fade, though thou hast not thy bliss,
     For ever wilt thou love, and she be fair!

III

Ah, happy, happy boughs! that cannot shed
   Your leaves, nor ever bid the Spring adieu;
And, happy melodist, unwearied,
   For ever piping songs for ever new;
More happy love! more happy, happy love!
   For ever warm and still to be enjoy'd,
     For ever panting, and for ever young;
All breathing human passion far above,
    That leaves a heart high-sorrowful and cloy'd
      A burning forehead, and a parching tongue.

IV

Who are these coming to the sacrifice?
   To what green altar, O mysterious priest,
Lead'st thou that heifer lowing at the skies,
   And all her silken flanks with garlands drest?
What little town by river or sea shore,
   Or mountain-built with peaceful citadel,
     Is emptied of this folk, this pious morn?
And, little town, thy streets for evermore
   Will silent be; and not a soul to tell
     Why thou art desolate, can e'er return.

V

O Attic shape! Fair attitude! with brede
   Of marble men and maidens overwrought,
With forest branches and the trodden weed;
   Thou, silent form, dost tease us out of thought
As doth eternity: Cold Pastoral!

When old age shall this generation waste,
    Thou shalt remain, in midst of other woe
Than ours, a friend to man, to whom thou say'st,
    "Beauty is truth, truth beauty,"—that is all
        Ye know on earth, and all ye need to know.

One may begin a more detailed exploration of the poem's calligraphy with two observations and consequently two intriguing questions. It has long been generally accepted that the impulse behind the
poem came from the general notoriety surrounding the Elgin Marbles and that Keats may not even have seen the actual sculptures, that
at best he may possibly have seen but a sketch of some of the pieces.
Why, then, is the poem not "about" the Marbles themselves, about a
sculpture, a frieze, a bas-relief? Why did Keats's imagination supply
an urn, memory image from some other perception, with its woman
shape and funerary aura? Explicitly or implicitly, commentary has
long explained the funerary aura as essential to the antithesis in the
poem between the fleeting quality of such human existence as the
poet's and the eternal stillness of the Cold Pastoral:

When old age shall this generation waste,
    Thou shalt remain, in midst of other woe
Than ours. . . .

But this is only a partial answer to the question, for the antithesis can
just as easily be achieved with a sculpture or bas-relief, as Shelley's
"Ozymandias" beautifully illustrates. The question thus becomes:
What does the urn add that a sculpture, frieze, or bas-relief cannot?
The second question has to do with the overt pattern of the poem, the
arrangement of stanzas and lines. The poem is comprised of five
stanzas of ten lines each, the first and the fifth of one rhyme scheme;
the second, third, and fourth of another, thus:

I: A B A B C D E D C E
II: A B A B C D E C D E
III: A B A B C D E C D E
IV: A B A B C D E C D E
V: A B A B C D E D C E

What has the poet's sense of form accomplished with this particular
pattern of stanzas and rhyme schemes?

The answer to both questions begins to emerge as one notices the
motive for metaphor visible in the opening lines. To say that the initial
address, "Thou still unravish'd bride of quietness," is a personification

of the urn is to be so general as to be dangerously imprecise. More carefully examined, the metaphor reveals an imaginative mingling of objects of decidedly different molecularities in a common animation or vivification: an inanimate marble urn, a flesh and blood bride, and her groom, the abstract and immaterial "quietness." One may conclude that the "contour" of this art object is to be found along the gradient of animation or vivification, a conclusion borne out by the fact that the impulse to animate manifests itself coherently throughout the poem, endowing the urn itself and the figures in its "leaf-fring'd legend" with a life every bit the equal of that of the poet-observer—except for the stillness, attribute of the Attic shape, the calm, serene enduring which the poet-observer does not, cannot possess because his fate is a stillness of another sort. The metaphoric movement presents, then, what is best described as an intersection of, on the one hand, the "Bold Lover" with his forever fair, never fading beloved within the "leaf-fring'd legend," the decorative band that "haunts about" the urn-shape and, on the other hand, the poet-observer with his "still unravish'd bride" as he haunts about the silent form, the "Fair attitude." It is, of course, this intersection which informs the doubled significance of the title, "Ode on a Grecian Urn." It is also this intersection which imparts multiple meanings to the word *still* and converts it to sign, especially at the point of intersection in the third stanza where the reader is constrained to ask whose is the

> More happy love! more happy, happy love!
>   For ever warm and still to be enjoy'd. . . ?

Is it the Bold Lover's of the "leaf-fring'd legend"—or the poet's as he responds to the voluptuous curves of the shape before him? At this point, *still* comprises both the intention of the Bold Lover and the perception of the poet.

The metaphoric movement of the poem climaxes in the last stanza with the clear emergence of the urn-shape, the "silent form," "Cold Pastoral," behind the bride-shape with which the poem began. The initial apostrophe of the stanza, "O Attic shape! Fair attitude," may, in the lover-poet intersection, refer either to the lover's or the poet's beloved, and this doubled reference imparts multiple dimensions to the remainder of the clause with a particular focus on *brede* and *over-wrought:*

> O Attic shape! Fair attitude! with brede
>   Of marble men and maidens overwrought,
> With forest branches and the trodden weed. . . .

One must ask at this point, precisely why did Keats in choosing from the lexicon available to him, prefer the words *brede* and *overwrought?* The bride-urn metaphor and the passion-still antithesis inherent in the metaphor suggest an answer. In the context of the gathering metaphor and its centripetality, *overwrought* may be read as referring to the fact that the marble surface of the urn is wrought over with figures of men and maidens, branches and trodden weed, but it may also be read in the passion-still antithesis as referring to the commotion among the marble men and women (possible on the gradient of vivification) as opposed to the calm, the serenity of the "still un-ravish'd bride." But this word-become-sign, interesting as it is, offers none of the high excitement one finds in *brede,* homonym of *breed,* denotative of an embroidered or plaited decoration on a woman's person or dress. (One should notice as well how *brede* echoes the *bride* of the first line of the poem, differing from it in but the one letter.) The coupling of *brede* with *overwrought* brings forth in turn a doubled dimension to *generation:* they look forward, that is, to the fate of man of woman born "when old age shall this generation waste," bringing the reader to the full span, the alpha to omega of *still.* This process in turn brings the reader to the urn, the isomorph of woman, as pregnant with significance in the ashes it was made to contain as is the bride in the life she was made to contain. Insofar as the bride's beauty is of the sort "warm and still to be enjoy'd," hers is a beauty signifying a truth, the truth of human generation; insofar as the urn's truth is also one of stillness it is a truth signifying the innate birthright of that human generation. The beauty-truth of the bride merges into, becomes interchangeable with, the truth-beauty of the urn.

With this perception one is in a position to perceive the overt figure the poem makes, the figural in the arrangement of the stanzas. The first and last stanzas, differentiated as they are from the three interior stanzas, are something more than beginning and end, opening and close. They embrace or contain the interior stanzas. And the interior stanzas continue the pattern of containment in that they focus on the middle stanza with its "more happy, happy love!" One has, then, reading outward from this ultimate content in either direction (to Stanzas II and IV) the two sides of the urn, the "leaf-fring'd legend" with the love scene on the one side (Stanza II) preceding the "happy, happy love" and the sacrificial scene on the other (Stanza IV) culminating in the image of the little town emptied of life, silent and desolate. Finally, embracing this circumference of the urn are the two "containing" stanzas, I and V. In short, the poem is circumferential, forming a container for all the significance of the urn's message

"Beauty is truth, truth beauty," a message in which *beauty,* which in the
syntax of the message both begins and ends it, literally encompasses
truth and consequently as Attic shape contains both seed and ashes.

Commenting upon such modern novelists as Robbe-Grillet and the
use of words as if they have no connection with the history of the
language, Roland Barthes wrote:

> The Word is no longer guided *in advance* by the general intention of
> a socialized discourse; the consumer of poetry, deprived of the
> guide of selective connections, encounters the Word frontally, and
> receives it as an absolute quantity, accompanied by all its possible
> associations. The Word, here, is encyclopaedic, it contains simulta-
> neously all the acceptations from which a relational discourse might
> have required it to choose. It therefore achieves a state which is
> possible only in the dictionary or in poetry—places where the noun
> can live without its article—and is reduced to a sort of zero degree,
> pregnant with all past and future specifications. The word here has
> a generic form; it is a category. Each poetic word is thus an unex-
> pected object, a Pandora's box from which fly out all the poten-
> tialities of language; it is therefore produced and consumed with a
> peculiar curiosity, a kind of sacred relish.[18]

Although it is true that the consumer of poetry "encounters the Word
frontally, and receives it as an absolute quantity," that he consequently
consumes poetry "with a peculiar curiosity, a kind of sacred relish,"
the calligraphy of Keats's ode suggests that Barthes's comment must
be massively revised. As argued here, the poetic sign exists in the
surreal world as mythos expanded beyond the selective connections
previously provided by the logos—indeed the first reading of the
poem is precisely for the reader the process of breaking the bounds of
those connections, but one must also recognize that the technique
here defined as the precision which creates movement, the fundamental and natural tropism of the human organism, the transformational process itself and the consequent syntax of verbal-visual
metaphors, in short the self-regulating structure, provide in their
concatenation a new set of selective connections which guides the
reader upon his entry into the surreal world and its mythos. The
poetic sign, for example Keats's *still, beauty,*or *truth,* is most definitely
not encyclopedic. Instead of containing simultaneously all the relational possibilities of the logos, the complete range of lexical possibilities in the dictionary entry for that vocable as word, it partakes of
a contour, is of a mythos-form which makes its polysemy "polyrela-
tional" within the mythos: it is isomorphic, it is calligraphic. To fall
back upon the metaphor with which Gertrude Stein expressed the

idea, we have the word, not as Pandora's box—that would be true ambiguity—but as cube, its dimensions well defined and formed by its values, in its selected place within the total form. The sense which results for the reader as he becomes naturalized in the new language, as the signs are juxtaposed the one to the other, is then quite accurately described as Gertrude Stein described it: cubistic.

The effect, as in the case of Stephen Spender and John Keats—had one the space one could equally well demonstrate it with Hawthorne's *The Scarlet Letter*, William Faulkner's *Absalom, Absalom!*, or Robbe-Grillet's *La Jalousie*—is what one may best describe as a "volumetric" reading. The polysemy and the polyrelationalism leave the alert reader no choice but to accept the total range of significance within the individual signs in a simultaneity of apprehension: the reading of the poem advances not on various levels at once but rather in several dimensions at once. One is tempted to say in three dimensions, but a necessary consequence of the polyrelationalism within the calligraphy is the appearance during the volumetric reading of a special temporal dimension which transforms the normal "cube" into something closer to a Necker cube. The simultaneity of the volumetric reading occurs both forward and backward as one reads in the temporal-spatial plane of the verbal event. For example, *still,* the second vocable in the verbal event of Keats's ode, does not reveal its full volume until one reaches the "silent form" paradoxically "speaking" its enigmatic message in the last stanza. The volumetric reading is not only introspective, into the interior of the word-cube immediately present in the temporal-spatial plane of the verbal event, but also retrospective and prospective to expanded relationships in the past and the future of that temporal-spatial plane. The volumetric reading is, then, necessarily a synchronous reading which becomes almost literally a backward reading at what would be the end in the Aristotelian concept of the story line.

At this point, the sign, indeed the poem or the novel, as Archibald MacLeish insisted, does not mean: It merely *is* in the total being of a form. In the works of Gertrude Stein or other overtly Cubist writers the form is presented in a manner similar to that in Picasso's portrait of Kahnweiler.[19] But just as one often forgets, in the shock of the frontal encounter with the cube in painting, to see the Rembrandt in Picasso, so too one often forgets, in the shock of encounter with eye and nose, lip and brow, to see the Picasso in Rembrandt. Picasso and Rembrandt, Gertrude Stein and Shakespeare, from the cave artists of the Upper Paleolithic to William Faulkner it has always been true that, in the words of Matisse, "Il faut étudier longtemps un objet pour

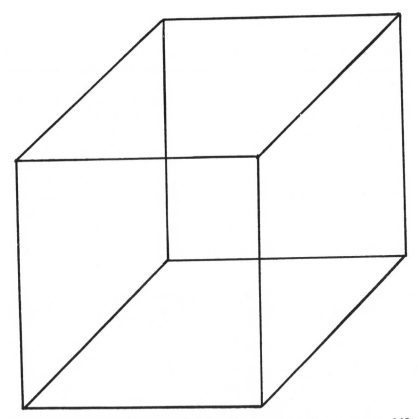

The Necker cube: When regarded fixedly its orientation seems to shift alternately to the right and left or vice versa, so that the "front" becomes the "back," the "back" becomes the "front."

savoir quel est son signe. Encore que dans une composition l'objet devienne un signe nouveau qui fait partie de l'ensemble en gardant sa force. En un mot, chaque oeuvre est un ensemble de signes inventés pendant l'exécution et pour le besoin de l'endroit. Sortis de la composition pour laquelle ils ont été créés, ces signes n'ont plus aucune action [It is necessary to study an object at length in order to know what is its sign. Although, in a composition the object becomes a new sign which forms a part of the whole while retaining its own force. In a word, each work is a whole of signs invented during the execution and for the needs of the locale. Away from the composition for which they have been created, these signs no longer have any active power]."[20] So it is, too, with the signs of the literary language; the significance begins in a long and careful study of so much as one is enabled to perceive of the object Absolute, a study culminating in a

transformational vision by virtue of which the perceived object becomes a surreal image, a composition, its word in the logos becoming
a new sign in the calligraphy of the mythos. In a very real sense, the
vocable of a literary text is neither chosen nor borrowed from the
logos: it is invented during the construction and has significance
specifically in response to the needs of the form-space it both occupies
and shapes. Away from this composition, it no longer has the active
power of the imaged-action fusion which quickened it. Instead, it falls
back across the gap from the surreal world to the "real," a shattered
fragment to be stored, lifeless, in the dictionaries of the logos, until
once again, in the hands of another artist it is shaped anew into the
poetic sign, the cubic sign, or as Whitman put it, the word *en masse.*

9

The Pleasure of Ulteriority

*T*o begin our inquiry into the role of the visual in that calligraphy we call poetry, we noted in the first pages of Chapter 1 how Hemingway, in the years of his apprenticeship in Paris, went almost daily to the Musée du Luxembourg to study the paintings exhibited there, above all to study the paintings of Cézanne. We began our inquiry with the same question with which Hemingway faced Cézanne: "How did he see?" or as Nick Adams phrased it, "How may a writer live right with his eyes?" In pursuit of an answer, we have been tracing the steps in artistic creation which lead from the archetropic fusion of two images in a transformational perception—such a fusion as that experienced by the prehistoric artist who looked at a rocky protuberance in the "meander field" of the rocky walls and ceiling of the cave now called Altamira and saw a bison shape—from such a fusion to the "concerted ensemble" of the verbal and the visual, the calligraphy, which is the Attic shape, the urn-bride, which Keats called the "Ode on a Grecian Urn." We have been climbing, that is, what Wallace Stevens called the *gradus ad Metaphoram*, the steps which lead in apparent paradox from metaphor to metaphor, from that sense of the word *metaphor* in which metaphor is "poetry at its source" to that other sense upon which Angus Wilson insisted when he asserted, "Everyone says as a commonplace that a novel is an extended metaphor, but too few, perhaps, insist that the metaphor is everything, the extension only the means of expression."[1] Stevens wrote:

> There is a gradus ad Metaphoram. The nature of a metaphor is, like the nature of a play, comic, tragic, tragic-comic, and so on. It

may be poetic. A poetic metaphor—that is to say, a metaphor poetic in a sense more specific than the sense in which poetry and metaphor are one—appears to be poetry at its source. It is. . . . But the steps to this particular abstraction, the gradus ad Metaphoram in respect to the general sense in which poetry and metaphor are one, are, like the ascent to any of the abstractions that interest us importantly, an ascent through illusion which gathers round us more closely and thickly, as we might expect it to do, the more we penetrate it.[2]

In the last chapter, to characterize the polysemy of individual signs in the literary language we adopted the verbal-figural metaphor of the cubist painters, with the image of the cube signifying the multidimensionality of the sign. But at least two poets, Robert Frost and Wallace Stevens, have offered a related but significantly different and more vivid image to characterize the effect, the consequence of metaphor at each end of the *gradus,* of metaphor both as the source of poetry and as the figure a poem makes. The image is that of a prism, the lens, triangular in cross section, which breaks down light into its constituents, the colors of the spectrum from red to violet. We will start with Frost's use of the image and turn to Stevens's later in the chapter.

Frost once said, "Education by poetry is education by metaphor. [Metaphor is] the prism of the intellect."[3] To see his prism in operation, one may look at such a painting as Matisse's *Tabac Royal* (1943), this because Matisse's painting advances our inquiry at least one step beyond Picasso's *Ma Jolie* and brings it to a conclusion. In *Ma Jolie,* the version discussed in the last chapter, the metaphor menu or dish/new mistress is carried out in an attributive interplay between figural and verbal forms. In *Tabac Royal* the metaphor exists in what at first glance appears to be a simple juxtaposition of figural forms (see color plate). On the left of the canvas and, in the perspective, pushed back in depth, is a woman in an angular chair, the woman dressed in a white, slightly blue-shaded dress. On the right of the canvas, in the foreground, is another chair, the curved back of which echoes the curve of the woman's shoulders. On the chair, painted in a warm ochre flesh tone, is a lute, placed as if it were seated, its neck resting against the back of the chair so that the configuration of the head and neck of the lute rising above the rounded chair-back echoes, despite the obvious differences, the woman's head and neck rising above her shoulders. The strings of the instrument are not represented, and the circular sounding hole and the bridge, its ends pulled up like the corners of a smiling mouth, are presented in the same value so that they both seem holes in the surface. As a consequence, the treatment of the lute causes one to tremble on the edge of a suggestion, a suggestion which causes the viewer to exclaim, "The lute has more expression than the woman!" A sheet of music trails half its width off the far edge of the chair seat. Between the two chairs is a table on which is a tobacco can, labeled *tabac royal,* containing flowers, and a vase also containing flowers, the vase voluptuously curved, these in a perspective on the table which echoes that of the two chairs; that is to say, the vase is farther forward than the can, but their lateral placement reverses that of the two chairs: the vase is to the left of the can. The painting thus troubles the eye, for one hovers, as noted a moment ago, on the edge of a suggestion, that suggestion twice made in the presentation of the flower containers, vase and can in a juxtaposition with the woman and curved lute—both seated in chairs, one chair angular, the other curved to constitute another juxtaposition. Beyond the suggestion in the treatment of the lute's bridge and surface and its placement in the chair, Matisse never tells us by attribute as did Picasso that the seated lute is the sign for a woman whose beauty sets his heart a-singing, as does the woman in the blue-shadowed silk for Peter Quince as he sits at his clavier. One's eye plays with the suggestion in the harmonies of curved vase, curved lute, curved chair over against the contrasting can, woman, and chair, and then returns to the individual objects as objects Absolute, as Emily Dickinson phrased it—only to come back once again to the edge of the suggestion. Whether the painter intends it or not, there is a truth to be learned here.

But obviously the truth to be learned is of a sort discernibly different from the truths with which science deals. "L'Art est fait pour troubler," Braque wrote in his notebook, "la science rassure [Art disturbs, science reassures]."[4] The difference may perhaps be best illustrated with a simple change in Matisse's composition: Suppose one were to change the placement of the lute and the sheet of music, place them both on the table, leaving the foreground chair vacant. The painting would then become the simple anecdote of an interrupted musical séance, the vacant chair and the laid-aside instrument and music indicative of the absent player. One is able, that is, to pull the elements of the painting together into a reassurance, a propositional statement: "The musician will be right back." But composed as it is, the painting forces the viewer, by virtue of its suggestive juxtapositions in an entirely different direction.

Of particular interest for the present purpose is the fact that the suggested modification changes our perception of other elements in the painting, elements which nevertheless have not been physically altered. This is especially true of the vase, the tobacco can, the white central square of the blue wall panel, the sheet of music, and the two red panels flanking the blue. In the painting as it stands, the vase and the can are linked by the fact that they both as containers contain flowers. The relationship between them is established not only by what they have in common, the contained flowers and the container function, not by what differentiates them, their color, value, and shape. But part of that which differentiates them serves to relate each of them to the lute/woman juxtaposition. The can is by its angularity related to the central square of the wall panel, the sheet of music and the background chair and by its color again to the central square and sheet of music and as well to the woman; the vase is by its color and curves related to the foreground chair. Thus the vase and the can eventually lead the viewer to consider the possibility of a relationship, something in common among all that differentiates them, between the woman and the lute. The suggestion is reinforced by the red wall panels which link the woman and the chair-lute combination across the intervening blue panel and by the overlapping, as it were, of the relationships in the fact that the axis formed by the vase and the chair-lute group overlaps the axis formed by the can and the seated woman, a compositional element underscored, as it were, by the patch of red rug on the floor.

The force of *Tabac Royal* resides in the simultaneity with which the juxtapositions are presented to the viewer's perception and the result- ant simultaneity of two possible perceptions of the painting. As Matisse painted it, it can be "read" anecdotally, but not so clearly anecdotally as the suggested changes would make it. Simultaneously, as Matisse painted it, it can be "read" metaphorically in terms of the lute/woman metaphor. This second possible reading plays as a kind of ghostly lambency over the surface of the anecdote. But with the sug- gested changes this lambency disappears. The difference in effect appears most clearly in the different "readings" of the two flower containers. In Matisse's version, the interrelations of the various jux- tapositions force the viewer to see them as synchronous in the cen- tripetality of the total composition, whereas in the suggested modification, a major result of the shift to pure anecdote is the fact that the flower containers become part of a temporal sequence. No longer seen as divergencies with something in common, they become indications of a pluperfect tense, an action performed by one or the other or both of the "characters," the seated woman and the absent lute-player, before the musical séance, now interrupted, began.

The shift from signification in *Tabac Royal* to meaning in the suggested modification reveals something of considerable importance about the force of the copula in such metaphors as that which Poe, borrowing from the Koran, incorporated in his poem "Israfel":

> In Heaven a spirit doth dwell
>   "Whose heart-strings are a lute";
>
> None sing so wildly well
>   As the angel Israfel.

Speaking of the tension in a metaphor between two interpretations, the literal and the figurative, the tension between identity and difference, Paul Ricoeur wrote, "In order to elucidate this tension deep within the logical force of the verb *to be*, we must expose an 'is not,' itself implied in the impossibility of the literal interpretation, yet present as a filigree in the metaphorical 'is.' Thus the tension would prevail between an 'is' and an 'is not.'"[5] According to this view the metaphor disturbs the reader because it presents him with a proposition which simultaneously affirms and denies an identity:

> In Heaven a spirit doth dwell
>   "Whose heart-strings $\frac{\text{are}}{\text{are not}}$ a lute. . . ."

But the evidence afforded by the analysis of *Tabac Royal* suggests that although the insight is of some value it is not quite precise enough to capture the complexity of the suggestion in metaphor. One element of Matisse's painting, not yet overtly considered, throws considerable light on this issue: the table itself, the form of which is a kind of hyphen in the painting, for, although the table does separate the woman from the lute, it as well is in the composition a connective element which links the woman and the lute, a kind of visual bridge, a bridge for the eyes, which leads the viewer's regard from the one to the other. Greater precision would result, then, if one were to regard the copula as little more than a hyphen, as, for example, in the metaphor "heart-strings," for the hyphen, like the table in the painting, all in conjoining the two expressed elements of the metaphor, serves nevertheless as a strut to hold the two apart. It is, of course, the force of this linkage which constitutes the central strategy of Gerard Manly Hopkins's poetry, for Hopkins overtly reduced a large number of his copulative metaphors to hyphenated compounds as, for example, in the case of "fire-folk," "gold-dew," and—most breathtakingly vivid—"flake-doves" in his poem "The Starlight Night":

Look at the stars! look, look up at the skies!
O look at all the fire-folk sitting in the air!
The bright boroughs, the quivering citadels there!
The dim woods, quick with diamond wells; the elf-eyes!
The gray lawns cold where quaking gold-dew lies!
Wind-beat white-beam; airy abeles all on flare!
Flake-doves sent floating out at a farmyard scare!—
Ah well! it is a purchase and a prize.
Buy then! Bid then!—What?—Prayer, patience, alms, vows.—
Look, look! a May-mess, like on orchard boughs;
Look! March-bloom, like on mealed-with-yellow sallows.—
These are indeed the barn; within-doors house
The shocks. This piece-bright paling hides the Spouse
Christ, and the mother of Christ and all his hallows.

But even greater precision would result from the adoption of a term offered by Wallace Stevens when he wrote, "There is always an analogy between nature and the imagination, and possibly poetry is merely the strange rhetoric of that parallel: a rhetoric in which the feeling of one man is communicated to another in words of the exquisite appositeness that takes away all their verbality."[6] In the metaphor "flake-doves," the relationship between the two words which constitute the metaphor, the relationship which Stevens calls an "exquisite appositeness," is an apposition in two senses, i.e., an apposition in that the two terms of the metaphor are, like the woman and the lute in *Tabac Royal*, no more than placed side by side; an apposition as well in that the two terms are happily appropriate, suitable, in that way specified by the remainder of the sentence: ". . . sent floating out at a farmyard scare!" The word *floating* is appropriate more for "flake" than for "doves," but possible for either. It brings at least to this reader's eyes the image of glistening snow flakes lifting and spreading in a swirl of wind. But the words "farmyard scare" are specifically appropriate for doves. They bring to this reader's eyes an image of doves, their wings flashing with reflected sunlight as the flock bursts upward, curving, sweeping and spreading in unison, from the dovecote. Thus the combination of "floating" and "farmyard scare" functions much like the vase and tobacco can in *Tabac Royal* to form an interlocking which holds "flake" and "doves" in a metaphoric relationship which, although presented in verbal signs, goes far beyond the verbal, goes far beyond to a vivid visual image of the Milky Way sweeping, a gust of snowflakes, a flight of doves, across the midnight sky.

In an entry in his notebook which simultaneously takes us back to the bison paintings in Altamira and to Keats's "Ode on a Grecian

Urn," Georges Braque wrote, "Rechercher le commun qui n'est pas le semblable. C'est ainsi que le poëte peut dire: Une hirondelle poignarde le ciel, et fait d'une hirondelle un poignard [Seek out the common which is not the similar. It is in this manner that the poet is able to say, 'A swallow stabs the sky,' and makes a dagger of a swallow]."[7] The drawing with which he illustrated this *à propos* evokes once again the woman-vase metaphor. That is, he drew a vase, and, partially superimposed upon it, overlapping its right side, he drew a woman's head. It is, of course, possible that the drawing is merely an etymological comment upon the fact that the French word for "head," *tête,* is derived from colloquial Low Latin *testa,* "little pot." But several particulars militate against such an interpretation. First of all, there is the overlapping which suggests only a partial relationship between the two signs of the drawing. Then, too, there is the fact that the separateness of the two signs is reinforced by the fact that the vase is completely shaded, but the area of overlap is not. This area is left paper-white as is the portion of the head which falls outside the outline of the vase. And finally, the vase is not head-shaped. Thus Braque indicates that he is not dealing with a similarity. What he is dealing with appears in the fact that he has given to his vase the same shape which Keats's urn acquires from the still unravish'd bride; that is, Braque drew the vase with a flaring rim, a smooth curving, first inward to the "waist," then outward to the wide "hips," and then a gentle taper to a smaller base. The drawing thus invites the viewer to see in terms of what is not similar but rather of what is in common between a woman and a vase. In the overlapping itself, an overlapping which recalls that which ties together the metaphorical elements in *Tabac Royal,* Braque has figured that aspect of metaphor which is obscured by Ricoeur's image of the filigree, for the filigree suggests that in one sense, a somewhat "ornamental" sense, the metaphor "is," is true in its entirety as a proposition, whereas in another sense, the literal sense, it "is not," that is to say, the "is" is false. But the lesson of Altamira, of *Tabac Royal,* of the woman-vase, and of Hopkins's "flake-doves" is that the "is" and the "is not" both reside in the literal aspect of the metaphor. That which is in common in woman and in vase "is" in the most literal sense of the woman-vase metaphor, while simultaneously, obviously, again in the most literal sense of the metaphor, that which woman and vase do not have in common "is not." Once again, the evidence from both painting and poetry brings us to the topological model, the Riemann-Hugoniot surface derived from René Thom's mathematical theory, for the topological model permits a clear visualization of both the "is" and the "is not." The "is not" is figured in the two opposite extremes of the surfaces where woman is woman, a being of blood and flesh, and vase is vase, an inanimate object of clay, each at its own level. The "is" is centered in the overlap area, the area of bimodality and synchronicity where, as we have seen in Keats's ode, the woman and vase as vessels—for Keats, vessels of life and of death—are one in the same time-space continuum. In this area the poet's metaphor, in its surreality, figures a truth about "reality" which is itself a "reality," a truth which the current lexicon is unable to express denotatively.

Or to state the matter in other terms, those employed by I. A. Richards, metaphor is not a matter of one tenor and one vehicle but rather a matter of two vehicles, each of which contributes a portion of itself, a portion which is in common with the corresponding portion of the other, to the constitution of a tenor. Ricoeur applauded Richards's terminology, saying, ". . . The advantage of this esoteric terminology [*tenor* and *vehicle*] is precisely that it combats every allusion to a proper meaning, every return to a non-contextual theory of ideas, but also and above all, anything borrowed from the notion of mental image."[8] Indeed Richards is to be applauded insofar as he did combat the tendency to see metaphor as a decorative or pretty way of saying what allegedly could otherwise have been said more straightforwardly in a presumed "rhetoric degree zero," the concept of metaphor which holds that it is translatable into "plain language." But if indeed Richards's text may be so read as to preclude any return to the notion of mental images, the evidence from Altamira to *Tabac Royal,* from at least 35,000 years ago to the present, strongly argues that the literary language will not be fully grasped in its total significance unless one does return to the image, that image which is here called the archetropic image.

In fairness to Richards, it should be noted that it is not altogether clear that he in fact intended, as Ricoeur assumes, to rule out any role for visuo-spatial images in the functioning of metaphor. To support his interpretation, Ricoeur quotes from Richards's discussion of a passage from Coleridge's Appendix C to *The Statesman's Manual.* However, the essence of Coleridge's discussion is not a rejection of visuo-spatial images per se, but a rejection of a certain misuse of images. For poetic purposes he rejects those images furnished by the Fancy in favor of those furnished by the Imagination, *Fancy* and *Imagination* having those specific meanings which Coleridge assigned to them. In *Table Talk* he wrote, "The Fancy brings together images which have no connexion natural or moral, but are yoked together by the poet by means of some accidental coincidence; as in the well-known passage in Hudibras:—

> The sun had long since in the lap
> Of Thetis taken out his nap,
> And like a lobster boyl'd, the morn
> From black to red began to turn.

The Imagination modifies images, and gives unity to variety; it sees all things in one, *il più nell' uno*." Throughout his works, the word *image* tends to vary in meaning from a percept—a visuo-spatial image which is a construct, according to Coleridge's remarkably modern notion of perception, of the external "reality"—to a construct formed totally in the artist's mind, where as construct it may vary from the kind of forced fusion here decried in *Hudibras* to those which have a connection natural and moral as in an image which Coleridge gleaned from Shakespeare's *Venus and Adonis* where Adonis's flight from Venus is described:

> Look! how a bright star shooteth from the sky
> So glides he in the night from Venus' eye.

But in all his uses of the word, the visuo-spatial aspect either as sensory percept or as memory construct is rarely, if ever, absent. In the context of poetic creation, however, as we have seen in Chapter 2, he was quite as dependent as any other poet upon transformational perception and that image which is just such a fusion of the common in dissimilarities, the archetropic image, as is present in either *Tabac Royal* or Braque's notebook.

Indeed, to return to Richards and the possibility that Ricoeur may have misunderstood him, in one passage in *The Philosophy of Rhetoric*, Richards comes close to the very terminology used here to describe the archetropic image. Richards wrote, "The processes of metaphor in language, the exchange between the meanings of words which we study in explicit verbal metaphors, are superimposed upon a *perceived world* [my emphasis] which is itself a product of earlier or unwitting metaphor, and we shall not deal with them justly if we forget that this is so."[9] That is, explicit verbal metaphors are founded on metaphoric perception, that perception which is here called transformational perception.

Metaphor, that metaphor which is both the source and the substance of poetry, is then first of all a particular mode of perception, and to forget this fact, to attempt to deal with metaphor as uniquely a verbal phenomenon, is to become trapped in that dilemma which Jacques Derrida described in "White Mythology," the fact that in language there is no nonmetaphorical verbal form, no "rhetoric degree zero," which may be used for the analysis of metaphor, with the result that the attempt to explicate figurative language is self-defeating. One must "recognize," he asserts, "the *conditions which make it in principle impossible* to carry out such a project," the fact that even at the most fundamental level, the first philosophical elements "cannot be subsumed" because it, that level itself, is metaphorical.[10] This is the trap into which the "deconstructionists" as a group have fallen.

The trap has its origins in part in Heidegger's attempt to subsume the metaphorical in the metaphysical. In approaching Heidegger's concept of metaphor, one must first notice that he clung to the now quite obsolete notion of a proper sense which is in the metaphor expressed through figurative means. Metaphor, for Heidegger, is a verbal transaction in which the sensory is transposed to the nonsensory level, that is, to the realm of thought. To make his point, he discusses the metaphorical use of such terms as *grasping* by way of *seeing* and *hearing* to express the functioning of thought and concludes that when these words, *grasping, seeing, hearing,* are so used one does not understand them as merely a metaphorical transposition but also "as a transposition of the allegedly sensible to the non-sensible (. . .als Übertragung des vermeintlich Sinnlichen in das Nichtsinnliche)." This metaphysical transfer of the sensible to the nonsensible is the basis, then, for the metaphorical transfer of the literal to the figurative. Thus he is led to the well-known declaration that "the metaphorical exists only within the bounds of the metaphysical (Das Metaphorische gibt es nur innerhalb der Metaphysik)."[11]

As a logical proposition this has been rather thoroughly demolished by Paul Ricoeur,[12] but one aspect of Heidegger's argument is, in the light of the evidence afforded by this study, susceptible to further demolition on firmer grounds than those offered by Ricoeur. Ricoeur dismisses the argument because Heidegger goes so far as to assert that "the separation of sensible from non-sensible is 'at the root of the meaning of the term *metaphysics,* and has become a determining norm for Western thought,'" to which Ricoeur replies, "I am afraid that only a reading forced beyond any justification can make Western philosophy lie on this Procrustean bed."[13] The objection is, of course, well taken, but one may object on the further grounds that Heidegger and Gadamer attempt to treat metaphor as uniquely a linguistic, a rhetorical phenomenon in which words, either singly or in larger semantic structures, are used in an "impertinent" manner. For them a trope is not the "turning back" in transformational perception which precedes the words but rather a deviant use of the word, a turning from the normal lexical pattern. This concept of metaphor, of course, is dictated by the more fundamental assumption which Hans-Georg Gadamer expressed when he wrote, "We can only think in a language, and just this residing of our thinking in a language is the profound enigma that language presents to thought [Das eigentliche Rätsel der Sprache ist aber dies, das wir das in Wahrheit nie ganz können. Alles Denken über Sprache ist vielmehr von der Sprache schon immer wieder eingeholt worden]."[14] Indeed, if one makes the appropriate adjustments to take into account the much deeper penetration into the phenomenon we call language, one nevertheless finds that, for all the subtleties with which he surrounds his central concept, Jacques Derrida in essence falls into a very similar misconception. One may, as does Derrida in *De la Grammatologie,* refine or "deconstruct" the concepts of language, writing, and speech until one arrives at *la brisure,* "the hinge," that which is articulation, the "spacing" which structures, the interstices between the units of a sequence. But, call these spaced units what one will, the model of the "spacing," of the articulation is that of a verbal language with its sequentiality and its linearity. It is but the pattern of beginnings, middles, and ends, the "succeeding" which Gertrude Stein denounced as inimical to the art of the poet. Indeed, the dilemma which Derrida describes in "White Mythology," the assumption that there is no nonmetaphorical language with which to discuss metaphor, is dilemma only if one accepts the basic assumption that thought is a representation in a medium which is an articulated sequence. But the evidence presented here, the evidence afforded by the poet and the painter, confirmed by the neurophysiologist and the topologist, establishes beyond doubt that the human being is quite capable of conceptualizing in a nonsequential, nonarticulated fusion of visuo-spatial images, can, indeed, through the "concerted ensemble" of words and visuo-spatial images, convert a sequence, an articulation of words into a single form, what Mallarmé called the "signe pur général." It is worth emphasizing here that the archetropic fusion characteristic of this morphogenesis is quite different from that which is fundamental to the traditional semiologist's concept of the sign, for that fusion is still a linear and horizontal fusion of separable elements in an articulation. The sign as redefined here is a vertical fusion, a superimposition to form a surreality, a "being in the present," as, again, Gertrude Stein phrased it, which has no temporality, no "spacing." And, more directly to the point, the evidence adduced here indicates that metaphor is not at all a matter of language and its sequences. Rather—the point must be reiterated—it is a matter of perception, that particular kind of perception which makes possible the calligraphy of the poetic language. The "is" of that perception is the truth of poetic truth.

Ricoeur touches obliquely upon this fact when he makes of metaphor a matter of gain in meaning where ". . .every gain in meaning [by means of metaphor] is at one and the same time a gain in sense and a gain in reference."[15] However, because he approaches the question of metaphor by way of such a poetics as Aristotle's, he misses a most important point which becomes abundantly clear when one sees how metaphor functions in such a painting as *Tabac Royal*. In his study, Ricoeur is led to conclude that ". . . the metaphorical utterance functions in two referential fields at once. This duality explains how two levels of meaning are linked together in the symbol [metaphor]. The first meaning relates to a known field of reference, that is to the sphere of entities to which the predicates considered in their established meaning can be attached. The second meaning, the one that is to be made apparent, relates to a referential field for which there is no direct characterization, for which we consequently are unable to make identifying descriptions by means of appropriate predicates."[16]

But, as Braque, Keats, and Picasso make clear in the woman/vase metaphor, verbal metaphor functions in at least three referential fields, two known (*woman* and *vase*) and one to be made apparent, that one which is figured in the area of bimodality and synchronicity in the topological model. The two known referential fields, for all their dissimilarities, nevertheless contain elements which they have in common, elements which, when superimposed the ones over the others constitute a "cubic" sign with a reference to a referential field for which there is, in the lexicon, no currently available means for direct reference. But the matter is even more complex than that. As *Tabac Royal* and Poe's heart-strings/lute metaphor make clear, other metaphors both visual and verbal form the new referential signs in a complex of three or more known referential fields. In *Tabac Royal* the ultimate metaphor, woman/lute, is the consequence of a dynamic system which begins with the flower containers, the vase and the tobacco can. From thence the ultimate metaphor develops through an intermediate stage in which the tobacco can/woman juxtaposition is as a unit juxtaposed to the vase/lute juxtaposition. There is a "logic" to this sort of thing as Frost said, a logic which in a "surrealistic" way echoes the logic of a syllogism. One finds a similarly complex dynamic system in the opening lines of Stevens's "Peter Quince at the Clavier":

> Just as my fingers on these keys
> Make music, so the self-same sounds
> On my spirit make a music, too.
>
> Music is feeling, then, not sound;
> And thus it is that what I feel,
> Here in this room, desiring you,
>
> Thinking of your blue-shadowed silk,
> Is music. . . .

For the topologist, every object or physical form, *Tabac Royal,* for example, or Stevens's "Peter Quince at the Clavier," can be represented as an *attractor* of a dynamic system on a space of internal variables. Following the topologist in this line of analysis and applying it specifically to what we have seen in the preceding chapters, we may say that the morphogenesis of the art object—indeed, for the topologist, of any object or form—in the words of René Thom, "peut être décrite par la disparition des attracteurs représentant les formes initiales et leur remplacement par capture par les attracteurs représentant les formes finales [can be described as the disappearance of the attractors representing the initial forms and their replacement by capture by the attractors representing the final forms]."[17] This is the process which Thom calls catastrophe, the process which we have been pursuing in the preceding chapters. In the case of *Tabac Royal,* the morphogenesis can best be perceived in the dynamic process which leads from that which is represented by the suggested anecdotal version to that which is represented by Matisse's metaphorical version. The suggested anecdotal version is the "attractor" representing what one might call the "reality" form, the initial form (one may substitute here the rock protuberance in Altamira or any other such stimulus form—say the Elgin Marbles for Keats—prior to the occurrence of the transformational perception), whereas Matisse's version, which has its origins in a "reality" form, is nevertheless the "attractor" representing a "surreality" form. As we have seen, such structurally stable morphological processes may be described by a structurally stable "catastrophe" (the rock protuberance become bison in Altamira) or by a system of structurally stable "catastrophes" as in *Tabac Royal* or Spender's "Air Raid across the Bay at Plymouth" or Keats's "Ode on a Grecian Urn"—indeed as in any painting or literary work. Stevens's staircase, the *gradus ad Metaphoram,* is but the image of such systems. It is this description which disengages the poem or painting from or defines it within what van Gogh called the "dizzy whirl and chaos" of the receptible environment or, in the case of literature, the general linguistic medium, what the topologist calls "a space of external variables" as opposed to the space of internal variables of the dynamic system of which the painting or poem is the "attractor."

As the analysis of *Tabac Royal* makes manifest, the morphological process, the system of structurally stable catastrophes from vase/tobacco can to woman/lute may be decomposed into structurally stable subsets (vase/tobacco can; tobacco can/woman; vase/lute; woman/lute) figuring in a multidimensional "syntax" which controls their positions in the composition. To designate what I here call subsets, Thom, borrowing from the geneticist C. H. Waddington of the University of Edinburgh, uses the term *chreod*. A chreod differs from the more general concept of morphogenetic field in that it adds to morphogenetic field the hyperplane time with that particular orientation expressed by the word *forward* and the consequent concept of irreversibility.[18] Roughly speaking, in the case of the rock protuberance in Altamira, the whole cave surface is a morphogenetic field, but any one protuberance, say the one which has figured throughout this study, becomes chreod as soon as it becomes the initiator of the transformational process with consequently a space-time particular to that process. When any one of these subsets is considered as a "word" in the multidimensional syntax, the system figured in the *gradus ad Metaphoram*, the signification of the "word"—as the last chapter argues, "sign" is a more appropriate term—the signification of the sign, then, is precisely that of the global topology of the associated "attractor," in this particular case, Matisse's *Tabac Royal*. More precisely, the signification of the total form is defined by the geometry of its domain of existence on or within the space of external variables, the "dizzy whirl and chaos," and the topology of those catastrophes which assure and reveal the systematic functioning of the dynamic system—the topology, that is, of the defining isomorphic metaphors as discussed in Chapter 5, the catastrophes which bound that domain of existence, the metaphors which provide the discontinuity which is the contour of the surreality.

As Thom notes, when the mathematical analysis is applied to the general phenomenon of language one rediscovers "l'axiome cher aux linguistes de l'école formaliste, selon lequel la signification d'un mot n'est rien de plus que l'usage de ce mot [the axiom dear to the formal linguists: that the meaning of a word is nothing more than the use of the word]. . . ."[19] Taken in conjunction with the testimony of both poets and painters, the mathematical analysis confirms the conclusion already reached here about the referential field of the metaphor which is poetry at its source, that the referential field in the surreality is figured by what is in common in the two referential fields in the two "realities" which participate in the transformational perception.

The mathematical analysis also points forward to a valuable conclusion about the referential field of that extended metaphor which is the poem as a whole. One is tempted to say that the metaphor which is poetry at its source and, consequently, the metaphor which is the poem as a whole not only figure but actually create the referential field manifested in the area of bimodality and synchronicity, the area of surreality. But to do so would be to forget the truth of the "is" in transformational perception and, consequently, the truth of the "is" in the literal reading of the verbal metaphor. That is to say, one would forget that metaphor as archetropic image is directly dependent upon "reality" and simultaneously, in that which we call "poetic truth" in the surreality, turns us back to that "reality." This is the point of another comment by Wallace Stevens:

> The study of the activity of resemblance is an approach to the understanding of poetry. Poetry is a satisfying of the desire for resemblance. As the mere satisfying of a desire, it is pleasurable. But poetry if it did nothing but satisfy a desire would not rise above the level of many lesser things. Its singularity is that in the act of satisfying the desire for resemblance it touches the sense of reality, it enhances the sense of reality, heightens it, intensifies it. If resemblance is described as a partial similarity between two dissimilar things, it complements and reinforces that which the two dissimilar things have in common. It makes it brilliant. When the similarity is between things of adequate dignity, the resemblance may be said to transfigure or to sublimate them.[20]

Stevens's word "brilliant" brings us back, equipped for greater insight, to the "clarification of life" which, according to Frost, one gains by means of the "prism of the intellect," for the discussion is tending from a central truth about poetry, the role of transformational perception in the creation of metaphor/poetry, to a central truth about poetic truth itself. For if the steps leading there are through an illusion, the goal is nevertheless "reality" itself. Even more, implicit in another comment by Stevens is the fact that through the structure of poetry one learns something of the structure of "reality." He wrote, "We have been trying to get at a truth about poetry, to get at one of the principles that compose the theory of poetry. It comes to this, that poetry is a part of the structure of reality. If this has been demonstrated, it pretty much amounts to saying that the structure of poetry and the structure of reality are one or, in effect, that poetry and reality are one, or should be."[21] In support of this proposition Stevens insists that poetic truth is a factual truth seen, however, "it may be," by those, the poets, whose perception of "reality" is in some way greater than that of the nonpoet. The poet both desires and strives to avoid falsity, and he can only do that by writing that which is in agreement with "reality." Such an agreement necessarily makes poetic truth a factual truth. But, once again, it must be emphasized, poetry is no mere reportage, no mere statement of bare fact. Rather it is a statement of facts which exist beyond the normal range of the nonpoet's perception and sensibility. "What we have called elevation and elation on the part of the poet, which he communicates to the reader, may be not so much elevation as an incandescence of the intelligence. . . ."[22] For the ordinary person, the nonpoet, transformational perception satisfies the desire for resemblance and he is content with the resulting pleasure, but, as Stevens notes, poetry does this and more: By figuring and thus reinforcing that which the poem has in common with the real, by reinforcing the *real* in the *surreal* of the poem, the poet enhances and intensifies the sense of reality, if only by discovering to the eyes of his readers new patterns of relationships among the elements of the "real" and thus new significations for those elements.

The transfiguration or sublimation of things so perceived appears clearly in a passage from Thomas Wolfe's *You Can't Go Home Again* in which Wolfe, through the persona of George Webber, describes how he learned, as Nick Adams put it, "to live right with the eyes." In his attempt to discern the significance of his experience, "to extract the whole, essential truth of it," and to learn how to write about that experience, the neophyte novelist tried to recapture in his imagination the entirety of what he had seen down to the smallest detail. He spent, as he said, weeks and months trying to express on paper the "exactitudes" of the various fragments in his memory:

> It was a process of discovery in its most naked, literal and primitive terms. He was just beginning really to see thousands of things for the first time, to see the relations between them, to see here and there whole series and systems of relations. He was like a scientist in some new field of chemistry who for the first time realizes that he has stumbled upon a vast new world. . . .[23]

For Wolfe/Webber, then, poetic perception is a process of discovery which involves the perception of an entirely different taxonomy than the one which is the basis for the currently accepted lexicon, a taxonomy which, nevertheless, must find its mode of expression through the means afforded by the current lexicon. It is this truth about poetic truth that Stevens pointed toward when he wrote, "We come . . . to understand that the moment of exaltation that the poet experiences when he writes a poem that completely accomplishes his purpose, is a moment of victory over the incredible, a moment of purity that does not become any the less pure because, as what was incredible is eliminated, something newly credible takes its place."[24] But we must understand as well that this victory over the incredible involves a conjunction which is incredible only according to the currently lexicalized taxonomy. Because of the newly perceived taxonomy, the conjunction is quite credible. This is why so many metaphors become enshrined in the language of discourse as so-called "dead" metaphors. The conjunctions they figure have become so credible that one forgets the preceding taxonomy according to which they were once incredible. The perception of this fact led Ricoeur to assert, "But if metaphor is a statement, it is possible that this statement would be untranslatable, not only as regards its connotation, but as regards its very meaning, thus as regards its denotation. It teaches something, and so it contributes to the opening up and the discovery of a field of reality other than that which ordinary language lays bare."[25] But once again one must insist that metaphor is not the untranslatable statement but rather the perception which is not denotatively expressible in the current language. The point is again visible in another of Ricoeur's statements. He wrote, ". . . The goal of poetry is to establish a new pertinence by means of an alteration in the language."[26] But the evidence requires a reversal of the statement: The goal of poetry is to express a new pertinence by means of an adaptation of the old language. *Adaptation* is, however, the wrong word in this context, for the newly perceived pertinence leads, as we have seen, to a new creation in language. It is not, as so many have argued, that the language creates a new "reality." Rather it is that the newly perceived "reality" leads to the creation of new signs in the language. One might even argue within the limitations established in this study that in effect the newly perceived "reality" leads to the creation of a new language, the Chinese which Henry Miller claimed he wrote. Nelson Goodman in his discussion of metaphor proposed an image which, if modified to fit the evidence adduced here, permits greater precision. He wrote, "The shifts in range that occur in metaphor . . . usually amount to no mere distribution of family goods but to an expedition abroad. A whole set of alternative labels, a whole apparatus of organization, takes over new territory. What occurs is a transfer of a schema, a migration of concepts, an alienation of categories. Indeed, a metaphor might be regarded as a calculated category-mistake—or rather as a happy and revitalizing, even if bigamous, second marriage."[27] The evidence, of course, dictates a modification in the image of a bigamous second marriage. Like Ricoeur, Goodman sees metaphor as involving only two categories, the two terms overtly expressed in the metaphor, one of which, properly "married," nevertheless enters into a union with the other, the "spouse," from another category. The image, revised according to the evidence manifested in such paintings as *Tabac Royal*, should be that of two categories, each, although properly "married," here mated, copulating, if you will, in an adulterous union to produce an offspring, a third category, which, bastard though it may be according to the old taxonomy, is an incontrovertible fact in the new taxonomy which now exists, which now is true, if only by virtue of the offspring's birth.

The perception, then, upon which verbal metaphor is founded is the perception of a taxonomic factor not previously perceived, the perception of a relationship, a *rapport de grand écart*, as Picasso phrased it, which links together, by what is common between them, two entities which are, according to the accepted taxonomy, sharply differentiated. It is this that permits Stevens to say that the poet's perception "enhances the sense of reality, heightens it, intensifies it." Or, as he elsewhere put it, poetry is "capable of bringing about fluctuations in reality" because poetry "is one of the enlargements of life."[28] The enlargement results, of course, from a perception which is an enlargement of the view of "reality." The imagination, Stevens wrote, "is always attaching itself to a new reality, and adhering to it. It is not that there is a new imagination but that there is a new reality."[29]

With his metaphors, then, the poet describes his voyage into the surreal world in order to report to his reader the discovery of a new world, a new world which is a metamorphosis of the one about which science reassures us. This new world is a magical one of shifting, fleeting illusions, like those created by a flicking lamp light on the walls of a cave, shapes which sometimes fuse—the heart leaps up when it happens—to form a new certainty, a new permanence, among the old or the ephemeral, the "supreme fictions" as Wallace Stevens called them, for they form the shape of "the world in which we shall come to live."[30] Through poetry one lives a life of perpetual revelation, as Georges Braque phrased it in a memorable statement of what the artist achieves with his transformational perception, revelations which never will occur for the reader of poetry until he is willing to suspend his disbelief in the "chinese" which the poet has created for him. In explanation of his assertion that "art disturbs; science reas-

sures," he said, "If there is no mystery then there is no 'poetry'. . . ."
Then, to define "poetry" he evoked the element "most important for
my work": metamorphosis, that transformational perception of which
we have been treating, the fact that "no object can be tied down to any
one sort of reality." The consequences of the resultant metamorphic
confusion are striking:

> You see, I have made a great discovery: I no longer believe in
> anything. Objects don't exist for me except in so far as a *rapport*
> exists between them, and between them and myself. When one
> attains this harmony, one reaches a sort of intellectual non-
> existence—what I can only describe as a state of peace—which
> makes everything possible and right. Life then becomes a perpetual
> revelation.[31]

The painter, if he is a Braque, a Picasso, a Matisse, can present this
perpetual revelation to the alert, the happy viewer. When he does, the
viewer, his eyes at the moment rapt with the artist's surreality, his
memory filled with images from his own "reality," makes for himself a
discovery about that "reality," a discovery attained in his own state of
peace which makes everything possible and right. Wallace Stevens
reached the same conclusion as Braque and, in doing so, extended
Frost's image of the "prism of the intellect." In analyzing the difference between the two insistent allegory of Bunyan's *Pilgrim's Progress*
and the much more evenly balanced demands of the anecdotal and
the allegorical in La Fontaine's "The Crow and the Fox," he found the
double sense of Bunyan's analogy to be distracting: One is more engaged by what is symbolized than by the means of symbolization. That
which is symbolized "divides our attention and this diminishes our
enjoyment of the story." In the case of such an indisputable masterpiece as Bunyan's, however, one can hypothesize two readers, one of
whom, oblivious of the symbolic meaning, reads of Christian's adventures merely for the story, the other of whom, oblivious of the story,
reads of them merely for the symbolic meaning. Stevens, however,
argues for a third reader in terms which again bring us close to those
employed in this study: "But there is a third reader, one for whom the
story and the other meaning [the allegorical] should come together
like two aspects that combine to produce a third or, if they do not
combine, inter-act, so that one influences the other and produces an
effect similar in kind to the prismatic formations that occur about us
in nature in the case of reflections and refractions." In the case of La
Fontaine's fable, there is no distraction, for the reader's attention is
focused upon the symbol. The symbolized meaning is not overtly

present, and consequently the reader is not particularly conscious of it. Instead, "it is like a play of thought, some trophy that we ourselves gather, some meaning that we ourselves supply. It is like a pleasant shadow, faint and volatile."[32] The prismatic effect thus becomes the product of an interaction between the story overtly present in the fable and a meaning, the pleasant shadow, in the reader's thoughts. La Fontaine's fable thus becomes, in Stevens's argument, the means of approaching poetry in general, that great body of literature which in Archibald MacLeish's phrase does not mean but is.

The effect of this vast body of literature, this vast body of analogies, like the effect of such paintings as *Tabac Royal,* again derives from the interaction of two aspects: that aspect which is the poet's view of the world in which he lives and that aspect which is the reader's sense of the world in which he, in his own right, lives. And these lead us, then, to the identification of a fourth reader "for whom the effect of analogy is the effect of the degree of appositeness, for whom the imaginative projection, the imaginative deviation, raises the question of rightness, as if in the vast association of ideas there existed for every object its appointed objectification. In such a case, the object and its image become inseparable. It follows that for this fourth reader the effect of analogy is the effect of consummation."[33] We arrive, that is, at that "strange rhetoric" which is "words of [an] exquisite appositeness that takes away all their verbality." We arrive there, however, much better equipped now to understand what that exquisite appositeness is when all the verbality is stripped away. For we now have the poet's and the painter's prism, two senses of the "real," ours and the artist's, interacting to produce prismatically a third entity, a surreality. Or, perhaps, one may draw an analogy from the prehistoric art with which this study began: The artist's work, poem or painting, provides an illumination, a flame, with which we, the viewers, the readers, now equipped to see as the artist sees, may enter upon our own lives as the prehistoric artist entered into the caves. We, too, then, equipped for discovery, knowing now what Braque called that state of peace which makes everything possible and right—surely Keats would recognize this as Negative Capability—, find life a perpetual revelation. We, like Frost's Pertinax, can now

> Let chaos storm!
> Let cloud shapes swarm!
> [And] wait for form.

Notes

Chapter 1. The Painter

1. *A Moveable Feast* (New York: Scribners, 1964), p. 13.

2. Ernest Hemingway, "On Writing," *The Nick Adams Stories* (New York: Scribners, 1972), p. 239.

3. *Treatise on Painting*, trans. Philip McMahon (Princeton: Princeton University Press, 1956), p. 50.

4. Quoted in E. H. Gombrich, *Art and Illusion: A Study in the Psychology of Pictorial Representation* (London: Phaidon Press, 1959), p. 158.

5. Tokuzo Masaki, *Honami Gyojoki* (Tokyo: Chukoron Bijutsu Shuppan, 1965), pp. 70–71. Translation of the passage by Professor Yorimasa Nasu, Dōshisha University, Kyoto, personal letter to the author, 26 May 1977.

6. *La Signification de l'art rupestre paléolithique* (Paris: A. & J. Picard et Cie., 1962), p. 26.

7. There has been some discussion as to whether the accidental rock shapes dictated to the prehistoric artist's imagination or the artist, already committed to figuring a certain animal, sought out the rock form which would best provide the bas-relief required. On this point see G.-H. Luquet, *L'Art et la religion des hommes fossiles* (Paris: Masson et Cie., 1926), pp. 160–65, whose conclusions represent the position adopted by most modern prehistorians and accord generally with those advanced here.

8. Peter J. Ucko and Andrée Rosenfeld, *Paleolithic Cave Art* (New York: McGraw-Hill Book Co., 1967), p. 49.

9. Annette Laming, *Lascaux: Paintings and Engravings*, trans. Eleanore Frances Armstrong (Harmondsworth: Penguin Books, 1959), pp. 28–29.

10. Letter to *The Amherst Student*, 1935, repr. in Elaine Barry, *Robert Frost on Writing* (New Brunswick, N.J.: Rutgers University Press, 1973), p. 113.

11. The suggestion here that the meanders and the found forms of prehistoric art are late and highly sophisticated techniques goes somewhat counter to G.-H. Luquet's thesis that they represent the earliest manifestation of man's artistic bent. See Luquet, pp. 136–46.

12. For the general chronology in the formation of this drawing I am indebted to Professor André Leroi-Gourhan, Chaire de Préhistoire, Collège de France, and Conservateur, Musée de l'Homme, Paris, personal interview, 14 May 1976.

13. "Inspiration to Order," quoted in Brewster Ghiselin, *The Creative Process: A Symposium* (Berkeley and Los Angeles: University of California Press, 1952), p. 58.

14. *Victor Hugo dessinateur* (Paris: Éditions du Minotaure, 1963), p. 37.

15. *Treatise on Painting*, p. 59.

16. Brassaï, *Picasso and Company*, trans. Francis Price (Garden City, N.Y.: Doubleday, 1966), p. 70.

17. "Pictorial Conceits," *Verve: An Artistic and Literary Quarterly* 1 (1939): 104.

18. *Écrits et propos sur l'art*, ed. Dominique Fourcade (Paris: Hermann, 1972), p. 61.

19. Gaston Bachelard, *L'Air et les songes* (Paris: José Corti, 1943), p. 7.

20. Brassaï, *Picasso and Company*, p. 112.

21. André Verdet, *Prestiges de Matisse . . .* (Paris: Editions Emile-Paul, 1952), pp. 75–76.

22. "Pensées et réflexions sur l'art," quoted in *Artists on Art, from the XIV to the XX Century*, ed. Robert Goldwater and Marco Treves (New York: Pantheon Books, 1945), p. 422.

23. Others have already commented on this fact in respect to several of the bison at Altamira. For example, Luquet comments: "L'attitude forcée de certains animaux d'Altamira, notamment les trois bison ramassés. . . , que l'on interprète d'ordinaire comme une manifestation de manièrisme ou de convention d'école, pourrait bien être due simplement à la forme naturelle des bosses rocheuses utilisées pour les figures, que se limitent presque à leur surface, à part les cornes, les pieds et la queue [The forced attitude of certain animals at Altamira, notably the three crouching bison. . . , which is ordinarily interpreted as a manifestation of mannerism or school convention, could well be due simply to the natural form of the rocky outcroppings used for the figures, which are contained almost totally within the limits of their surfaces, apart from the horns, feet and tail]" (p. 165).

24. *Dear Theo: The Autobiography of Vincent van Gogh*, ed. Irving Stone (Garden City, N.Y.: Doubleday & Company, 1946), p. 344.

25. *Letters to an Artist: From Vincent van Gogh to Anton Ridder van Rappard, 1881–1885*, trans. Rela van Messel (New York: Viking Press, 1936), p. 107.

26. *Letters to an Artist*, p. 107 (van Gogh's emphasis).

27. *Letters to an Artist*, p. 106.

28. *Letters to an Artist*, p. 107.

29. Émile Bernard, as quoted in Maurice Malingue, *Gauguin: Le peintre et son oeuvre* (Paris: Presses de la Cité et Londres, 1948), p. 35.

30. *Biographia Literaria, Edited with His Aesthetical Essays*, by J. Shawcross (London: Oxford University Press, 1967), 1 : 69, note.

31. "Inspiration to Order," quoted in Brewster Ghiselin, *The Creative Process: A Symposium* (Berkeley and Los Angeles: University of California Press, 1952), p. 59.

32. *Das bildnerische Denken*, ed. Jurg Spiller (Basel: Benno Schwabe & Co., Verlag, 1956), p. 4; English translation: *The Thinking Eye*, ed. Jurg Spiller (New York: George Wittenborn, 1964), p. 4.

Chapter 2. The Poet

1. *Discours prononcés dans les conférences de l'Académie Royale de Peinture et de Sculpture*, as quoted in *Artists on Art, from the XIV to the XX Century*, ed. Robert Goldwater and Marco Treves (New York: Pantheon Books, 1945), p. 161.

2. Françoise Gilot and Carlton Lake, *Life with Picasso* (New York: McGraw-Hill Book Company, 1964), p. 120.

3. *The Necessary Angel* (London: Faber and Faber, 1951), p. 160.

4. *Treatise on Painting*, trans. Philip McMahon (Princeton: Princeton University Press, 1956), p. 17.

5. "A Transatlantic Interview, 1946," in *A Primer for the Gradual Understanding of Gertrude Stein*, ed. Robert B. Haas (Los Angeles: Black Sparrow Press, 1971), p. 31.

6. Letter to Afanasi Afanas'evich Fet, Paris 6/18 April 1862, *Letters: A Selection*, trans. and ed. Edgar H. Lehrman (New York: Alfred A. Knopf, 1961), p. 134.

7. Stephen Spender, *The Making of a Poem* (London: Hamish Hamilton, 1955), p. 45.

8. Quoted in Ivan Turgenev, *The Portrait Game*, ed. Marion Mainwaring (London: Chatto and Windus, 1973), pp. 12–13.

9. Quoted in Victor Hugo, *Victor Hugo dessinateur* (Paris: Éditions du Minotaure, 1963), p. 10.

10. "Making Pictures," in his *Assorted Articles* (New York: Alfred A. Knopf, 1930), pp. 202–3.

11. Quoted in Rosamond Harding, *An Anatomy of Inspiration* (New York: Barnes and Noble, 1940), p. 28.

12. *The Complete Writings of William Blake*, ed. Geoffrey Keynes (London: Oxford University Press, 1966), p. 605.

13. Raymond Escholier, *Matisse, ce vivant* (Paris: Librairie Arthème Fayard, 1956), p. 153.

14. *The Human Metaphor* (Notre Dame: University of Notre Dame Press, 1964), p. 53.

15. "The Language of Chinese Literature," *New Literary History* 4 (Autumn 1972): 141–50.

16. Yujiro Nakata, *The Art of Japanese Calligraphy*, trans. Alan Woodhull with the collaboration of Armins Nikovskis (Tokyo: Heibonsha, 1967; New York: Weatherhill, 1973), p. 27.

17. Chiang Yee, *Chinese Calligraphy: An Introduction to Its Aesthetic and Technique*, 3rd edition (Cambridge: Harvard University Press, 1973), p. 207.

18. *Picasso on Art: A Selection of Views*, ed. Dore Ashton (New York: Viking, 1972), p. 131.

19. Wilhelm Boeck and Jaime Sabartés, *Picasso* (New York and Amsterdam: Harry N. Abrams, 1955), p. 304.

20. "The Art of Fiction," in his *The Art of Fiction and Other Essays* (New York: Oxford University Press, 1948), p. 5.

21. *Painting and Reality* (New York: Meridian, 1959), pp. 208–9. Gilson quotes from Maurice de Vlaminck, *Portraits avant décès* (Paris: Flammarion, 1943), p. 177.

22. *Das bildnerische Denken*, ed. Jurg Spiller (Basel: Benno Schwabe & Co., Verlag, 1956), p. 17; English translation: *The Thinking Eye*, ed. Jurg Spiller (New York: George Wittenborn, 1964), p. 17.

23. *Proust* (New York: Grove Press, 1970), p. 67.

24. "Some Aspects of the Grotesque in Southern Fiction," in her *Mystery and Manners: Occasional Prose*, ed. Sally and Robert Fitzgerald (New York: Farrar, Straus & Giroux, 1969), p. 42.

25. *What Are Masterpieces?* (New York: Pitman Publishing Corp., 1970), pp. 103–4.

26. *The Common Asphodel: Collected Essays on Poetry, 1922–1949* (London: Hamish Hamilton, 1949), p. 295.

27. *A Writer's Diary, Being Extracts from the Diary of Virginia Woolf*, ed. Leonard Woolf (London: Hogarth Press, 1954), p. 306.

28. *The Wild Garden* (Berkeley and Los Angeles: University of California Press, 1963), p. 149.

29. "Preface" to *The Portrait of a Lady, Novels and Tales,* The "New York Edition" (New York: Scribners, 1922), 3:vii. Another comment to the same effect appears in his essay "Ivan Turgénieff," in *The Art of Fiction and Other Essays,* p. 111.

30. Turgenev, as quoted by James in "Preface" to *The Portrait of a Lady, Novels and Tales,* 3:viii.

31. *Henry Moore on Sculpture,* ed. Philip James (New York: Viking Press, 1966), p. 141.

32. Letter to George and Thomas Keats, Hampstead, 28 December 1817, in *The Letters of John Keats,* ed. Maurice Buxton Forman (Oxford: Oxford University Press, 1931), 1:77.

33. *The Notebooks of Samuel Taylor Coleridge,* ed. Kathleen Coburn, Bollingen Series 50 (Princeton: Princeton University Press, 1961), II, entry no. 2013, April 1804.

34. *Poetic Unreason and Other Studies* (London: Cecil Palmer, 1925), pp. 49–56.

35. *Proust,* pp. 20–21.

36. "The Figure a Poem Makes," *The Complete Poems of Robert Frost* (New York: Holt, Rinehart and Winston, 1964), pp. vii–viii.

37. "A Course in Poetics, First Lesson," *Southern Review* 5 (1940): 411–12.

38. Samuel L. Clemens, *Mark Twain in Eruption,* ed. Bernard DeVoto (New York: Harper & Brothers, 1940), pp. 196–97.

39. The same process may be traced in numerous sequences throughout Twain's published and unpublished works. For several examples, see *Mark Twain's Satires & Burlesques,* ed. Franklin R. Rogers (Berkeley and Los Angeles: University of California Press, 1967; London: Cambridge University Press, 1967).

40. Henri Matisse, letter to Pierre Matisse, Nice, 1 September 1940, in Pierre Schneider, *Henri Matisse, Exposition du Centenaire, Grand Palais, Avril–Septembre 1970* (Paris: Ministère d'Etat, Affaires Culturelles, Réunion des Musées Nationaux, 1970), p. 300.

41. *The Art of Letters; Lu Chi's "Wen Fu," A.D. 302,* trans. E. R. Hughes (New York: Pantheon Books, 1951), pp. 96–97.

42. *On Poetry: Arthur Skemp Memorial Lecture* (Bristol: University of Bristol, 1939), p. 19.

43. "The Art of Fiction," p. 17.

44. "The Nature and Aim of Fiction," in her *Mystery and Manners,* p. 7.

45. "The Fiction Writer and His Country," in her *Mystery and Manners,* pp. 34–35.

46. "A Course in Poetics," pp. 416–17.

47. *The Art of Letters,* pp. 95, 98.

48. "Preface" to *The Spoils of Poynton, Novels and Tales,* 10:v–vi.

49. "The Art of Fiction," p. 11.

50. *A Writer's Diary,* pp. 105–106.

51. *The Necessary Angel,* pp. 164–65.

52. *The Making of a Poem,* pp. 55–57.

53. *The Necessary Angel,* p. 165.

54. *Das Bildnerische Denken,* p. 82; *The Thinking Eye,* p. 82.

Chapter 3. Archetrope and Transformation

1. *The New Landscape in Art and Science* (Chicago: Paul Theobald and Co., 1956), pp. 229–30.

2. *The Necessary Angel: Essays on Reality and the Imagination* (London: Faber and Faber, 1951), p. 73.

3. Quoted in E. H. Gombrich, *Art and Illusion: A Study in the Psychology of Pictorial Representation* (London: Phaidon Press, 1959), pp. 154–55.

4. Gaston Bachelard, *The Poetics of Reverie,* trans. Daniel Russell (Boston: Beacon Press, 1971), p. 1.

5. *Assorted Articles* (New York: Alfred A. Knopf, 1930), pp. 205–6.

6. Letter to T. W. Higginson, n.d., *The Letters of Emily Dickinson,* ed. Thomas H. Johnson, associate ed. Theodora Ward (Cambridge: The Belknap Press of Harvard University Press, 1958), 2:473.

7. "Miró: An Interview in Mallorca," *Arts Magazine* 43 (November 1968): 17.

8. *The Name and Nature of Poetry* (Cambridge: Cambridge University Press, 1950), pp. 45–46.

9. *The Name and Nature of Poetry,* pp. 48–49.

10. Bernard Leach, *Hamada, Potter* (Tokyo: Kodansha, 1975), p. 123.

11. Françoise Gilot and Carlton Lake, *Life with Picasso* (New York: McGraw-Hill Book Co., 1964), p. 284.

12. To get the strength of the object depicted, such as tiger's claws or the beak and talons of a predatory bird, the strength of the subject's movement must be in the strength of the single brush stroke which depicts it *(fude no chikara, fude no ikioi).* The moment the brush touches the paper the artist must invoke the sentiment of strength throughout his entire being so that it is transmitted through his arm and hand to the brush and thus to the painted subject. See Henry P. Bowie, *On the Laws of Japanese Painting* (San Francisco: P. Elder & Co., 1911), pp. 35, 77–79.

13. *The New Landscape,* p. 24.

14. Sen Shoshitsu and Sen Shoshu, *Sado Zenshu (9)* (Tokyo: Sogensha, 1941), p. 555, passage trans. Professor Yorimasa Nasu, Dōshisha University, Kyoto, in personal letter to the author, 26 May 1977.

15. Georges Charbonnier, *Le Monologue du peintre* (Paris: René Juillard, 1960), 2:7–8.

16. *La Formation du symbole chez l'enfant: imitation, jeu et rêve, image et représentation* (Neuchâtel-Paris: Delachaux et Niestlé, 1976), p. 294.

17. *L'Image mentale chez l'enfant: étude sur le développement des représentations imagées* (Paris: Presses Universitaires de France, 1966), pp. 2–9.

18. *L'Image mentale chez l'enfant,* pp. 429–32.

19. *Cognitive Psychology* (New York: Appleton-Century-Crofts, 1967), p. 64.

20. "Preface" to *The Tragic Muse, Novels and Tales of Henry James,* The "New York Edition" (New York: Scribners, 1922), 7:v.

21. Gaston Bachelard, *L'Air et les songes* (Paris: José Corti, 1943), p. 78.

22. *L'Image mentale chez l'enfant,* p. 69.

23. *Imagination* (Berkeley and Los Angeles: University of California Press, 1976), p. 115.

24. As quoted in *Artists on Art, from the XIV to the XX Century,* ed. Robert Goldwater and Marco Treves (New York: Pantheon Books, 1945), p. 435.

25. *Lectures in America* (New York: Random House, 1935), pp. 86, 212. It should be noted that she reserved nouns and adjectives for poetry, which should have in her view less movement and more the solidity of substances.

26. *Hommage à Henri Matisse* (Paris: Société Internationale d'Art, 1970), p. 114.

27. Henri Matisse, *Portraits* (Monte Carlo: André Sauret, Editions du Livre, 1954), p. 12.

28. Henri Matisse, "Notes d'un peintre sur son dessin," *Le Point,* no. 21 (July 1939): 14(110).

29. E. Tériade, "Constance du Fauvisme," *Minotaure* 2, no. 9 (1936): 3.

30. *The Notebooks of Samuel Taylor Coleridge,* ed. Kathleen Coburn (New York: The Bollingen Foundation, 1957–1973), vol. 2, entry no. 2061.

31. *Prefaces to His Works* (London: J. M. Dent and Sons, 1937), pp. 106–8.

32. *A Writer's Diary, Being Extracts from the Diary of Virginia Woolf,* ed. Leonard Woolf (London: Hogarth Press, 1954), pp. 100–101.

33. *A Writer's Diary,* p. 169.

34. *The Waves* (New York and London: Harcourt Brace Jovanovich, 1978), p. 284.

35. *The Waves,* p. 297.

36. "Preface" to *The Tragic Muse, Novels and Tales* 7 : v.

37. *The Common Asphodel, Collected Essays on Poetry, 1922–1949* (London: Hamish Hamilton, 1949), p. 117.

38. *The Common Asphodel,* pp. 117–18.

Chapter 4. The Literary Art Object

1. *What Are Masterpieces?* (New York: Pitman Publishing Corp., 1970), p. 26.

2. *The Wild Garden* (Berkeley and Los Angeles: University of California Press, 1963), pp. 149–50.

3. Henri Matisse, "Notes d'un peintre," *La Grande Revue* 52 (25 December 1908): 739.

4. *What Are Masterpieces?* p. 98.

5. *Écrits et propos,* p. 243.

6. *On Poetry: Arthur Skemp Memorial Lecture* (Bristol: University of Bristol, 1939), pp. 10, 25.

7. *The Complete Writings of William Blake,* ed. Geoffrey Keynes (London: Oxford University Press, 1966), p. 585.

8. *Stabilité structurelle et morphogénèse* (Reading: W. A. Benjamin, 1972), p. 37; *Structural Stability and Morphogenesis,* trans. D. H. Fowler (Reading: W. A. Benjamin, 1975), p. 20.

9. *The Perception of the Visual World* (Boston: Houghton Mifflin Co., 1950), p. 191.

10. Thom, *Stabilité structurelle et morphogénèse,* p. 25; trans., p. 9.

11. R. L. Gregory, "Cognitive Contours," *Nature* 238 (7 July 1972): 52.

12. "Subjective Contours," *Scientific American* 234 (April 1976): 48–49.

13. Jean Piaget and Bärbel Inhelder, *L'Image mentale chez l'enfant: étude sur le développement des représentations imagées* (Paris: Presses Universitaires de France, 1966), pp. 86–104; see especially Tables 27 (p. 88) and 32 (p. 102).

14. Gregory, "Cognitive Contours," p. 52.

15. Kanizsa, "Subjective Contours," pp. 49–51.

16. Brassaï, *Picasso and Company,* trans. Francis Price (Garden City, N.Y.: Doubleday & Co., 1966), p. 241.

17. Bernard Leach, *Hamada, Potter* (Tokyo: Kodansha, 1975), p. 89.

18. Joseph Joubert, *Pensées* (Paris: Bloud & Cie., 1909), p. 80.

19. *Das bildnerische Denken,* ed. Jurg Spiller (Basel: Benno Schwabe & Co., Verlag, 1956), p. 7; English translation: *The Thinking Eye,* ed. Jurg Spiller (New York: George Wittenborn, 1964), p. 7.

20. André Verdet, *Prestiges de Matisse* (Paris: Editions Emile-Paul, 1952), p. 71.

21. *Structural Anthropology,* trans. Claire Jacobson and B. G. Schoepf (New York: Basic Books, 1963), p. 260 and pp. 248–66 passim.

22. "Littérature et discontinu," in his *Essais critiques* (Paris: Éditions du Seuil, 1964), pp. 185–86.

23. "L'Activité structuraliste," in his *Essais critiques,* p. 217.

24. "The Hero in the New World: William Faulkner's *The Bear,*" *Kenyon Review* 13 (Autumn 1951): 648.

25. Roland Barthes, *Writing Degree Zero,* trans. Annette Lavers and Colin Smith (New York: Hill and Wang, 1968), pp. 30–31.

26. *Writing Degree Zero,* pp. 9–14.

27. Thom, *Stabilité structurelle,* p. 152; trans., p. 145.

28. *Proust* (New York: Grove Press, 1970), p. 66.

29. *Lectures in America* (New York: Random House, 1935), p. 147.

30. *What Are Masterpieces?* p. 31.

31. "A Transatlantic Interview," in her *A Primer for the Understanding of Gertrude Stein,* ed. Robert B. Haas (Los Angeles: Black Sparrow Press, 1971), p. 20.

32. *Interviews with Robert Frost,* ed. Edward C. Lathem (New York: Holt, Rinehart and Winston, 1966), p. 19.

33. "The Profitable Reading of Fiction," in *Life and Art,* ed. Ernest Brennecke, Jr. (New York: Books for Libraries Press, 1968), p. 68.

Chapter 5. Literary Form

1. *Lectures in America* (New York: Random House, 1935), pp. 74–75.

2. As quoted in E. H. Gombrich, *Art and Illusion: A Study in the Psychology of Pictorial Representation* (London: Phaidon Press, 1959), p. 98.

3. *The Educated Imagination* (Bloomington: Indiana University Press, 1964), p. 91.

4. "To *The Amherst Student,*" reprinted in Elaine Barry, *Robert Frost on Writing* (New Brunswick: Rutgers University Press, 1973), p. 113.

5. "The Figure a Poem Makes," preface to *Complete Poems of Robert Frost* (New York: Holt, Rinehart and Winston, 1964), p. vi.

6. Wallace Stevens, *The Necessary Angel: Essays on Reality and the Imagination* (London: Faber and Faber, 1951), pp. 78–79.

7. F. E. Sparshott, "'As,' or The Limits of Metaphor," *New Literary History* 6 (Autumn 1974): 83.

8. *L'Imaginaire: psychologie phénoménologique de l'imagination* (Paris: Gallimard, 1940), p. 87.

9. "Mind and Metaphor: A Commentary," *New Literary History* 6 (Autumn 1974): 213–14.

10. *The Necessary Angel,* pp. 72–73.

11. Max Ernst, "Inspiration to Order," in Brewster Ghiselin, *The Creative Process: A Symposium* (Berkeley and Los Angeles: University of California Press, 1952), pp. 60–61.

12. Quoted in André Breton, *Manifeste du surréalisme* (Paris: Éditions du Sagittaire, [1924]), p. 34.

13. Brassaï, *Picasso and Company,* trans. Francis Price (Garden City, N.Y.: Doubleday & Co., 1966), p. 28.

14. *Picasso on Art: A Selection of Views,* ed. Dore Ashton (New York: Viking Press, 1972), p. 18.

15. Brassaï, p. 33.

16. See Gina Bari Kolata, "Catastrophe Theory: The Emperor Has No Clothes," *Science* 196, no. 4287 (15 April 1977): 287, 350–51.

17. René Thom, *Stabilité structurelle et morphogénèse* (Reading, Mass.: W. A. Benjamin, 1972), pp. 31–32; *Structural Stability and Morphogenesis,* trans. D. H. Fowler (Reading, Mass.: W. A. Benjamin, 1975), p. 14.

18. For the requisite mathematical operations, see Thom, pp. 78–80, 118–19 (English version, pp. 62–63, 110–12). See also E. C. Zeeman, "Catastrophe Theory," *Scientific American* 234 (April 1976): 65–83, for a more simplified discussion of the entire theory.

19. *The Necessary Angel*, p. 73.

20. *Models and Metaphors: Studies in Language and Philosophy* (Ithaca: Cornell University Press, 1962), p. 41.

21. *Lectures in America*, p. 73.

22. Jacques Guenne, "Entretien avec Henri Matisse," *L'Art Vivant*, no. 18 (15 September 1925): 5.

23. *Dear Theo: The Autobiography of Vincent van Gogh*, ed. Irving Stone (Garden City, N.Y.: Doubleday & Co., 1946), p. 116.

24. *Dear Theo*, p. 197.

25. *Picasso on Art*, p. 66.

26. Brassaï, pp. 69–70.

27. E. Tériade, "Emancipation de la peinture," *Minotaure* 1, nos. 3–4 (1933): 10.

28. Erich Neumann, *The Archetypal World of Henry Moore* (New York: Harper & Row, 1965), p. 83.

29. *Picasso on Art*, p. 128.

30. Roman Jakobson and Morris Halle, *Fundamentals of Language* (The Hague: Mouton & Co., 1956), pp. 76–82.

31. "Langage poétique et symbole," *Études philosophiques* 26 (1971): 343–52.

32. "À propos du 'Langage des images,'" *La Revue d'aesthétique* 22 (1969): 33.

33. Gaston Bachelard, *Psychoanalysis of Fire*, trans. Alan C. M. Ross (Boston: Beacon Press, 1968), p. 109.

34. *L'Air et les songes* (Paris: José Corti, 1943), p. 284.

35. Susan Peterson, *Shoji Hamada, A Potter's Way and Work* (Tokyo: Kodansha International, 1974), p. 188.

36. *The Thinking Eye*, ed. Jurg Spiller (New York: George Wittenborn, 1964), pp. 4, 21.

37. *The Making of a Poem* (London: Hamish Hamilton, 1955), p. 54.

38. "The Figure a Poem Makes," *Complete Poems*, p. vi.

39. "Conversations on the Craft of Poetry with Cleanth Brooks and Robert Penn Warren," as quoted in Elaine Barry, *Robert Frost on Writing*, p. 157.

40. Jerome S. Bruner, *On Knowing: Essays for the Left Hand* (Cambridge: The Belknap Press of Harvard University Press, 1962), p. 74.

41. *Proust* (New York: Grove Press, 1970), pp. 67–68.

Chapter 6. The Perception of Poetic Form

1. *Structuralism*, trans. and ed. Chaninah Maschler (New York: Basic Books, 1970), pp. 127–28.

2. *Style and Proportion: The Language of Prose and Poetry* (Boston: Little, Brown and Co., 1967), p. 127.

3. Françoise Gilot and Carlton Lake, *Life with Picasso* (New York: McGraw-Hill Book Co., 1964), p. 59.

4. Ibid., p. 77.

5. René Thom, *Stabilité structurelle et morphogénèse* (Reading, Mass.: W. A. Benjamin, 1972), p. 77; *Structural Stability and Morphogenesis*, trans. D. H. Fowler (Reading, Mass.: W. A. Benjamin, 1975), p. 60.

6. *Dialogues*, trans. B. Jowett (New York: Random House, 1937), 1:235.

7. Jean Paulhan, *Les Fleurs de Tarbes, ou la terreur dans les lettres* (Paris: Gallimard, 1941), pp. 28, 174.

8. Gaston Bachelard, *La Terre et les rêveries de la volonté* (Paris: José Corti, 1948), p. 320.

9. Bachelard, *The Poetics of Reverie*, trans. Daniel Russell (Boston: Beacon Press, 1971), p. 53.

10. Natsume Kinnosuke [Sōseki], *The Three-Cornered World*, trans. Alan Turney and Pete Owen (Chicago: Henry Regnery Co., 1967), p. 48.

11. Ibid., pp. 48–49.

12. *The Common Asphodel: Collected Essays on Poetry, 1922–1949* (London: Hamish Hamilton, 1949), p. 121.

13. "The Constant Symbol," Preface to *Poems* (1946), reprinted in Elaine Barry, *Robert Frost on Writing* (New Brunswick: Rutgers University Press, 1973), p. 131.

14. Benjamin Lee Whorf, *Language, Thought, and Reality*, ed. John B. Carroll (Cambridge: The M.I.T. Press, 1956), pp. 145–46.

15. Solomon E. Asch, "The Metaphor: A Psychological Inquiry," in *Person Perception and Interpersonal Behavior*, ed. Renato Tagiuri and Luigi Petrullo (Stanford, Calif.: Stanford University Press, 1958), pp. 87–91.

16. "White Mythology: Metaphor in the Text of Philosophy," *New Literary History* 6 (Autumn 1974): 27.

17. *Language and Myth*, trans. Susanne K. Langer (New York: Dover Publications, 1946), p. 11.

18. *Écrits et propos sur l'art*, ed. Dominique Fourcade (Paris: Hermann, 1972), p. 105.

19. "Mind and Metaphor: A Commentary," *New Literary History* 6 (Autumn 1974): 215.

20. H. Werner and B. Kaplan, *Symbol Formation: An Organismic-Developmental Approach to the Psychology of Language and the Expression of Thought* (New York: Wiley, 1963), p. 49.

21. Allan Paivio falls into the same trap in the same context: see his *Imagery and Verbal Processes* (New York: Holt, Rinehart and Winston, 1971), p. 61. For an almost exhaustive exploration of the concrete-abstract fallacy, see Rudolf Arnheim, *Visual Thinking* (Berkeley and Los Angeles: University of California Press, 1969), pp. 153–87.

22. James Deese, "Cognitive Structure and Affect in Language," in Patricia Pliner et al., *Communication and Affect: Language and Thought* (New York: Academic Press, 1973), pp. 16–17.

23. Joseph Conrad, "Preface" to *The Nigger of the "Narcissus,"* in *Prefaces to His Works* (London: J. M. Dent and Sons, 1937), p. 52, and Max Black, *Models and Metaphors: Studies in Language and Philosophy* (Ithaca: Cornell University Press, 1962), pp. 25–47.

24. *Structuralism*, p. 5.

25. *Henry Moore on Sculpture*, ed. Philip James (New York: Viking Press, 1966), p. 80.

26. *Écrits et propos*, pp. 172–73.

27. Gaston Bachelard, *La Terre et les rêveries du repos* (Paris: José Corti, 1948), pp. 173–74.

28. B. Rand in *The Classical Psychologist* (1912), as quoted by Allan Paivio, "Imagery and Synchronic Thinking," *Canadian Psychological Review* 16 (1975): 149.

29. As quoted in Samuel Beckett, *Proust* (New York: Grove Press, 1970), pp. 41–42.

30. *La Terre et les rêveries de la volonté*, p. 262.

31. *S/Z*, trans. Richard Miller (New York: Hill and Wang, 1974), p. 16.

32. Elaine Barry, *Robert Frost on Writing*, p. 33.

33. *Biographia Literaria, edited with His Aesthetical Essays*, by J. Shawcross (London: Oxford University Press, 1967), 2:56.

34. *L'Eau et les rêves* (Paris: José Corti, 1942), p. 64.

35. *Dear Theo: The Autobiography of Vincent van Gogh*, ed. Irving Stone (Garden City, N.Y.: Doubleday & Co., 1946), p. 63.

36. *Dear Theo*, p. 344.

37. *The Making of a Poem* (London: Hamish Hamilton, 1955), pp. 51–52.

38. *Faulkner in the University*, ed. Frederick L. Gwynn and Joseph Blotner (Charlottesville: University Press of Virginia, reprinted 1977), p. 31.

39. *The Notebooks of Henry James*, ed. F. O. Matthiessen and K. B. Murdock (New York: Oxford University Press, 1947), p. 18.

40. *Écrits et propos*, pp. 131–32.

Chapter 7. Logos and Mythos

1. *The Wisdom of the Heart* (Norfolk, Conn.: New Directions, 1941), p. 4.

2. *The Art of Letters; Lu Chi's "Wen Fu," A.D. 302*, trans. E. R. Hughes (New York: Pantheon Books, 1951), pp. 96–97.

3. *The Wisdom of the Heart*, p. 23.

4. "Langage poétique et symbole," *Études philosophiques* 26 (1971): 346–47.

5. *Biographia Literaria, Edited with His Aesthetical Essays*, ed. J. Shawcross (London: Oxford University Press, 1967), 2:53.

6. *Henry Moore on Sculpture*, ed. Philip James (New York: Viking Press, 1966), pp. 62–64.

7. *A Giacometti Portrait* (New York: Museum of Modern Art, 1965), p. 60.

8. *The Book of Tea*, ed. Everett F. Bleiler (New York: Dover Publications, 1964), p. 24.

9. Françoise Gilot and Carlton Lake, *Life with Picasso* (New York: McGraw-Hill Book Co., 1964), p. 219.

10. *Lectures in America* (New York: Random House, 1935), p. 51.

11. *What Are Masterpieces?* (New York: Pitman Publishing Corp., 1970), p. 65.

12. *Lectures in America*, pp. 21–22.

13. *Écrits et propos sur l'art*, ed. Dominique Fourcade (Paris: Hermann, 1972), pp. 103–4.

14. Maurice Merleau-Ponty, *Signs*, trans. R. C. McCleary (Evanston: Northwestern University Press, 1964), p. 46.

15. "A Transatlantic Interview, 1946," in her *A Primer for the Gradual Understanding of Gertrude Stein*, ed. Robert B. Haas (Los Angeles: Black Sparrow Press, 1971), p. 19.

16. "A Course in Poetics, First Lesson," *Southern Review* 5 (1940): 416.

17. *Stabilité structurelle et morphogénèse* (Reading, Mass.: W. A. Benjamin, 1972), p. 152; *Structural Stability and Morphogenesis*, trans. D. H. Fowler (Reading, Mass.: W. A. Benjamin, 1975), p. 145.

18. For a survey of the initial investigations and subsequent results, see Roger W. Sperry, "Cerebral Organization and Behavior," *Science* 133 (June 1961): 1749–57; Michael S. Gazzaniga, J. E. Bogen, and Roger W. Sperry, "Some Functional Effects of Sectioning the Cerebral Commissures in Man," *National Academy of Sciences Proceedings* 48 (1962): 1765–69; Michael S. Gazzaniga, Joseph E. Bogen, and Roger W. Sperry, "Observations on Visual Perception after Disconnexion of Cerebral Hemispheres in Man," *Brain* 88, Part 2 (1965): 221–36; Michael S. Gazzaniga, *The Bisected Brain* (New York: Appleton-Century-Crofts, 1970); Michael S. Gazzaniga, "The Split Brain in

Man," in *Altered States of Awareness,* ed. Timothy J. Teyler (San Francisco: W. H. Freeman, 1972), pp. 119–24, reprinted from *Scientific American* (August 1967); and Michael S. Gazzaniga, "One Brain—Two Minds?" *American Scientist* 60 (1972): 311–17.

19. *Structuralism,* trans. and ed. Chaninah Maschler (New York: Basic Books, 1970), p. 93.

20. Seymour Axelrod, *Effects of Early Blindness: Performance of Blind and Sighted Children on Tactile and Auditory Tasks* (New York: American Foundation for the Blind, 1959), p. 72.

21. Edmund J. Rubin, *Abstract Functioning in the Blind* (New York: American Foundation for the Blind, 1964), p. 43.

22. Ibid., p. 46.

23. For more detailed information see Richard F. Cromer, "Conservation by the Congenitally Blind," *British Journal of Psychology* 64 (1973): 241–50; Sally Rogow, "Perceptual Organization in Blind Children," *New Outlook for the Blind* 69 (1975): 226–33; Herman A. Witkin et al., "Cognitive Patterning in Congenitally Totally Blind Children," *Child Development* 39 (1968): 767–86; and I. Zweibelson and C. Fisher Barg, "Concept Development of Blind Children," *New Outlook for the Blind* 61 (1967): 218–22.

24. "Dominant and Nondominant Hemispherectomy," in *Hemispheric Disconnection and Cerebral Function,* ed. Marcel Kinsbourne and W. Lynn Smith (Springfield, Ill.: Charles G. Thomas, 1974), p. 15.

25. See Jerre Levy and Colwyn Trevarthen, "Metacontrol of Hemispheric Function in Human Split-Brain Patients," *Journal of Experimental Psychology* 2 (August 1976): 299–312.

26. *The Bilingual Brain: Neuropsychological and Neurolinguistic Aspects of Bilingualism* (New York: Academic Press, 1978), pp. 253–54.

27. The literature concerning the hemispheric specializations in the asymmetric brain is rich and varied, scores of articles appearing yearly since the first announcements of the work of Sperry et al. The following will suffice for a general orientation: Stuart J. Dimond and J. Graham Beaumont, eds., *Hemisphere Function in the Human Brain* (London: Elek Science, 1974).

28. "The Other Side of the Brain, II: An Appositional Mind," *Bulletin of the Los Angeles Neurological Societies* 34 (July 1969): 157–58.

29. "The Asymmetry of the Human Brain," *Scientific American* 228 (March 1973): 70.

30. Allan Paivio, "Imagery and Long-Term Memory," in *Studies in Long Term Memory,* ed. Alan Kennedy and Alan Wilkes (London: John Wiley & Sons, 1975), p. 62. See also John G. Seamon and Michael S. Gazzaniga, "Coding Strategies and Cerebral Laterality Effects," *Cognitive Psychology* 5 (1973): 256.

31. "Mental Imagery and Associative Learning," in *Cognition in Learning and Memory,* ed. Lee W. Gregg (New York: John Wiley & Sons, 1972), p. 83.

32. See Allan Paivio, *Imagery and Verbal Processes* (New York: Holt, Rinehart and Winston, 1971), pp. 242, 278. See also Paivio, "Imagery and Long-Term Memory," p. 65.

33. Allan Paivio, "Imagery and Synchronic Thinking," *Canadian Psychological Review* 16 (1975): 161.

34. Michael S. Gazzaniga, "Cerebral Dominance Viewed as a Decision System," in *Hemisphere Function in the Human Brain,* ed. Stuart J. Dimond and J. Graham Beaumont (London: Elek Science, 1974), p. 374.

35. "Experimental Studies of Hemisphere Function in the Human Brain," in *Hemisphere Function in the Human Brain,* p. 75.

36. See Dorothy Lee, *Freedom and Culture* (Englewood Cliffs, N.J.: Prentice-Hall,

1959), pp. 90ff., and Bronislaw Malinowski, *Soil-Tilling and Agricultural Rites in the Trobriand Islands, Coral Gardens and Their Magic,* vol. 1 (Bloomington: Indiana University Press, 1965), pp. 172–73.

37. Clementina Kuhlman, "Visual Imagery in Children" (Ph.D. diss., Harvard University, 1960), as quoted in Jerome S. Bruner, "On Cognitive Growth," in *Studies in Cognitive Growth,* ed. Jerome S. Bruner et al. (New York: John Wiley & Sons, 1966), p. 27.

38. Hans G. Furth, *Thinking without Language: Psychological Implications of Deafness* (New York: Free Press, 1966), pp. 146–47, 152.

39. *Imagery and Verbal Processes,* p. 27.

40. *Writing Degree Zero,* trans. Annette Lavers and Colin Smith (New York: Hill and Wang, 1968), pp. 10–11.

41. "Metaphor and the Main Problem of Hermeneutics," *New Literary History* 6 (Autumn 1974): 103.

42. "The Constant Symbol," *Atlantic Monthly* 178 (October 1946): 50.

43. Louis Aragon, *Henri Matisse, roman* (Paris: Gallimard, 1971), 1:110.

44. William Fifield, "Miró: An Interview in Mallorca," *Arts Magazine* 43 (November 1968): 19.

45. *Lectures in America,* pp. 43–44.

46. *The Case of Wagner,* in *The Complete Works of Friedrich Nietzsche,* ed. Oscar Levy (New York: Russell & Russell, 1964), pp. 19–20.

47. *Narration: Four Lectures* (New York: Greenwood Press, 1935), pp. 22–23.

48. Claude Lévi-Strauss, *The Savage Mind* (Chicago: University of Chicago Press, 1966), p. 263.

Chapter 8. Words and Signs

1. *Stories and Texts for Nothing* (New York: Grove Press, 1967), p. 111.

2. *The Necessary Angel: Essays on Reality and the Imagination* (London: Faber and Faber, 1951), p. 32.

3. Françoise Gilot and Carlton Lake, *Life with Picasso* (New York: McGraw-Hill Book Co., 1964), pp. 72–73, 270.

4. *L'Imaginaire: psychologie phénoménologique de l'imagination* (Paris: Gallimard, 1940), pp. 90–91.

5. *The Making of a Poem* (London: Hamish Hamilton, 1955), pp. 54–55.

6. "A Transatlantic Interview, 1946," in her *A Primer for the Gradual Understanding of Gertrude Stein,* ed. Robert B. Haas (Los Angeles: Black Sparrow Press, 1971), p. 18.

7. "What Is Meant by Knowing a Language?" in *Communication and Affect: Language and Thought,* ed. Patricia Pliner, Lester Krames, and Thomas Alloway (New York: Academic Press, 1973), p. 6.

8. Ernst Cassirer, *Language and Myth,* trans. Susanne K. Langer (New York: Dover Publications, 1946), p. 9.

9. *The Necessary Angel,* pp. 49–50.

10. "The Constant Symbol," *Atlantic Monthly* 178 (October 1946): 151.

11. *The Necessary Angel,* pp. 117–18.

12. *Picasso on Art: A Selection of Views,* ed. Dore Ashton (New York: Viking Press, 1972), pp. 27, 101.

13. *Essays on Style, Rhetoric, and Language,* ed. F. N. Scott (Boston: Allyn and Bacon, 1893), p. 119.

14. William Empson, *Seven Types of Ambiguity* (New York: New Directions, 1947), pp. 90, 92, 94.

15. *A Window to Criticism: Shakespeare's Sonnets and Modern Poetics* (Princeton: Princeton University Press, 1964), pp. 15–16.

16. Empson, *Seven Types*, p. 170.

17. *On Poetry: Arthur Skemp Memorial Lecture* (Bristol: University of Bristol, 1939), p. 18.

18. *Writing Degree Zero*, trans. Annette Lavers and Colin Smith (New York: Hill and Wang, 1968), p. 48.

19. The similitude suggested here is akin to that which Eric Sellin discerned between Reverdy's symbolism and Picasso's postcubist paintings of mixed perspective. See Eric Sellin, "The Esthetics of Ambiguity: Reverdy's Use of Syntactic Simultaneity," in *About French Poetry from DADA to "TEL QUEL": Text and Theory*, ed. Mary Ann Caws (Detroit: Wayne State University Press, 1974), p. 118.

20. Maria Luz, "Témoignages: Henri Matisse," *XXᵉ Siècle*, no. 2 (January 1952): 66.

Chapter 9. The Pleasure of Ulteriority

1. *The Wild Garden* (Berkeley and Los Angeles: University of California Press, 1963), p. 150.

2. *The Necessary Angel: Essays on Reality and the Imagination* (London: Faber and Faber, 1951), p. 81.

3. Elaine Barry, *Robert Frost on Writing* (New Brunswick: Rutgers University Press, 1973), p. 32.

4. *Illustrated Notebooks, 1917–1955*, trans. Stanley Applebaum (New York: Dover Publications, 1971), p. 10. Applebaum translates the French as "Art is meant to upset people, science reassures them." But by making the verbs definitively transitive and by supplying the unexpressed objects, Applebaum changes the suggestiveness and thus the force of Braque's French.

5. *The Rule of Metaphor: Multi-Disciplinary Studies of the Creation of Meaning in Language*, trans. Robert Czerny (Toronto and Buffalo: University of Toronto Press, 1977), p. 248.

6. *The Necessary Angel*, p. 118.

7. *Illustrated Notebooks, 1917–1955*, p. 70.

8. *The Rule of Metaphor*, p. 81.

9. *The Philosophy of Rhetoric* (New York: Oxford University Press, 1936), p. 109.

10. "White Mythology," trans. F. C. T. Moore, *New Literary History* 6 (Autumn 1974): 18.

11. *Der Satz vom Grund* (Pfulligen: Neske, 1957), pp. 85–89.

12. *The Rule of Metaphor*, pp. 282–83.

13. *The Rule of Metaphor*, p. 282.

14. "Mensch und Sprache," in *Kleine Schriften* (Tübingen: J. C. B. Mohr [Paul Siebeck], 1967), 1:95; "Man and Language," in *Philosphical Hermeneutics*, trans. and ed. David Linge (Berkeley and Los Angeles: University of California Press, 1976), p. 62.

15. *The Rule of Metaphor*, p. 297.

16. *The Rule of Metaphor*, p. 299.

17. *Stabilité structurelle et morphogénèse; Essai d'une théorie générale des modèles* (Reading, Mass.: W. A. Benjamin, 1972), p. 321. English translation: *Structural Stability and Morphogenesis*, trans. D. H. Fowler (Reading, Mass.: W. A. Benjamin, 1975), p. 320.

18. See *Stabilité structurelle et morphogénèse*, pp. 121–22; English trans., pp. 114–15.

19. *Stabilité structurelle et morphogénèse*, pp. 321–22; English trans., p. 321.

20. *The Necessary Angel*, p. 77.

21. *The Necessary Angel*, pp. 80–81.

22. *The Necessary Angel*, pp. 59–60.

23. *You Can't Go Home Again* (New York: Dell Publishing Co., 1960), pp. 380–81.

24. *The Necessary Angel*, p. 53.

25. *The Rule of Metaphor*, p. 148.

26. *The Rule of Metaphor*, p. 155.

27. *Languages of Art, An Approach to a Theory of Symbols* (Indianapolis: Bobbs-Merrill Co., 1968), p. 73.

28. *The Necessary Angel*, p. vii.

29. *The Necessary Angel*, p. 22.

30. *The Necessary Angel*, p. 31.

31. J. Richardson, "Voice of the Artist: The Power of Mystery," *The Observer* (London), 1 December 1957, p. 16, reprinted in Douglas Cooper, *Braque: The Great Years* (Chicago: Art Institute of Chicago, 1972), pp. 100–101.

32. *The Necessary Angel*, p. 109.

33. *The Necessary Angel*, p. 114.

Works Cited

Abastado, Claude. *Expérience et théorie de la création poétique chez Mallarmé. Archives des lettres modernes,* no. 119. Paris: Lettres Modernes, 1970.

Alajouanine, Th. "Aphasia and Artistic Realization." *Brain* 71 (1948): 229–41.

Albert, Martin L., and Loraine K. Obler. *The Bilingual Brain: Neuropsychological and Neurolinguistic Aspects of Bilingualism.* New York: Academic Press, 1978.

Aragon, Louis. *Henri Matisse, roman.* 2 vols. Paris: Gallimard, 1971.

Arnheim, Rudolf. *Art and Visual Perception: A Psychology of the Creative Eye: The New Version.* Berkeley and Los Angeles: University of California Press, 1974.

———. *Toward a Psychology of Art, Collected Essays.* Berkeley and Los Angeles: University of California Press, 1966.

———. *Visual Thinking.* Berkeley and Los Angeles: University of California Press, 1969.

Axelrod, Seymour. *Effects of Early Blindness: Performance of Blind and Sighted Children on Tactile and Auditory Tasks.* New York: American Foundation for the Blind, 1959.

Bachelard, Gaston. *L'Air et les songes: essai sur l'imagination du mouvement.* Paris: José Corti, 1943.

———. *L'Eau et les rêves: essai sur l'imagination de la matière.* Paris: José Corti, 1942.

———. *The Poetics of Reverie.* Translated by Daniel Russell. Boston: Beacon Press, 1971.

———. *The Poetics of Space.* Translated by Maria Jolas. Boston: Beacon Press, 1969.

———. *Psychoanalysis of Fire.* Translated by Alan G. M. Ross. Boston: Beacon Press, 1968.

———. *La Terre et les rêveries de la volonté.* Paris: José Corti, 1948.

———. *La Terre et les rêveries du repos.* Paris: José Corti, 1948.

Bandi, Hans-Georg, and Johannes Maringer (en reprenant un projet de

Hugo Obermaier). *L'Art préhistorique: les cavernes, le levant espagnol, les régions arctiques.* Translated by Jean Descoullayes and François Lachenal. Paris: Éditions Charles Massin, 1952.

Barry, Elaine. *Robert Frost on Writing.* New Brunswick, N.J.: Rutgers University Press, 1973.

Barthes, Roland. *Critique et vérité, essai.* Paris: Éditions du Seuil, 1966.

———. *Elements of Semiology.* Translated by Annette Lavers and Colin Smith. New York: Hill and Wang, 1968.

———. *Essais critiques.* Paris: Éditions du Seuil, 1964.

———. *Mythologies.* Paris: Éditions du Seuil, 1957.

———. *The Pleasure of the Text.* Translated by Richard Miller. New York: Hill and Wang, 1975.

———. *S/Z.* Translated by Richard Miller. New York: Hill and Wang, 1974.

———. *Writing Degree Zero.* Translated by Annette Lavers and Colin Smith. New York: Hill and Wang, 1968.

Bataille, Georges. *La Peinture préhistorique: Lascaux ou la naissance de l'art. Les Grands siècles de la peinture.* Geneva: Skira, 1955.

Bauman, Richard. *Verbal Art as Performance,* with supplemental essays by Barbara A. Babcock et al. Rowley, Mass.: Newbury House Publishers, 1977.

Beckett, Samuel. *Proust.* New York: Grove Press, 1970.

———. *Stories and Texts for Nothing.* New York: Grove Press, 1967.

Begouen, Comte Henri. "Les Bases magiques de l'art préhistorique." *Scientia* 65, no. 324 [Série IV, vol. 33] (1 avril 1939): 206–16.

Birch, Cyril. "The Language of Chinese Literature." *New Literary History* 4 (Autumn 1972): 141–50.

Black, Max. *Models and Metaphors: Studies in Language and Philosophy.* Ithaca: Cornell University Press, 1962.

Blake, William. *The Complete Writings of William Blake.* Edited by Geoffrey Keynes. London: Oxford University Press, 1966.

Boeck, Wilhelm, and Jaime Sabartés. *Picasso.* New York: Harry N. Abrams [1955].

Bogen, Joseph E. "The Other Side of the Brain II: An Appositional Mind." *Bulletin of the Los Angeles Neurological Societies* 34 (July 1969): 135–62.

———. "The Other Side of the Brain III: The Corpus Callosum and Creativity." *Bulletin of the Los Angeles Neurological Societies* 34 (October 1969): 191–220.

Bonvicini, G. "Die Aphasie der Malers Vierge." *Wiener Medizinische Wochenschrift* 76 (1926): 88–91.

Bowie, Henry P. *On the Laws of Japanese Painting.* San Francisco: P. Elder, 1911.

Braque, Georges. *Illustrated Notebooks, 1917–1955.* Translated by Stanley Applebaum. New York: Dover Publications, 1971.

Brassaï. *Picasso and Company.* Translated by Francis Price. Garden City, N.Y.: Doubleday, 1966.

Breton, André. *Manifeste du surréalisme.* Paris: Éditions du Sagittaire [1924].

Breuil, Henri. *Quatre cents siècles d'art pariétal: les cavernes ornées de l'age du renne.* 1952. Reprinted Paris: Editions Max Fourny, 1974.

Bruner, Jerome S. *On Knowing: Essays for the Left Hand.* Cambridge: Belknap Press of Harvard University Press, 1962.

Bruner, Jerome S., et al. *Studies in Cognitive Growth.* New York: Wiley, 1966.

Bruter, C. P. *Bases philsophiques et mathématiques.* Vol. 1 of his *Topologie et perception.* Paris: Doin-Maloine, 1974.

Capitan, Louis, Henri Breuil, and D. Peyrony. *La Caverne de Font-de-Gaume aux Eyzies (Dordogne).* Monaco: Vve A. Chène, 1910.

Cassirer, Ernst. *Language and Myth.* Translated by Susanne K. Langer. New York: Dover-Harper, 1946.

Caws, Mary Ann, ed. *About French Poetry from DADA to "TEL QUEL": Text and Theory.* Detroit: Wayne State University Press, 1974.

Cézanne, Paul. *Correspondence.* Edited by John Rewald. Paris: Bernard Grasset, 1937.

Charbonnier, Georges. *Le Monologue du peintre.* 2 vols. Paris: René Juillard, 1960.

Chiang Yee. *Chinese Calligraphy: An Introduction to Its Aesthetic and Technique.* 3d ed. Cambridge: Harvard University Press, 1973.

Chomsky, Noam. *The Logical Structure of Linguistic Theory.* New York: Plenum Press, 1975.

Clemens, Samuel L. *Mark Twain in Eruption.* Edited by Bernard DeVoto. New York: Harper, 1940.

———. *Mark Twain to Mrs. Fairbanks.* Edited by Dixon Wecter. San Marino, Calif.: The Huntington Library, 1949.

———. *Mark Twain's Mysterious Stranger Manuscripts.* Edited by William M. Gibson. Berkeley and Los Angeles: University of California Press, 1969.

———. *Mark Twain's Satires & Burlesques.* Edited by Franklin R. Rogers. Berkeley and Los Angeles: University of California Press, 1967; London: Cambridge University Press, 1967.

Coleridge, Samuel T. *Biographia Literaria, with His Aesthetical Essays.* Edited by J. Shawcross. 2 vols. London: Oxford University Press, 1967.

———. *The Notebooks of Samuel Taylor Coleridge.* Edited by Kathleen Coburn, Bollingen Series 50. 3 vols. New York: The Bollingen Foundation; Princeton: Princeton University Press, 1957–73.

Conrad, Joseph. *Prefaces to His Works.* London: Dent, 1937.

Cooper, Douglas. *Braque: The Great Years.* Chicago: Art Institute of Chicago, 1972.

Copeland, Carolyn Faunce. *Language & Time & Gertrude Stein.* Iowa City: University of Iowa Press, 1975.

Coren, Stanley. "Subjective Contours and Apparent Depth." *Psychological Review* 79 (July 1972): 359–67.

Corot, Jean-Baptiste Camille. *Corot raconté par lui-même et par ses amis: pensées et écrits du peintre.* 2 vols. Vésenaz-Genève: Pierre Cailler, 1946.

Cromer, Richard F. "Conservation by the Congenitally Blind." *British Journal of Psychology* 64 (1973): 241–50.

cummings, e. e. *CIOPW.* New York: Covici-Friede, 1931.

———. *is 5.* New York: Horace Liveright, 1926.

Deese, James. "Mind and Metaphor: A Commentary." *New Literary History* 6 (Autumn 1974): 211–17.

Deikman, Arthur J. "Bimodal Consciousness." *Archives of General Psychiatry* 25 (December 1971): 481–89.

DeQuincey, Thomas. *Essays on Style, Rhetoric, and Language.* Edited by F. N. Scott. Boston: Allyn and Bacon, 1893.

Derrida, Jacques. "White Mythology: Metaphor in the Text of Philosophy." *New Literary History* 6 (Autumn 1974): 5–74.

Deutsch, Diana. "Musical Illusions." *Scientific American* 233 (October 1975): 92–104.

Dickinson, Emily. *The Letters of Emily Dickinson.* Edited by Thomas H. Johnson; Associate Editor Theodora Ward. Cambridge: The Belknap Press of Harvard University Press, 1958.

———. *The Poems of Emily Dickinson.* Edited by Thomas H. Johnson. 3 vols. Cambridge: The Belknap Press of Harvard University Press, 1955.

Dimond, Stuart J., and J. Graham Beaumont, editors. *Hemisphere Function in the Human Brain.* London: Elek Science, 1974.

Di San Lazzaro, G., editor. *Hommage à Henri Matisse. XXᵉ Siècle,* special number. Paris: Société Internationale d'Art, 1970.

Durand, Gilbert. "'Les Chats, les rats, et les structuralistes': symbole et structuralisme figuratif." *Cahiers internationaux de Symbolisme* 17–18 (1969): 13–38.

———. *L'Imagination symbolique.* Paris: Presses Universitaires de France, 1968.

———. *Les Structures anthropologiques de l'imaginaire.* Paris: Bordas, 1969.

Empson, William. *Seven Types of Ambiguity.* New York: New Directions, 1947.

Enciso, Jorge. *Design Motifs of Ancient Mexico.* New York: Dover Publications, 1953.

———. *Designs from Pre-Columbian Mexico.* New York: Dover Publications, 1971.

Escholier, Raymond. *Matisse, ce vivant.* Paris: Librairie Arthème Fayard, 1956.

Faulkner, William. *Faulkner in the University.* Edited by Frederick L. Gwynn and Joseph Blotner. Charlottesville: University Press of Virginia, reprinted 1977.

Fenollosa, Ernest. *The Chinese Written Character as a Medium for Poetry.* Edited by Ezra Pound. San Francisco: City Light Books, 1936.

Fifield, William. "Miró: An Interview in Mallorca." *Arts Magazine* 43 (November 1968): 17–19.

Freud, Sigmund. *On Creativity and the Unconscious.* Edited by Benjamin Nelson. New York: Harper, 1958.

Frost, Robert. *Complete Poems of Robert Frost.* New York: Holt, Rinehart and Winston, 1964.

———. "The Constant Symbol." *Atlantic Monthly* 178 (October 1946): 50–52.

Frye, Northrop. *Anatomy of Criticism.* Princeton: Princeton University Press, 1957.

———. *The Educated Imagination.* Bloomington: Indiana University Press, 1964.

Furth, Hans G. *Thinking without Language: Psychological Implications of Deafness.* New York: Free Press, 1966.

Gadamer, Hans-Georg. "Mensch und Sprache." In *Kleine Schriften.* Vol. 1. Tübingen: J. C. Mohr (Paul Siebeck), 1967, pp. 93–100; English translation: "Man and Language." In *Philosophical Hermeneutics.* Translated and edited by David E. Linge. Berkeley and Los Angeles: University of California Press, 1976.

Gardner, Howard. *The Shattered Mind: The Person after Brain Damage.* New York: Alfred A. Knopf, 1975.

Gazzaniga, Michael S. *The Bisected Brain.* New York: Appleton-Century-Crofts, 1970.

———. "One Brain—Two Minds?" *American Scientist* 60 (1972): 311–17.

Gazzaniga, Michael S., Joseph E. Bogen, and Roger W. Sperry. "Observations on Visual Perception after Disconnexion of the Cerebral Hemispheres in Man." *Brain* 88 (1965): 221–36.

———. "Some Functional Effects of Sectioning the Cerebral Commissures in Man." *National Academy of Sciences Proceedings* 48 (1962): 1765–69.

Ghiselin, Brewster. *The Creative Process: A Symposium.* Berkeley and Los Angeles: University of California Press, 1952.

Gibson, James J. *The Perception of the Visual World.* Boston: Houghton Mifflin, 1950.

Gilot, Françoise, and Carlton Lake. *Life with Picasso.* New York: McGraw-Hill, 1964.

Gilson, Etienne. *Painting and Reality.* New York: Meridian, 1959.

Goldwater, Robert, and Marco Treves, eds. *Artists on Art, from the XIV to the XX Century.* New York: Pantheon Books, 1945.

Gombrich, E. H. *Art and Illusion: A Study in the Psychology of Pictorial Representation.* London: Phaidon Press, 1959.

Goodman, Nelson. *Languages of Art, An Approach to a Theory of Symbols.* Indianapolis: Bobbs-Merrill, 1968.

Graves, Robert. *The Common Asphodel, Collected Essays on Poetry, 1922–1949.* London: Hamish Hamilton, 1949.

———. *Poetic Unreason and Other Studies.* London: Cecil Palmer, 1925.

Gregg, Lee W., ed. *Cognition in Learning and Memory.* New York: Wiley, 1972.

Gregory, R. L. "Cognitive Contours." *Nature* 238 (7 July 1972): 51–52.

Guenne, Jacques. "Entretien avec Henri Matisse." *L'Art Vivant,* no. 18 (15 September 1925): 1–6.

Harding, Rosamond. *An Anatomy of Inspiration.* New York: Barnes and Noble, 1940.

Hardy, Thomas. *Life and Art.* Edited by Ernest Brennecke, Jr. 1925. Reprinted New York: Books for Libraries Press, 1968.

Harley, Randall K., Jr. *Verbalism among Blind Children.* New York: American Foundation for the Blind, 1963.

Heidegger, Martin. *Der Satz vom Grund.* Pfulligen: Neske, 1957.

Hemingway, Ernest. *A Moveable Feast.* New York: Scribners, 1964.

———. *The Nick Adams Stories.* New York: Scribners, 1972.

Hess, Thomas B. *Willem de Kooning.* New York: George Braziller, 1959.

Housman, A. E. *The Name and Nature of Poetry.* Cambridge: Cambridge University Press, 1950.

Hugo, Victor. *Victor Hugo dessinateur.* Paris: Editions du Minotaure, 1963.

Ittelson, William H. *Visual Space Perception.* New York: Springer, 1960.

Ittelson, William, and F. P. Kilpatrick. "Experiments in Perception." *Scientific American* 185 (August 1951): 50–55.

Jakobson, Roman, and Morris Halle. *Fundamentals of Language.* The Hague: Mouton, 1956.

James, Henry. *The Art of Fiction and Other Essays.* New York: Oxford University Press, 1948.

———. *The Notebooks of Henry James.* Edited by F. O. Matthiessen and K. B. Murdock. New York: Oxford University Press, 1947.

———. *The Novels and Tales of Henry James.* New York Edition. 26 vols. New York: Scribners, 1922.

Joubert, Joseph. *Pensées.* Paris: Bloud & Cie., 1909.

Jung, Carl G. *The Archetype and the Collective Unconscious.* Translated by R. F. C. Hull. Vol. 9, pt. 1 of *The Collected Works of C. G. Jung.* New York: Bollingen Foundation, 1959.

———. *Psychological Types.* Vol. 6 of *The Collected Works of C. G. Jung.* Princeton: Princeton University Press, 1971.

Jung, Carl G. et al. *Man and His Symbols.* Garden City, N.Y.: Doubleday, 1964.

Kakuzo Okakura. *The Book of Tea.* Edited by Everett Bleiler. New York; Dover Publications, 1964.

Kanizsa, Gaetano. "Contours without Gradients or Cognitive Contours?" *Italian Journal of Psychology* 1 (April 1974): 93–112.

———. "Subjective Contours." *Scientific American* 234 (April 1976): 48–52.

Keats, John. *The Letters of John Keats.* Edited by Maurice Buxton Forman. 2 vols. Oxford: Oxford University Press, 1931.

Kennedy, Alan, and Alan Wilkes, eds. *Studies in Long Term Memory.* London: Wiley, 1975.

Kepes, Gyorgy. *The New Landscape in Art and Science.* Chicago: Paul Theobald, 1956.

Kimura, Doreen. "The Asymmetry of the Human Brain." *Scientific American* 228 (March 1973): 70–78.

Kinsbourne, Marcel, and W. Lynn Smith, eds. *Hemispheric Disconnection and Cerebral Function.* Springfield, Ill.: Charles C. Thomas, 1974.

Klee, Paul. *Das bildnerische Denken.* Edited by Jurg Spiller. Basel: Benno Schwabe & Co., 1956. English translation: *The Thinking Eye.* New York: George Wittenborn, 1964.

Koestler, Arthur. *The Act of Creation.* New York: Macmillan, 1964.

Kolata, Gina Bari. "Catastrophe Theory: The Emperor Has No Clothes." *Science* 196 (15 April 1977): 287, 350–51.

Krieger, Murray. *A Window to Criticism: Shakespeare's Sonnets and Modern Poetics.* Princeton: Princeton University Press, 1964.

Laming [-Emperaire], Annette. *Lascaux: Paintings and Engravings.* Translated by Eleanore Frances Armstrong. Harmondsworth, England: Penguin Books, 1959.

Laming-Emperaire, Annette. *La Signification de l'art rupestre paléolithique.* Paris: A. & J. Picard, 1962.

Langer, Susanne K. *Philosophy in a New Key: A Study in the Symbolism of Reason, Rite, and Art.* Cambridge: Harvard University Press, 1951.

Lathem, Edward C., editor. *Interviews with Robert Frost.* New York: Holt, Rinehart and Winston, 1966.

Lawrence, D. H. *Assorted Articles.* New York: Knopf, 1930.

Lawson, R. B., and W. L. Gulick. "Stereopsis and Anomalous Contour." *Vision Research* 7 (March 1967): 271–97.

Leach, Bernard. *Hamada, Potter.* Tokyo: Kodansha, 1975.

Lee, Dorothy. *Freedom and Culture.* Englewood Cliffs, N.J.: Prentice-Hall, 1959.

Leonardo da Vinci. *Treatise on Painting.* Translated by Philip McMahon. Princeton: Princeton University Press, 1956.

Leroi-Gourhan, André. *Préhistoire de l'art occidental.* Paris: Editions d'Art Lucien Mazenod, 1965.

Lévi-Strauss, Claude. *The Savage Mind.* Chicago: University of Chicago Press, 1966.

———. *Structural Anthropology.* Translated by Claire Jacobson and B. G. Schoepf. New York: Basic Books, 1963.

Levy, Jerre, and Colwyn Trevarthen. "Metacontrol of Hemispheric Function in Human Split-Brain Patients." *Journal of Experimental Psychology: Human Perception and Performance* 2 (August 1976): 299–312.

Lewis, R. W. B. "The Hero in the New World: William Faulkner's *The Bear.*" *Kenyon Review* 13 (Autumn 1951): 641–60.

Loran, Erle. *Cézanne's Composition: Analysis of His Form with Diagrams and Photographs of His Motifs.* Berkeley and Los Angeles: University of California Press, 1950.

Lord, James. *A Giacometti Portrait.* New York: Museum of Modern Art, 1965.

Lu Chi. *The Art of Letters; Lu Chi's "Wen Fu," A.D. 302.* A Translation and Comparative Study by E. R. Hughes. Bollingen Series 29. New York: Pantheon Books, 1951.

Luquet, G. -H. *L'Art et la religion des hommes fossiles.* Paris: Masson, 1926.

Luria, A. R. *The Working Brain: An Introduction to Neuropsychology.* Translated by Basil Haigh. New York: Basic Books, 1973.

Luz, Maria. "Témoignages: Henri Matisse; propos recueillis par Maria Luz et approuvés par Henri Matisse." *XXe Siècle,* no. 2 (January 1952): 66–67.

Lyman, R. S., S. T. Kwan, and W. H. Chao. "Left Occipito-Parietal Brain Tumor with Observations on Alexia and Agraphia in Chinese and in English." *The Chinese Medical Journal* 54 (December 1938): 491–516.

Lyotard-May, Andrée. "A Propos du 'Langage des images.'" *La Revue d'aesthétique* 22 (1969): 29–36.

MacLeod, Robert B., and Herbert L. Pick, Jr., eds. *Perception: Essays in Honor of James J. Gibson.* Ithaca: Cornell University Press, 1974.

Malingue, Maurice. *Gauguin, le peintre et son oeuvre.* Paris: Presses de la Cité et Londres, 1948.

Malinowski, Bronislaw. *The Language of Magic and Gardening.* Vol. 2 of his *Coral Gardens and Their Magic.* Bloomington: Indiana University Press, 1965.

———. *Soil-Tilling and Agricultural Rites in the Trobriand Islands.* Vol. 1 of his *Coral Gardens and Their Magic.* Bloomington: Indiana University Press, 1965.

Matisse, Henri. *Ecrits et propos sur l'art.* Edited by Dominique Fourcade. Paris: Hermann, 1972.

———. "Notes d'un peintre." *La Grande Revue,* no. 52 (25 December 1908): 731–45.

———. "Notes d'un peintre sur son dessin." *Le Point,* no. 21 (July 1939): 8(104)–15(111).

———. *Portraits.* Monte Carlo: André Sauret, Editions du Livre, 1954.

Merleau-Ponty, Maurice. *Signs.* Translated by R. C. McCleary. Evanston: Northwestern University Press, 1964.

Michaud, Guy. "Langage poétique et symbole." *Etudes philosophiques* 26 (1971): 343–52.

Miles, Josephine. *Style and Proportion: The Language of Prose and Poetry.* Boston: Little, Brown, 1967.

Miller, Henry. *The Wisdom of the Heart.* Norfolk, Conn.: New Directions, 1941.

Moore, Henry. *Henry Moore on Sculpture.* Edited by Philip James. New York: Viking, 1966.

Nakata, Yujiro. *The Art of Japanese Calligraphy.* Translated by Alan Woodhull in collaboration with Armins Nikovskis. Tokyo: Heibonsha, 1967; New York: Weatherhill, 1973.

Natsume Kinnosuke [Sōseki]. *The Three-Cornered World* [*Kusa Makura*]. Translated by Alan Turney and Pete Owen. Chicago: Henry Regnery Co., 1967.

Neisser, Ulric. *Cognitive Psychology.* New York: Appleton-Century-Crofts, 1967.

Neumann, Erich. *The Archetypal World of Henry Moore.* New York: Harper & Row, 1965.

Nietzsche, Friedrich. *The Case of Wagner.* In *The Complete Works of Friedrich Nietzsche,* edited by Oscar Levy. New York: Russell & Russell, 1964.

O'Connor, Flannery. *Mystery and Manners: Occasional Prose.* Selected and edited by Sally and Robert Fitzgerald. New York: Farrar, Straus & Giroux, 1969.

Paivio, Allan. "Imagery and Synchronic Thinking." *Canadian Psychological Review* 16 (1975): 147–63.

———. *Imagery and Verbal Processes.* New York: Holt, Rinehart and Winston, 1971.

Paulhan, Jean. *Les Fleurs de Tarbes, ou la terreur dans les lettres.* Paris: Gallimard, 1941.

Peterson, Susan. *Shoji Hamada: A Potter's Way and Work.* Tokyo: Kodansha International, 1974.

Piaget, Jean. *The Child's Conception of the World.* Translated by Joan and Andrew Tomlinson. Norwich, England: Jarrold and Sons, 1929.

———. *La Construction du réel chez l'enfant.* 5ème éd. Neuchâtel: Delachaux et Niestlé, 1973.

———. *La Formation du symbole chez l'enfant: imitation, jeu et rêve, image et représentation.* 6ème éd. Neuchâtel-Paris: Delachaux et Niestlé, 1976.

———. *Structuralism.* Translated and edited by Chaninah Maschler. New York: Basic Books, 1970.

Piaget, Jean, and Bärbel Inhelder. *L'Image mentale chez l'enfant: étude sur le développement des représentations imagées.* Paris: Presses Universitaires de France, 1966.

Picasso, Pablo. *Picasso on Art: A Selection of Views.* Edited by Dore Ashton. New York: Viking, 1972.

Plato. *Dialogues.* Translated by B. Jowett. 2 vols. New York: Random House, 1937.

Pliner, Patricia, Lester Krames, and Thomas Alloway. *Communication and Affect: Language and Thought.* New York: Academic Press, 1973.

Raphael, Max. *Prehistoric Cave Paintings.* Translated by Norbert Guterman. Bollingen Series IV. New York: Pantheon, 1945.

Richards, I. A. *The Philosophy of Rhetoric.* New York: Oxford University Press, 1936.

———. *Principles of Literary Criticism.* London: Routledge & Kegan Paul, 1949.

Richardson, Alan. *Mental Imagery.* New York: Springer, 1969.

Richardson, J. "Voice of the Artist: The Power of Mystery." *The (London) Observer,* 1 December 1957, 16.

Ricoeur, Paul. *The Conflict of Interpretations: Essays in Hermeneutics.* Edited by Don Ihde. Evanston: Northwestern University Press, 1974.

———. "Metaphor and the Main Problem of Hermeneutics." *New Literary History* 6 (Autumn 1974): 95–110.

———. *The Rule of Metaphor: Multi-Disciplinary Studies of the Creation of Meaning in Language.* Toronto and Buffalo: University of Toronto Press, 1977.

Rogow, Sally. "Perceptual Organization in Blind Children." *New Outlook for the Blind* 69 (1975): 226–33.

Rosenfield, John M., and Shūjirō Shimada. *Traditions of Japanese Art: Selections from the Kimiko and John Powers Collection.* Cambridge: Fogg Art Museum, Harvard University, 1970.

Rouault, Georges. "Pictorial Conceits." *Verve. An Artistic and Literary Quarterly* 1 (1939): 104.

Rubin, Edmund J. *Abstract Functioning in the Blind.* New York: American Foundation for the Blind, 1964.

Sartre, Jean-Paul. *L'Imaginaire: Psychologie phénoménologique de l'imagination.* Paris: Gallimard, 1940.

Sasanuma, Simiko, and Osamu Fujimura. "An Analysis of Writing Errors in Japanese Aphasic Patients: Kanji versus Kana Words." *Cortex* 8 (1972): 265–82.

———. "Selective Impairment of Phonetic and Non-Phonetic Transcription of Words in Japanese Aphasia Patients; Kana *vs.* Kanji in Visual Recognition and Writing." *Cortex* 7 (1971): 1–18.

Sassoon, Siegfried. *On Poetry: Arthur Skemp Memorial Lecture.* Bristol: University of Bristol, 1939.

Saussure, Ferdinand de. *Course in General Linguistics.* Edited by Bally and Sechehaye. Translated by Wade Baskin. New York: Philosophical Library, 1959.

Schneider, Pierre. With the collaboration of Tamara Préaud. *Henri Matisse: Exposition du Centenaire, Grand Palais, avril–septembre 1970.* Paris: Ministère d'Etat, Affaires Culturelles. Réunion des Musées Nationaux, 1970.

Seamon, John G., and Michael S. Gazzaniga. "Coding Strategies and Cerebral Laterality Effects." *Cognitive Psychology* 5 (1973): 249–56.

Sen Soshitsu and Sen Soshu. *Sado Zenshu (9).* Tokyo: Sogensha, 1941.

Sewell, Elizabeth. *The Human Metaphor.* Notre Dame: University of Notre Dame Press, 1964.

Shakespeare, William. *The London Shakespeare.* Edited by John Munro. 6 vols. New York: Simon and Schuster, 1957.

Sitwell, Dame Edith. *A Poet's Notebook.* Boston: Little, Brown, 1950.

Sparshott, F. E. "'As,' or The Limits of Metaphor." *New Literary History* 6 (Autumn 1974): 75–94.

Spender, Stephen. *Collected Poems: 1928–1953*. New York: Random House, 1955.

———. *The Making of a Poem*. London: Hamish Hamilton, 1955.

———. *Poems of Dedication*. New York: Random House, 1947.

Sperry, Roger W. "Cerebral Organization and Behavior." *Science* 133 (June 1961): 1749–57.

Stadler, Michael, and Jürgen Dieker. "Untersuchungen zum problem virtueller Konturen in der visuellen Wahrnehmung." *Zeitschrift für experimentelle und angewandte Psychologie* 19, no. 2 (1972): 325–50.

Stein, Gertrude. *The Autobiography of Alice B. Toklas*. New York: Harcourt, Brace, 1933.

———. *Lectures in America*. New York: Random House, 1935.

———. *Narration: Four Lectures*. New York: Greenwood Press, 1935.

———. *Picasso*. Boston: Beacon Press, 1959.

———. *A Primer for the Gradual Understanding of Gertrude Stein*. Edited by Robert B. Haas. Los Angeles: Black Sparrow Press, 1971.

———. *Two and Other Early Portraits*. New Haven: Yale University Press, 1951.

———. *What Are Masterpieces?* New York: Pitman, 1970.

Stevens, Wallace. *The Collected Poems of Wallace Stevens*. New York: Alfred A. Knopf, 1955.

———. *The Necessary Angel: Essays on Reality and the Imagination*. London: Faber and Faber, 1951.

Tagiuri, Renato, and Luigi Petrullo, eds. *Person Perception and Interpersonal Behavior*. Stanford: Stanford University Press, 1958.

Tériade, E. "Constance du Fauvisme." *Minotaure* 2, no. 9 (1936): 1–9.

———. "Emancipation de la peinture." *Minotaure* 1, nos. 3–4 (1933): 9–21.

Teyler, Timothy J., ed. *Altered States of Awareness: Readings from Scientific American*. San Francisco: W. H. Freeman, 1954–72.

Thom, René. *Stabilité structurelle et morphogénèse*. Reading, Mass.: W. A. Benjamin, 1972. English Translation: *Structural Stability and Morphogenesis*. Translated by D. H. Fowler. Reading, Mass.: W. A. Benjamin, 1975.

Tokuzo, Masaki. *Hon'ami Gyojoki*. Tokyo: Chuokoron Bijutsu Shuppan, 1965.

Turgenev, Ivan. *Letters, A Selection*. Edited and translated by Edgar H. Lehrman. New York: Knopf, 1961.

———. *Literary Reminiscences and Autobiographical Fragments*. Translated by David Magarshack. New York: Farrar, Straus and Cudahy, 1958.

———. *The Portrait Game*. Edited by Marion Mainwaring. London: Chatto and Windus, 1973.

Ucko, Peter J., and Andrée Rosenfeld. *Paleolithic Cave Art*. New York: McGraw-Hill, 1967.

Valéry, Paul. "A Course in Poetics, First Lesson." *Southern Review* 5 (1940): 401–18.

Van Gogh, Vincent. *Dear Theo: The Autobiography of Vincent Van Gogh.* Edited by Irving Stone. Garden City, N.Y.: Doubleday, 1946.

―――. *Letters to an Artist: From Vincent Van Gogh to Anton Ridder von Rappard, 1881–1885.* Translated by Rela van Messel. New York: Viking, 1936.

Verdet, André. *Prestiges de Matisse, précédé de Visite à Matisse. Entretien avec Matisse avec quatorze hors-textes dont trois en couleurs. Couverture spécialement composée par Matisse.* Paris: Editions Emile-Paul, 1952.

Vlaminck, Maurice de. *Portraits avant décès.* Paris: Flammarion, 1943.

Warnock, Mary. *Imagination.* Berkeley and Los Angeles: University of California Press, 1976.

Werner, H., and B. Kaplan. *Symbol Formation: An Organismic-Developmental Approach to the Psychology of Language and the Expression of Thought.* New York: Wiley, 1963.

Whorf, Benjamin Lee. *Language, Thought, and Reality.* Edited by John B. Carroll. Cambridge: The M.I.T. Press, 1956.

Wilson, Angus. *The Wild Garden.* Berkeley and Los Angeles: University of California Press, 1963.

Witkin, Herman A., et al. "Cognitive Patterning in Congenitally Totally Blind Children." *Child Development* 39 (1968): 767–86.

Wolfe, Thomas. *You Can't Go Home Again.* New York: Dell Publishing Co., 1962.

Woolf, Virginia. *The Waves.* New York and London: Harcourt Brace Jovanovich, 1978.

―――. *A Writer's Diary, Being Extracts from the Diary of Virginia Woolf.* Edited by Leonard Woolf. London: Hogarth Press, 1954.

Zaimov, K., D. Kitov, and N. Kolev. "Aphasie chez un peintre." *Encephale* 63 (1969): 377–417.

Zeeman, E. C. "Catastrophe Theory." *Scientific American* 234 (April 1976): 65–83.

Zweibelson, I., and C. Fisher Barg. "Concept Development of Blind Children." *New Outlook for the Blind* 61 (1967): 218–22.

Index

243